7/1/12

P9-CLN-335

ALSO BY ANDREW MARR

Making of Modern Britain

A History of Modern Britain

My Trade: A Short History of British Journalism

THE REAL ELIZABETH

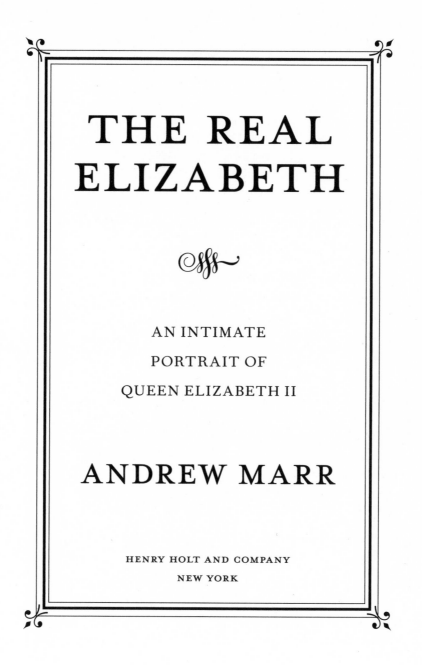

THE REAL ELIZABETH

AN INTIMATE PORTRAIT OF QUEEN ELIZABETH II

ANDREW MARR

HENRY HOLT AND COMPANY
NEW YORK

Henry Holt and Company, LLC
Publishers since 1866
175 Fifth Avenue
New York, New York 10010
www.henryholt.com

Henry Holt® and ® are registered trademarks of Henry Holt and Company, LLC.

Copyright © 2012 by Andrew Marr
All rights reserved.

Originally published as *Diamond Queen: Elizabeth II and Her People* in
Great Britain in 2011 by Macmillan UK, London

Library of Congress Cataloging-in-Publication Data
Marr, Andrew.
  [Diamond Queen]
  The real Elizabeth : an intimate portrait of Queen Elizabeth II /
Andrew Marr.—1st U.S. ed.
      p.   cm.
  "Originally published as Diamond Queen: Elizabeth II and her people in
Great Britain in 2011 by Macmillan UK, London."
  Includes bibliographical references and index.
  ISBN 978-0-8050-9416-9
  1. Elizabeth II, Queen of Great Britain, 1926–   2. Queens—Great Britain—
Biography.   3. Great Britain—History—Elizabeth II, 1952–   I. Title.
  DA590.M35 2012
  941.085092—dc23
  [B]   2011035155

Henry Holt books are available for special promotions and premiums.
For details contact: Director, Special Markets.

First U.S. Edition 2012

Designed by Meryl Sussman Levavi

Printed in the United States of America
1   3   5   7   9   10   8   6   4   2

For my mother, Anne Valerie Marr,
sometimes mistaken for . . .

Contents

Preface to the U.S. Edition

Why should Americans be interested in Queen Elizabeth II, monarch of the United Kingdom and fifteen other countries, from Canada and Australia to tiny Tuvalu? It is a good question. She is a kind of anti-celebrity, a woman happiest in scarf, old coat and rubber boots, out with her dogs or horses. Though enormously wealthy, she eats frugally, keeping her breakfast cereals in plastic boxes and switching off unnecessary lights as she passes through rooms. She has a wonderful smile when she chooses to use it, but otherwise her face falls naturally into a rubbery solemnity she herself has likened to Miss Piggy. Her formal power is very small, and almost entirely irrelevant to the lives of those who are not her subjects.

Her son Charles—who as he approaches his own old age looks increasingly like his Hanoverian ancestor George III, the King who lost the American colonies—is hardly a celebrity either. The last time Americans became fixated by his story was when he separated from his far more media-friendly wife Diana, who was later killed in a Paris road accident. Now, with Kate Middleton, the middle-class woman whose wedding to Prince William, the Queen's grandson, was watched by a third of the world's television audience, the House of Windsor may have a new star. But the Queen herself has never played to the cameras and lives a life about as out of step as it's possible to be from the glossy, brash, fast-moving world of comtemporary culture.

This is exactly why she ought to fascinate anyone interested in American politics and history, as well as those simply curious about modern royalty. And since the Queen has no equivalent in the United States, her story presents a series of striking contrasts. The first, most obvious one is that she has been head of state for so very long. In 2012 she celebrates her Diamond Jubilee, marking the sixtieth anniversary of her accession to the British throne. Before our eyes, she has grown from the willowy, dark-haired young mother of the 1950s into the shrewd great-grandmother of today. Now, at eighty-five, she is the second-longest-reigning monarch in British history. Only her great predecessor Queen Victoria spent more time in London's palaces. That means she has known, personally and sometimes quite well, every U.S. President since Harry Truman. Of all of them, she was probably closest to Ronald Reagan, although she and her ninety-year-old husband Prince Philip have struck up an unlikely-seeming cordiality with the Obamas. Whatever one thinks about her, the Queen and her long reign have provided the British people with a sense of continuity unlike any that can be found in a democratic republic.

For many of us, she is the only British monarch we have ever known. Her father, King George VI, died on February 6, 1952, less than seven years after the end of World War II. She inherited the throne in the same year Stalin died, Truman announced the hydrogen bomb and the Rosenbergs were executed; it was also the year the first edition of *Playboy* magazine appeared, Elvis Presley graduated from high school, and Kinsey electrified America with his report on female sexuality. During her reign, the Queen saw the final transition of the British Empire into a Commonwealth of fifty-four countries—an organization that comprises about a third of

the world's population yet is unknown to most Americans. She met
the leaders of the post-Stalin Soviet Union, such as Khrushchev
and Bulganin, and became the first British monarch to visit Russia
since the killing of Tsar Nicholas and his family in 1917. She had a
ringside seat from which to witness the disastrous British and
French invasion of Nasser's Egypt and the terrifying Cuban missile
crisis. She remembers historic figures such as Charles de Gaulle
and Haile Selassie. She has seen her country go from being overwhelmingly white to a multiracial "world island" with hundreds of
new communities. She has reigned through the Korean and Vietnam wars, the worst stages of the Cold War, Perestroika, the fall of
the Berlin Wall, the Iraq and Afghan wars and the rise of China.

   Across all those years, the Queen has devoted a good part of
every day except Christmas to a close reading of the private paperwork of the British state, secret intelligence reports and paperwork
about humdrum appointments alike. She has a wicked enthusiasm
for mimicry and a phenomenal memory, so although she is deadlock-
discreet, her recall of the events and players of modern times is
probably unparalleled. This vast store of knowledge has proved
beneficial, particularly because of her role as a private counselor
and informal therapist to a long procession of prime ministers. The
early ones, including Winston Churchill, rather bullied her; the
later ones have mostly been in awe of her. In hard times she has
been able to talk them through earlier, parallel crises and so provide invaluable perspective.

   Monarchy can allow for the longer view. Americans, like the
British, live their politics on a four-year electoral cycle, but the biggest issues we face play out over much longer time spans than that.
Energy security, climate change, mass migration, long-term government debt and species extinction are hard for political leaders to
focus on, given that they tend to think only a year or two ahead. By
their nature, "Royals" think in generations, and it's useful to have
someone in a position of influence consider the long-term implications of a policy or a program.

Another contrast worth noting is Elizabeth II's own view of her role. Though we live in a secular and materialistic age, the Queen believes, quite literally, that she has a vocation—that her function is a religious calling she must answer every day of her life. When she was anointed with a secret recipe of oils at her Coronation in 1953, a tradition going back to ancient Jewish custom, she accepted a life-long position that can more easily be compared to religious service than to modern politics. This, perhaps more than anything, explains her remarkable humility. She is, in fact, a shy person whose nerves can still get a little shaky before she makes a speech, which is quite remarkable given that she spends most of her life meeting strangers and making speeches. No wonder her outspoken husband has said that no one in their right mind would choose to do her job.

The Real Elizabeth is, I hope, very different from most books about the British royalty that are published in the United States. There is an insatiable and entirely understandable appetite for gossip and scandal, and it must be said that even in a world so full of both, the House of Windsor has done its bit for splashy sensation. The essential outbreaks of royal mayhem are described and analyzed here too: without understanding the disastrous reign of Edward VIII or the breakdown of the marriage of Charles and Diana, we cannot possibly understand the Queen's reign. Further, I have spoken to many of those who know and work with the Queen, and I have tried to provide a rounded portrait of her as a woman as well as a monarch. My sources have included many of the politicians, officials and courtiers—as well as members of the Queen's close family—who never speak about the Queen and her role in public, and only rarely to outsiders, even in private.

My ultimate purpose here is to show how monarchy has actually worked, through the various political periods and crises of modern times, and to explain and make the case for a system of government that will strike most Americans as little short of bizarre. In other words, I have taken the Queen seriously, on her own terms. She is, after all, singular. No other ruler of a major country has lasted so long in modern times, or had to cope with such a mixture of international and family crises. It is a pretty safe prediction that there will never be anyone like her again. She is, in her own way, a major world figure whose story is both stranger and more complex than most people know.

THE REAL
ELIZABETH

Prologue: What the Queen Does

"She is never—you know—not the Queen."

A friend

"There's a lot of nonsense talked about what a terrible life she has. Nonsense! I think she loves it."

Senior politician

"I would earnestly warn you against trying to find out the reason for and explanation of everything. . . . To try and find out the reason for everything is very dangerous and leads to nothing but disappointment and dissatisfaction, unsettling your mind and in the end making you miserable."

Queen Victoria to a granddaughter, 1883

"Well . . . she knows what's going on. She has—a good nose for a story. *She would have been a good journalist."*

Senior member of the Royal Household, when asked by the author what he had missed about the Queen, 2011

She is a small woman with a globally familiar face, a hundred-carat smile—when she chooses to turn it on—and a thousand years of history at her back. She reigns in a world which has mostly left monarchy behind, yet the result of her reign is that two-thirds of British people assume their monarchy will still be here in a century's time. She is wry and knowing, but she feels a calling. She can brim with dry observations but she seems empty of cynicism.

There she is, in May 2011 and dressed in emerald green, arriving for her first visit to the Republic of Ireland. Aged eighty-five, she makes one of the most politically significant speeches of her life. "It is a sad and regrettable reality that through our history our islands have experienced more than their fair share of heartache, turbulence and loss. These events have touched many of us personally. . . . To all those who have suffered as a consequence of a troubled past I extend my sincere thoughts and deep sympathy." This is a highly emotional trip, recalling the murder of her relative Lord Mountbatten by the IRA in 1979, and centered on a visit to Croke Park, the stadium and headquarters of the Gaelic Athletic Association where in 1920, fourteen innocent people were shot by police and auxiliaries loyal to the Crown—to her grandfather—at the beginning of the bloody struggle for Irish independence.

This trip was a long time coming and security bosses on both sides of the Irish Sea had been pale-faced with worry. The visit was announced well in advance and the Queen does not cancel. As it happened, the vast majority of Irish people welcomed the visit; the Queen even shook hands with a representative of the die-hard republican and once pro-IRA Sinn Fein. So this was a small but significant page turn in history, recognizing that by 2011 what mattered to Irish and British citizens were their shared family, business, emotional and sporting connections, not the bloodied past. The Queen impresses on the Irish prime minister, Enda Kenny, that this is a visit she has waited much of her life to make, what he calls "a closing of the circle." In private she sits under the portrait of the Irish military leader Michael Collins. In public she bows her head in memory of the Irish rebels who died fighting the Crown.

Nobody else from Britain could have made such a visit of high-profile reconciliation, covered by more than a thousand journalists and reported all round the world. No British politician has served long enough, or been personally touched so closely, or could claim to speak for Britain itself. Ireland's President Mary McAleese is a class act, the first Northerner and the second woman to serve in the job. But no Briton other than the Queen has the authority to represent the British.

There she is again, a few days later, welcoming President Barack Obama to stay at Buckingham Palace. In the gusty sunshine over-looking the lawn there is picture-postcard pomp—a guard of Household Cavalry, marching soldiers, bagpipes, national anthems, the reverberations of artillery salutes. On the eve of his visit, speak-ing in Washington, Obama had gone out of his way to praise the Queen in lavish if not entirely politically accurate terms as "the best of England." His earlier visit had gone spectacularly well. Even so, this is a relationship which is also, in a gentler and more personal way, about friendship and reconciliation.

When Obama first became president a number of prominent people in London were uneasy. Here was a man who seemed cool about the (exaggerated) "special relationship" with Britain. He had no personal ties—or rather, just one, which was unhappy and about which he had written when younger. His grandfather had been arrested, imprisoned and tortured in what is now Kenya. The early years of the Queen's reign had been marked by a brutal war against the nationalist Mau-Mau there. Obama is a supremely professional politician, very unlikely to allow personal history to influence his decision making, but the unease was there. Once the pomp was over the Queen did her level best to make him and his wife, Michelle, feel especially welcome, showing the couple to their bedroom per-sonally.

On show was a shrewdly chosen selection of memorabilia from the Royal Archive—as there always is for a state visit. There was a note in George III's handwriting, from around 1780, lamenting "America is lost! Must we fall beneath the blow?" but going on to speculate about a future of trade and friendship. There were letters from Lincoln, Obama's hero, and from Queen Victoria to Lincoln's widow, as well as diary entries by Victoria showing her sympathy for black slaves and recording her excitement in meeting one, Josiah Henson, who she said had "endured great suffering and cruelty" before escaping to British Canada. There were records of a visit by the then Prince of Wales to Obama's home city of Chicago in 1860, and a handwritten note by the Queen Mother to the then Princess Elizabeth recording their visit to President Roosevelt in 1939 when they ate under the trees "and all our food on one plate . . . some ham, lettuce, beans and HOT DOGS too!" The image may have been homely, but it was a reminder of the vital wartime alliance which followed King George VI's most important overseas visit. Finally, there was a flag from Hawaii, Obama's birthplace.

This collection of archival items contained the essence of the case for monarchy. The Queen fulfills a constitutional role but also a personal one. By recalling American independence and the story of slavery, and by referring to places of particular interest to Obama, the array of memorabilia attempted to make an emotional connection—to find points of contact. (In return, Obama gave the Queen a book of photographs of her parents' visit to the United States on the eve of war.) Later during this visit, the president would hold important and potentially tricky talks with Prime Minister David Cameron about Libya, Afghanistan and their different approaches to economics, and the hope was that his visit with the Queen would put him in the warmest possible mood. As with the Irish visit, nobody else could do it. It must also be said, however, that the Queen can only work effectively because so many other people (such as the Royal Librarian, the Hon. Lady Roberts) work very hard behind the scenes, unknown to the public. This book is their story too.

But it is her story first. The best antidote to weariness or hostility about Queen Elizabeth II is to try to follow her around for a few months. From trade-based missions overseas to visits to small towns and hospitals, she endures a surprisingly grueling routine. It includes grand ceremonial occasions and light-footed, fast-moving trips to meet soldiers, business people, volunteers and almost every other category of citizen one can imagine. It eats up evenings, where at one palace or another thousands of people have been invited to be "honored" for their work or generosity. It involves the patient reading of fat boxes of serious paperwork, oozing from the governments who work under her name. In Whitehall, Britain's center of government, where they assess the most secret intelligence as it arrives, the Queen is simply "Reader No. 1."

Hers has been a life of showing up. But showing up is not to be underestimated. The Queen has a force-field aura that very few politicians manage to project today. An appearance by the British monarch creates an atmospheric wobble of expectation, a slight but helpless jitter. When she turns up, people find their heart rate rising, however much they try to treat her as just another woman. Somehow, despite being everywhere—in news bulletins, on postage stamps, on front pages—she has managed to remain mysterious. Her face moves from apparently grumpy to beaming, and back. Her eyes flicker carefully around. She gives little away.

After the rapids of family crisis and public controversy, the Queen now enjoys calmer waters. British royalty has become surprisingly popular around the world. She watched with great interest and some pleasure a recent film, featuring Colin Firth, about her father's struggle against his stutter and the man who helped him, the Australian Lionel Logue. (She remembers Logue vividly.) She herself was the subject of a blockbuster movie starring Helen Mirren. Her illustrious ancestress Elizabeth I was portrayed by Judi Dench in a film about Shakespeare. Firth, Mirren and Dench all won Oscars, as one of the Queen's children wryly notes.

The Queen is not an actor, but the popularity of the monarchy owes a lot to the way she performs. Life has taken her around the world many times and introduced her to leaders of all kinds, from the heroic to the monstrous; and to seas of soapy faces; and to forests of wiggling hands. Ever since she was a small girl, she has known her destiny. Though shy, she regards being Queen as a vocation, a calling which cannot be evaded.

Like any eighty-five-year-old she has been bereaved and suffered disappointment as well as enjoying success. She has lost a King, a Queen and Princesses—her father, mother, sister and the remarkable Diana—as well as close friends. She has borne four children and seen three of them divorced. Yet she can be satisfied. She knows her dynasty, unlike so many others, is almost certain to survive. Her heir and her heir's heir are waiting. With her, and her kind of monarchy, most of her people are content.

Those who can remember her as a curly-headed little girl are now a small platoon. On May 12, 2011, she became the second-longest-serving monarch in British history, having reigned for 21,645 days, beating George III's record. In September 2015, if she is still alive, she will outlast even Queen Victoria's record too. Her husband, now ninety, still has the gimlet stare and suspicious bearing of a man's man cast adrift in a world of progressives and liberals. He could have scaled most ladders. Instead, he chose to spend his life as "Consort, liege and follower."

The Duke of Edinburgh's life and the Queen's life have been lived in lockstep, through an annual circle of ritual and tradition, swiveling from palace to palace as the seasons change. Both of them dress up, often several times a day, for lunches, openings, speeches, military parades, investitures and dinners. The Queen's mornings begin as they have for most of her life, with BBC radio news, Earl Grey tea, the *Racing Post* and the *Daily Telegraph* and, while having breakfast toast with her husband, enjoying the music (ignorant people would call it noise) of her personal bagpiper in the garden. Near to her are the last truly dangerous members of the British monarchical system, the Queen's dogs—four corgis and three dorgis (a dachshund-corgi cross).

A discreet, protective staff she calls by their first names come and go. A typed sheet of engagements is waiting; soon the first of the red boxes of official papers, containing everything from minor appointments to alarming secret service reports, will arrive. The Queen may pay a visit upstairs to the domain of Angela Kelly, her personal assistant and senior dresser, who has suites off a narrow corridor just below the Buckingham Palace roof. A genial and down-to-earth Liverpudlian, she is one of the people closest to the Queen, family apart. She works with huge bolts of cloth, dummies and scissors to create many of the Queen's outfits. Before overseas or long domestic visits, she plans with the Queen the dresses, hats, bags and shoes she will bring with her. Outside designers are brought in from time to time. (One Scottish designer insisted on a full personal fitting. As she crouched down nervously with a tape measure, the Queen exclaimed: "Leg out! Arm out! Leg out!" and giggled as the measurements were taken.) A floor below Angela Kelly wait the old-fashioned leather suitcases and trunks for a Royal journey, each stamped simply with "The Queen." They have had a lot of use; the monarch is not a fan of the throwaway society.

Down in her office, the contents of the various official boxes are sorted out by her private secretary and carried upstairs to be scrutinized. She alone reads these; the Duke maintains a careful constitutional distance from some parts of her life, though he runs the estates and remains a very active nonagenarian, still often weaving through the London traffic at the wheel of his own, pleasantly anonymous taxi. Like anyone who has followed routines for so many years—the Queen is now the longest-lived monarch in her country's history—she hopes there will be a surprise today, if only a small one. As the day begins, she surely wonders, Now what? What will happen today?

THE JOB

Today, the Queen will dress and go out and do her job. Angela Kelly will have laid out clothes which will, they both hope, make the Queen stand out in a crowd and will be appropriate to whatever obligations lie ahead that day. At certain times of the year, of course, she will not be working. There are quiet family weekends and a long summer break, mostly at Balmoral in Scotland. Otherwise, however, the expectations of people—civil servants and politicians, tourists, presidents and the passing crowd—are so great that her duties never end.

As head of state, Queen Elizabeth is the living symbol of nations, above all that of the United Kingdom of Great Britain and Northern Ireland, but also fifteen others, including Australia, Canada, New Zealand and smaller countries, down to Tuvalu. She is different from most other constitutional monarchs. Unlike other states, Britain has neither a single written constitution nor any founding document. About a third of the Dutch constitution explains what the Dutch monarch's duties are. Spain's king is part of one of Europe's oldest and grandest royal houses, the Bourbons, but his job is strictly limited in the careful prose of the Spanish constitution.

The British Queen's authority is more like a quiet growl from ancient days, still thrumming and mysterious. She stands *for* the state—indeed, in some ways, at least in theory, she *is* the state. She is the living representative of the power structure that struggles to protect and sustain some 62 million people, and another 72 million in her other "realms."

She is not the symbol of the people. How could she or anyone represent the teeming millions belonging to many different ethnic groups and religions, and representing every political view, bias and age? Her enthusiasm for the Commonwealth of nations, which is not the private passion of many British politicians, has made her more interested in the lives of the new black and Asian Britons than one might expect. Receptions at Buckingham Palace are generally more socially and ethnically mixed than they are at Downing Street, or in the City. She is at her most relaxed and smiling with young people, nervous people and unflashy people. Watching her at official occasions, it is clear that the chores are the grand dinners and speeches.

Yet, like it or not, she is the symbol of the authority which drives the state servants and laws—the elections, armies, judges and treaties which together make modern life possible. For sixty years she has appeared in public to open *her* Parliament, to remember *her* nation's war dead, to review *her* troops or to attend services of *her* Church. "Britain" cannot go to the Republic of Ireland to finally heal a political breach that goes back to the Irish struggle for independence in the 1920s—but the Queen can. "Britain" cannot welcome a pope or a president. She can.

She has great authority and no power. She is a brightly dressed and punctual paradox. She is the ruler who does not rule her subjects but who serves them. The ancient meaning of kingship has been flipped; part of the purpose of this book is to explain how, and why, that has been done. Modern constitutional monarchy does not mean subjection, the hand pressed down on an unruly nation. Instead it offers a version of freedom. The Crown is not the government. There is a small, essential space between it and the day-to-day authority of ministers. It would be rude to say that those who govern are squatters in the state—for governments come from parliaments which are elected, and the ultimate bastions of our liberty. Nevertheless, governments are lodgers in the state. They are welcome for a while, but have no freehold rights.

The Queen stands for continuity. This may be a dull word, but when asked what the Queen is really about, "continuity" is the word used most often by other members of the royal family, by prime ministers, archbishops and senior civil servants. What do they mean? Not simply the continued existence of the country or the state. It is true that the state is a living and valuable presence before and after any one government. People look back to the past and imagine a future that outlives them: monarchy takes a real family and makes it the living symbol of that universal fact. A constitutional monarchy goes further. It claims to represent the interests of the people before they elected their current government, and after it has gone. A constitutional monarchy remembers. It looks ahead, far beyond the next election.

The distinction between state and government is an essential foundation of liberty. In Britain a pantomime of ritual has grown up to express it. At the annual State Opening of Parliament, the Queen reads out her prime minister's words, ventriloquizing for her government. She speaks with deliberate lack of emphasis or emotion: nobody must be able to hear her own feelings break through. A junior minister is taken hostage at Buckingham Palace to guarantee her safety and underline the separation of politics and state. When she leaves Westminster, he is released (after a decent drink) and normal politics resumes. The state and the government have come together, touched hands, and gone their separate ways. Other countries make a similar distinction, expressing it through written documents or powerless elected presidents; the British have long preferred a person.

In practice the Queen's job is a little harder than it looks. When the most important foreign leaders arrive for a state visit, the Queen greets them in the country's name with a smile and a gloved handshake and small talk, again deliberately designed never to offend. She offers lodging and pays kind attention to people she may privately regard as abominable or merely hideous bores. Guests at Buckingham Palace or at Windsor will be shown to their bedrooms by the Queen in person. Beforehand, she will have checked the rooms herself, making sure suitable books are left by the bed, that the flowers look good, and that everything is welcoming. At the grand dinners she will have checked the food, flowers and place settings: will everybody be satisfied with where they are seated, and get on with the people put beside them? She will have had her librarians dig up letters, photos or pictures which might particularly interest or amuse them.

When the guests arrive and the conversation starts she has to remember to dodge anything that might cause her ministers a head-ache. One former foreign secretary, Douglas Hurd, has watched her do it: "She's got quite an elaborate technique. When a visiting head of state, or whatever it is, begins to talk politics, begins to explain what's happening in his country, she says, 'That's very interesting Mr. President . . . and I'm sure the foreign secretary would very much like to discuss that with you.' And so you're shunted. The points change, and you're shunted onto a different line." Others talk about how she uses polite silence to deflect trouble, and when you ask people about their conversations with the Queen, they often bubble about her wit and insight—and then tell you only what *they* said to *her*. Clever.

Much the same seems to happen in her weekly audiences with her prime ministers, of whom there have been a dozen to date. Though these meetings are completely private (no note takers, no secretaries, no microphones), former premiers and civil servants talk about them as a kind of higher therapy, rather than a vivid exchange of views. For sixty years she has listened to whatever her prime ministers have said—self-justifying explanations, private whinges, a little malice about their rivals—without letting any of them know whose side she is on except, in the broadest sense, the side of the continuing government of the country. Sir Gus O'Donnell, a cabinet secretary who has worked with four prime ministers—Sir John Major, Tony Blair, Gordon Brown and now David Cameron, says: "They go out of their way not to miss it. It's a safe space where prime ministers and sovereigns can get together, they can have those sorts of conversations, which I don't think they can have with anybody else in the country . . . They come out of them better than they went in, let's put it that way."

She knows almost every state secret of the past sixty years. Gus O'Donnell again: "We give the Queen the minutes of cabinet, for instance, so she's up to date on the discussions, the decisions that have been made. She gets a lot of material about what the government's actually doing, in her red boxes." The Queen is very interested in issues involving the constitution—Sir Gus singles out current controversies about Britain's switch to fixed-term parliaments and the future of the House of Lords—and anything to do with Britain's military. She works hard, too, to support the civil service, who like her have to be neutral but get very little applause from the public or press. In public, in her Christmas broadcasts and many speeches, she generally takes great care to stay on the safe ground of general expressions of goodwill, although at Christmas she often touches on issues of the day. For decade after decade she has dodged traps that could have led the monarchy into serious danger. She has made mistakes, of course; everyone does. But overall she has managed this dance of discretion so adroitly that many people have concluded that she is herself almost without character—neutral, passive, even bland.

She is not. She has a long memory and shrewd judgment; she is a wicked mimic and is capable of sharp asides. She has been very frank about her children's scrapes. She has closely observed and drily described the oddities of foreign leaders and famous politicians. She has done it while playing patience during the evening at Balmoral, or with her legs tucked up under her on a sofa on the Royal Yacht, a glass of something cheerful in hand, or walking on beaches and hillsides. In private she has hugged and laughed; she has shown impatience with dawdlers and slow eaters. Though she does not like confrontation and has often subcontracted that out to her husband, she has strong views about people. But her job requires that she hide all this. Other people, celebrities and actors, are paid to have a "personality." She is required to downplay hers.

This does not mean her life is dull. "We're in the happiness business," whispers one of her ladies-in-waiting as the Queen heads for yet another line of shouting, waving children. It must be wonderful to cheer people up without cracking jokes or telling odd stories. She can do it simply by arriving, smiling, nodding and taking a posy or two. No one who has followed this now slightly stooping lady in her mid-eighties as she walks through small towns, foreign hotels, cathedrals and military barracks, casting sharp glances all around, and observed the grinning, pressing lines of people waiting for her, can doubt it. But in the happiness business, there is also a huge amount of ceremonial, religious and social business to be dealt with, week in, week out. (Some say too much, particularly for a woman of her age.)

The Queen stands atop the Anglican Church, that national breakaway from Rome hurriedly set up by her Tudor ancestor the beef-faced and priapic Henry VIII. She is called "Defender of the Faith" and "Supreme Governor of the Church of England." The former title is technically somewhat absurd since it was given to Henry by Pope Leo X before he rebelled. But the latter one certainly counts: the Queen appoints bishops and archbishops and takes her role as the fount of Anglican respectability very seriously, addressing the General Synod and talking regularly to its leading figures.

The current Archbishop of Canterbury, Rowan Williams, says she is formally the final court of appeal, the place where arguments stop. In practice, of course, she does not intervene in rows about the ordination of women priests or gay marriage, any more than she does in parliamentary arguments. But, says the Archbishop, "She believes that she has some responsibility for keeping an eye on the business of the church, some responsibility to support it, to get on the side of those who are administering the church, and she is herself very committed as a Christian." Williams says she was profoundly affected by being given a book of private prayers by his predecessor shortly before her Coronation, which she still uses. For her, Williams asserts, the Coronation was a vocation, "a calling, not a privilege but a calling. If it's costly, it's costly." As we shall see, at times it certainly has been.

The Queen is also "the fount of honors." She bestows medals, crosses, knighthoods and ribbons, mostly (but not always) on the advice of politicians, to those who are worthy (and sometimes not so worthy). Each one requires conversation, eye contact, briefing and time. She has so far bestowed 404,500 honors and awards, and personally held more than 610 investitures (the grand honor-giving ceremonies) since becoming Queen in 1952.

Then there are the armed forces. The Queen is Head of the Armed Forces. It is to the Queen that new soldiers, airmen and sailors pledge allegiance, and in whose name they fight and die. She has a special relationship with some regiments—her first official job was as a colonel-in-chief, and the Duke still is—and a general one with all. This role requires many more visits and ceremonies. She is also a patron of huge numbers of charities. They too lobby and plead for her time, often to encourage fund-raising. From time to time the royal family tries to organize their charitable work. After the death of her mother and sister, the family sat down at Sandringham around a card table and shared out the work they would have to take on. They discovered some charities had rather too many Royals associated with them, and others none at all, so some switching around was agreed.

Then there is Abroad. The Queen never forgets that she is Head of the Commonwealth, a title invented in 1949 to allow the newly independent republican India to keep its association with Britain. This responsibility obliges her to do a great deal of travel, all of which she undertakes in addition to visiting her other realms and the diplomatic and trade-boosting visits her government tells her each year she must make. In the Foreign Office, they draw up their wish list for state visits and other visits, arguing about which trading partner has priority over which, and which leader would be particularly gratified if the Queen arrived. And then they send the list to the Palace and another negotiation begins.

These visits are not jaunts. They involve a lot of planning, endless changes of dresses and hats and, above all, a staggering amount of listening, nodding and smiling. Most trying of all, there are the speeches. The Queen is a naturally shy and quiet person who even now, after all these years, gets no pleasure from public speaking whether the event is grand or modest. One journalist who has followed her for decades says, "Even if it is the Great Hall of the

People, or it is the Girl Guides' Association she gets nervous before the speech. And yet afterwards, once she's completed that speech and she's got marvellous congratulation and applause, then she's . . . really buzzing because it's out of the way. I've never seen her change once." As the Queen and Duke get older, they find these visits more tiring and trying. So far, they keep agreeing to go, in general twice a year.

Beyond all this, the Queen views the monarchy as a sort of national adhesive, making constant visits around the country to be seen, to greet and to thank people who are mostly ignored by the London power brokers and commercial grandees. She holds parties, lunches and charity gatherings at Buckingham Palace and Edinburgh's Palace of Holyroodhouse to thank or bring together other lists of good-doers, civic worthies and business strivers. At special themed receptions she honors all sorts of disparate groups—they might be Australians in Britain, or young people in the performing arts, or campaigners for the handicapped, or the emergency services. These events are meticulously planned. The Queen hangs over the lists of who may be invited, and why. She plans the evenings and the choreography, and manages to remember many of the names. Only by watching the delight of elderly volunteers whom nobody else had thought to make much of, or struggling young musicians, can one understand the quiet power of this mostly unreported monarchical campaign.

Finally there are the mass celebrations, the royal jubilees and weddings. The jubilees are an invented tradition that allow the monarchy to dominate, however briefly, the crowded news agenda of a busy country and enable people to look back at the last twenty-five, fifty or sixty years, and to look forward, too, in a kind of national pause for thought. The marriages may turn out well or not, but the weddings allow the most fanatically royalist, and many others, to go briefly mad.

By now, I hope the reader is feeling a little exhausted. (And keep in mind that I have not yet mentioned her additional roles of mother, grandmother, wife, aunt, horse owner, manager of farms and estates, employer and overall accountant-in-chief that fill in the quiet moments.) The point is, for most of us the Queen seems always to have been there. She has done her job so well that she has come to seem part of the natural order of things, along with the seasons and the weather. One day, of course, she won't be there. And when that day comes, there will be a gaping, Queen-sized hole in the middle of British life.

PART ONE

Dynasty Is Destiny:
How the British Monarchy
Remade Itself

The Queen is only the fourth head of a fairly new dynasty. If you put brackets around her uncle Edward VIII, who lasted less than a year, she is only the third of the Windsors. Yet the British monarchy itself is one of the world's oldest: the Queen can trace tiny flecks of her bloodline back to bearded Anglo-Saxons and ancient Scottish warlords. More substantially, Hanoverian ancestry remains a strong influence. Both she and her eldest son have faces that recall monarchs of the eighteenth century, the solemn early Georges. But like other families, monarchies can reinvent themselves. Today's House of Windsor created itself less than a century ago, leaping away from the Hanoverians and their German connections in 1917.

The old British monarchy—of Victoria, the fecund Queen-Empress, and her son Edward, the louche and shrewd King-Emperor—had been at the center of a golden web of royalty stretching across Europe and Russia. Monarchy was a family club, largely closed to outsiders. Britain's segment of the web had particularly close connections with German royal houses, connections that went back to the eighteenth century and the Hanoverians. Kaisers came to tea and joined parades dressed in British military uniform. They raced their yachts against those of their British cousins at Cowes. There might be mutual suspicion, but it was family rivalry rather than political.

The closeness was symbolized by the last visit King George V and Queen Mary made to Germany before the Great War. Arriving in Berlin in May 1913 for the wedding of the Kaiser's daughter to their cousin the Duke of Brunswick-Luneburg, they were greeted by Queen Mary's aunt the Grand Duchess of Mecklenburg-Strelitz—a very old English-born lady who remained in her north German estate until 1916. They went on to meet the Kaiser, Tsar Nicholas II, endless other dynastic cousins and what the family called simply "the royal mob." The mob noted the presence of film cameras, or what they called "those horrid Kino-men," but felt themselves a family, whose connections remained essential to the future of the "civilized" world.

George V was particularly fond of his Austro-Hungarian fellow Royals, and of numerous princely German relatives. Sir Frederick Ponsonby, the King's private secretary, noted of the visit, "whether any real good is done, I have my doubts. The feeling in the two countries is very strong" and George's biographer rightly said that, in the coming of the Great War, "King George V was no more than an anguished and impotent spectator."[1] Others at the time took the opposite view, or diplomatically pretended to: the British ambassador to Berlin Sir Edward Goschen said he thought the visit would prove "of lasting good."[2] Either way, Queen Mary had a lovely time in Berlin. By contrast, she dreaded a visit to Paris the following year, primarily because France was to her above all an alien republic and there were no friendly family faces to welcome her.

By 1917, however, deep into the bloodied mud of total war, this royal web seemed likelier to strangle the British monarchy than protect it. Germans had become loathed in Britain, their shops destroyed, their brass bands expelled, even their characteristic dogs put down. To be a monarch with German connections was uncomfortable. Rising radical and revolutionary feeling across Europe had made monarchs unpopular too. King George was already well aware of the danger to him of revolutionary socialist feeling. During 1911–12 Britain had faced mass strikes and great unrest. At times it seemed that London would be starved of food by militant dockers, while radical Liberals had struck at the aristocratic principle when the House of Lords blocked their "People's Budget." In the streets, a more militant socialism was being taught, with the earliest Labour politicians often defining themselves as antimonarchists in a way few would today. Labour's much loved early leader Keir Hardie was a lifelong republican who was particularly hated by the Palace. Though an MP, he had been banned from the Windsor Castle garden-party list for criticizing Edward VII's visit to see his cousin Tsar Nicholas in 1908. Later, he described George V as "a street corner loafer . . . destitute of ordinary ability." The King responded by calling him simply "that beast." For monarchs, even before the war came, these were unsettling times.

George, however, was lucky in his advisers, one above all. Lord Stamfordham's story began colorfully. As Arthur Bigge, the son of a Northumberland parson, he was an artillery officer who fought in the Zulu War of 1879. One of his friends was the son of France's deposed emperor Napoleon III, and when this young man was killed by a Zulu, Bigge was chosen to show his bereaved mother where it had happened, and to visit Queen Victoria to tell her the story. Queen Victoria liked Bigge so much that she immediately appointed him her assistant private secretary, and he spent the rest of his life working for the monarchy. When Edward VII became king, Bigge served his son, first as Duke of Cornwall, then as Prince of Wales, then as King George V, at which point Bigge became Lord Stamfordham. He had enormous influence on George, who once said he could hardly write a letter without Bigge's help.

At the start, though, Stamfordham did not get everything right. He and the King both had instinctively strong conservative

views, and during the constitutional crisis of 1910–11, Stamfordham advised George to face down the Liberal prime minister, Her-
bert Asquith. The Liberals were confronted by the Tory-dominated
House of Lords, which was blocking the radical "People's Budget."
Asquith had secured a promise from Edward VII to allow a deluge
of Liberal peers to be created as a last-resort way of swamping the
upper house. George V instinctively hated the idea, which seemed
an assault on the notion of aristocracy. Had the newly crowned
George V gone with his instincts and backed the peerage rather than
the elected government, he would have forced an immediate general election that would have been in part about the right of the
monarch to interfere in politics—the very thing his granddaughter
has spent her reign carefully avoiding.

Looking back nearly a century, what we now imagine as
golden-hazed "Edwardian" Britain was in fact a confrontational
and seething nation, rife with revolutionary thinking and physical
opposition. The Liberals, though more moderate than the rising
Labour and socialist parties, were convinced that Stamfordham was
their implacable enemy, sitting at the center of the imperial state.
Feelings ran high. The then Liberal chancellor, later prime minister
Lloyd George, disliked him so much that when Stamfordham came
for meetings in Downing Street during the war, he made him wait
outside on a hard wooden chair.

Yet Stamfordham learned from his mistakes. Later King George
said he was the man who had taught him how to be a king. He did
it by telling truth to power, and by listening. Stamfordham was a
dry and difficult man but he prided himself on his honesty, and in
particular telling his king the facts, however alarming they might
seem. In the years before World War I, he worked hard to turn the
sea dog and countryman into a politically aware national leader. By
the outbreak of war, and then through its first hard years, George
V had become a vivid and popular rallying point.

In the spring of 1917, the truths brought to the King by his adviser seemed very alarming indeed. The war was going badly. There were strikes and growing complaints that the King was closer to his German cousin, the hated Kaiser, than to his own people. This was entirely untrue, but George V did make crucial mistakes. He had opposed stripping the Kaiser and his family of their honorary commands of British regiments and their British chivalric honors, not to mention their banners hanging at St. George's Chapel, Windsor. Royal solidarity and ancient hierarchy apparently counted, even in the throes of an industrial war. Early in the war, King George had been furious at the campaign against Admiral Prince Louis of Battenberg, born German, but married to one of Queen Victoria's granddaughters and now British First Sea Lord. Battenberg had to quit, to the despair of his son, then a naval cadet himself, who wrote to his mother about the latest rumor "that Papa has turned out to be a German spy. . . . I got rather a rotten time of it." (That boy grew up to be Lord Louis Mountbatten, and one of the most influential figures in the Queen's life.)

These instinctive flinches against the rampant anti-German feelings of wartime Britain had allowed the King's critics to paint him as not wholly patriotic. Lloyd George, summoned to Buckingham Palace in January 1915, wondered aloud "what my little German friend has got to say to me." London hostesses mocked the court's Hanoverian character. Street-corner agitators warned about "the Germans" in the Palace. In fact, George was an exemplary wartime monarch, carrying out hundreds of troop visits and cutting down heavily on the expenses and living standards of the monarchy while the country suffered. He even gave up alcohol when Lloyd George asked him to, in order to set an example to drunkards (not an example, it has to be said, that Lloyd George himself followed). But the whispering went on and then grew louder. On March 31, 1917, there was a mass meeting at the Albert Hall chaired by one of Labour's great heroes, George Lansbury, to celebrate the fall of Tsar Nicholas II, with much cat-calling against monarchy in general. At the time, the government's wartime censors kept news of this out of the papers, but George was given eyewitness reports of what was said.

Stamfordham made it his job to get as much information as possible and to pass it to the King. When Ramsay MacDonald, later Labour prime minister, called for a convention to be held in Leeds "to do for this country what the Russian revolution had accomplished in Russia," or the trade union leader Robert Williams called for a "to let" sign to hang outside Buckingham Palace, George was told about it. Stamfordham said a few weeks later, "There is no socialist newspaper, no libellous rag, that is not read and marked and shown to the King if they contain any criticism, friendly or unfriendly to His Majesty and the Royal Family."[3]

In April 1917 the writer H. G. Wells wrote to *The Times* calling for the establishment of republican societies; he was also reported to have complained that England suffered from an alien and uninspiring court, to which George famously retorted: "I may be uninspiring, but I'm damned if I'm an alien." Henry Hyndman, the eccentric, top-hatted editor of the Marxist newspaper *Justice*, argued that the royal family is "essentially German" and called for a British Republic. At the other end of the political scale, the editor of the *Spectator* magazine, John St. Loe Strachey, told Stamfordham that there was a spread of republican sentiment among coal miners who "feel kings will stand together" and that there was "a trade union of kings."[4] Lady Maud Warrender said that when George was told that it was whispered he must be pro-German because his family had German names, "he started and grew pale." Wells returned to the attack, this time in the *Penny Pictorial*, calling for the monarchy to sever its destiny "from the inevitable collapse of the Teutonic dynastic system upon the continent of Europe . . . we do not want any German ex-monarchs here." The file headed "Unrest in the Country" had begun to thicken at the Palace.

More than ninety years on, it might seem that all this was mere hysterical fluff, and that George and his advisers were wrong to take it seriously. Small magazines, reported conversations in the coalfields, publicity-seeking authors—did it really add up to the beginning of the end for the British monarchy? The truth is that in 1917, British society was stretched to breaking point. People were ready to believe the wildest claims about German plots and secret networks of sexual blackmail, stretching right up to the court itself. The armies in France faced defeat and the Atlantic seabed was a graveyard of supply ships. Russia had been engulfed, Germany was next and there was rising militancy in British factories. In Britain the key wartime leader was not the King, but the King-mocking Lloyd George, soon to be hailed as "the man who won the war." Aristocracy, which has always buttressed monarchy, was on its knees, its sons dead or maimed and its estates facing financial ruin. The monarchy, it seemed, had few powerful friends. Finally, George V decided that if the monarchy was to survive in Britain, it must be radically reformed.

Advised by Stamfordham, King George made a series of changes which have had a huge influence on the current Queen's reign. The first and most public was to change his name, and that of the dynasty. "Saxe-Coburg-Gotha" was not only a mouthful but rather obviously German. It had to go. Tellingly, George did not know what his own original surname might be: it was lost in the tangled skeins of monarchical bloodlines and uncontrolled hyphenation. The Royal College of Heralds was consulted. They told the King his surname was not Stewart. It might be Guelph. More probably it was Wipper or Wettin, neither of which sounded helpfully British. So the search began for an invented surname. Tudor-Stewart, Plantagenet, York and Lancaster were all discussed but cast aside, as was the too-obvious "England," which would hardly have pleased the Scots, Irish or Welsh. More obscure suggestions included D'Este and Fitzroy. Clever Lord Stamfordham went back to the place-name of the King's favorite palace and suggested "Windsor." Not only did it sound good, it later turned out that Edward III had once used the name too, so there was even a slender historical explanation.

Thus, on July 17, 1917, the Windsor dynasty was born. George V declared and announced "that We for Ourselves and for and on behalf of Our descendants . . . relinquish and enjoin the discontinuance of the use of the degrees, styles, dignities, titles and honours of Dukes and Duchesses of Saxony and Princes and Princesses of Saxe-Coburg and Gotha, and all other German degrees." A cascade of further name changes followed which confuse many people even today about who was really who. There were the Tecks, for instance. George V's wife, Queen Mary, or May, was the daughter of Francis, Duke of Teck, who had married one of George III's granddaughters, the famously substantial Mary Adelaide, known in the family as "fat Mary" and memorably described as being "like a large purple plush pincushion." George V's in-laws therefore included a lot of Tecks, and for de-Tecking, mellifluous British place-names were at a premium. One of Queen Mary's brothers became the Marquis of Cambridge and another, the Earl of Athlone. Similarly, the Battenbergs—descended from Queen Victoria and the Princes of Hesse, and connected to the Tsar's family— became Mountbattens, one being renamed Marquis of Milford Haven and another Marquis of Carisbrooke. Anything Germanic was briskly rubbed out.

Less publicized but more important than the name changes was an announcement by George V and Queen Mary that, as noted by the King in his diary, they "had decided some time ago that our children would be allowed to marry into British families. It was quite an historical occasion."[5] As far back as the eighteenth century, politicians and much of the British public had not liked the Hanoverian habit of marrying German princesses and princelings, since it seemed to mean that British taxes subsidized foreign families. Queen Victoria herself had pointed out that her family's dynastic marriage habits had caused "trouble and anxiety and are of no good" when European countries went to war with one another: "Every family feeling was rent asunder, and we were powerless."[6] Yet the habit had continued. Now Victoria's instinct that "new" blood—by which she meant blood from non-royal British families—would strengthen the throne morally and physically, became a settled policy.

In effect, the British monarchy was being nationalized. The Bishop of Chelmsford, an influential figure, had told Stamfordham that "the stability of the throne would be strengthened if the Prince of Wales married an English lady . . . she must be intelligent and above all full of sympathy." A little later, another churchman, Clifford Woodward, the Canon of Southwark, said to Stamfordham that the Prince of Wales should live for a year or two in some industrial city, perhaps Sheffield, and marry an Englishwoman, preferably "from a family which had been prominent in the war."[7] Though "David," the Prince of Wales, would later follow a very different path, the King's announcement in 1917 of this new policy paved the way for Elizabeth Bowes Lyon, a Scotswoman whose family had indeed been prominent in the war, to marry Albert, also known as "Bertie," the Duke of York and later George VI. The policy also made it possible for Prince Charles to marry Diana, and later Camilla; and it meant that Prince William could marry Kate Middleton. It may seem almost commonplace now, but marrying their subjects had hardly occurred to the old House of Saxe-Coburg-Gotha.

The King's next move was more brutal, some say cowardly. George V cut off his "Cousin Nicky," the deposed Tsar Nicholas II, and his entire family, leaving them to the tender mercies of Lenin's Bolshevik revolution. The Tsar, unlike the Kaiser, had been a loyal ally of Britain's until his empire collapsed. Though George cannot have known that the Romanovs would be assassinated in a cellar, he knew they were in serious danger, and that they hoped for refuge in Britain. Initially he agreed. But left-wing opinion was violently hostile to the Tsar and supportive of the revolution, and as Kenneth Rose, George V's biographer, revealed, the King panicked. At his request Stamfordham bombarded Number Ten with notes making it clear that the Tsar was not welcome after all. Much was made of petty issues, such as the lack of suitably grand accommodation. In the end, however, it seems that George was at least willing to look the other way while Nicholas and his family were imprisoned, moved and finally killed. (The current Queen read the evidence and wrote with a flourish across a manuscript of Rose's book: "Let him publish.")

No action could more eloquently show the radical change brought about by the war. Before it, in 1905, King George's father had refused the Tsar's plea for Britain to restore normal relations with Serbia, after the particularly brutal assassination of its king. In words that sound like those of George Bernard Shaw or even Oscar Wilde, Edward VII explained that his trade was simply "being a king. . . . As you see, we belonged to the same guild, as labourers or professional men. I cannot be indifferent to the assassination of a member of my profession or, if you like, a member of my guild. We should be obliged to shut up our business if we, the Kings, were to consider the assassination of kings as of no consequence at all."[8] Now his son had calmly refused to come to the aid of Nicholas II, which later resulted in the assassination of the Tsar himself. A revolution can focus the mind of a monarch as effectively as a judicial death sentence for lesser mortals.

⚜

The next change was to the honors system. Most countries have some such system; Britain's was both limited and tightly entwined with royal supporters. Of the ancient orders, the oldest is the Order of the Garter, established by Edward III probably in 1344 and limited to the monarch, the heir and up to twenty-four other members or "knights companions." Membership is in the monarch's gift. Today's Knights and Ladies of the Garter, who parade each June at Windsor for a ceremony during Royal Ascot week, wearing Tudor caps with ostrich and heron feathers, blue velvet capes and blue garters, are a mix of aristocrats, former prime ministers and retired civil servants. There are also "Stranger Knights" of the Garter who are foreign monarchs: in 1915, both Kaiser Wilhelm and the Austro-Hungarian emperor Franz Joseph were stripped of their memberships.

Other old orders include Scotland's Order of the Thistle, which goes back to 1687 and is limited to sixteen knights and ladies, and the Irish Order of St. Patrick, now defunct. Aside from these, the grandest is the Order of the Bath, founded by the first of the Hanoverians, George I, in 1725. Though the name refers to the ancient medieval practice of requiring that new knights be bathed for purification, the order has a less elevated origin: it was created partly because the first and infamously corrupt British prime minister Robert Walpole wanted a new form of patronage. Extended after the Napoleonic wars, today it is also used by Britain to honor eminent foreigners, from overseas generals to leaders. Two of them, the tyrants Nicolae Ceauşescu of Romania and Robert Mugabe of Zimbabwe, were eventually stripped of the honor.

For most of its history the British monarchy has been criticized by artists and intellectuals for being insufficiently interested in the arts, writing or ideas generally. This was considered a problem even during the early years of Queen Victoria's reign, when it was noticed that Britain had nothing like the Prussian Pour le Mérite decoration, or the French honors for cultural and scientific achievement. In 1902 Edward VII instituted the Order of Merit to mark his Coronation. Unlike most other honors, it carries no aristocratic handle and has no connection with the government; it is in the gift of the King or Queen alone, and is limited to twenty-four members. Perhaps as a result it is one of the few British systems of award with an almost faultless record. Of all the figures in science, the arts and politics during the twentieth century one might have expected and hoped to be represented, a surprising proportion actually have been. From figures of the Victorian Age still alive in the early days (such as Florence Nightingale and Thomas Hardy), through the great composers (Britten and Vaughan Williams), poets (T. S. Eliot and Ted Hughes), artists (Henry Moore and Lucien

Freud, writers (E. M. Forster and Henry James), and a wide range of scientists (Paul Dirac and Tim Berners-Lee), the roll call has been very impressive. There have been admirals aplenty and even the political choices, such as Attlee and Thatcher, have been well made.

In general, the Order of Merit is a club for people who need only their surname to describe them. They get the occasional lunch or dinner, all together with the Queen, and they get their portraits painted. But OM has nothing to do with pomp or pageantry. It is the nearest Britain has to a gathering of "the immortals"—though as one of them once put it to me, beaming happily, "There are, I think, rather more immortals than there are of us."

Until 1917, these, plus a special order for diplomats and another for personal service to the monarch, the Royal Victorian Order, comprised the honors system. There were military honors too, of course, but nothing for all those ordinary Britons who served in other ways—giving money, providing extraordinary service, doing something "above and beyond."

Up to George V's reign it could be argued that being honored and having "an honor" were two different things. The approval of fellow citizens and private marks of respect, plus the occasional gong from a charity or civic organization, were the most anyone could expect. George changed that when he instituted the Order of the British Empire on June 4, 1917. It has five classes, running from the Knight Grand Cross to the more humble Member. The top two classes create Knights or Dames, and whereas the higher ones are limited in number, the simple OBEs and MBEs are not. The order is divided into military and civilian wings, and the latter in particular has substantially increased the influence of the monarchy. Many of the 404,500 honors that have been conferred by the Queen are OBEs and MBEs: the twice-yearly lists of celebrities, sports stars and others have become a staple for newspaper comment, congratulation and disappointment. The notion of such an honor was almost certainly the idea of Lord Esher, a onetime Liberal MP whose long service as a courtier had started in Victorian times (he installed a lift for Queen Victoria at Windsor, and pushed her wheel-chair round Kensington Palace) and who was later heavily involved in Edward VII's reign. Esher was sinuous, bisexual and a bit too much of a flatterer for George's taste, but he was shrewd and saw the need for a more democratic honor.

The war had prompted the distribution of new military honors to vast numbers of frontline heroes, while at home the idea was that the OBE would go to people involved in the enormous voluntary efforts being made. Since it was impossible for the Palace to find and assign those to be honored, this became almost entirely in the gift of the government of the day. Among the first recipients were trade union officials, including the left-wing William Appleton of the General Federation of Trade Unions and Ben Turner of the textile workers. By the end of 1919, twenty-two thousand OBEs had been awarded, many to factory workers and charitable campaigners. The monarchy was putting down new roots in the very areas where it felt threatened. Unfortunately the postwar government of Lloyd George not only sold many peerages and knighthoods, but also treated the OBEs as a kind of bargain-basement offer; for a time they became as the Order of the Bad Egg. But in the decades since, the OBE has risen in status, rather than declined, and it is now at least as important to the British honors system as the Légion d'Honneur is in France.

⸎

The final founding act of the House of Windsor merely took a habit of earlier twentieth-century monarchy and pushed it further. Edward VII had understood the importance of being seen by his people and making regular visits to open hospitals, launch ships and inspect regiments. The Victorian royals had had their names appended to everything from children's hospitals to major charities. But George and Mary were in a different league. During the industrial strife of the prewar period they visited industrial areas of England, Scotland and Wales. George even went down a coal mine and called on bereaved miners' families. But war brought a far greater drive to get out and visit ordinary people. Wartime Britain depended on voluntary organizations in a way that is hard to appreciate today; from 1914 to 1918, about ten thousand new ones were formed. Having a royal patron or connection, or even a royal visit, helped raise money, and the renamed Windsors put themselves at the center of an endless flurry of fund-raising and morale boosting.

Recently George V has not had a good press. He is remembered as a philistine, obsessed by outdated rules of dress and etiquette, and criticized for being overenthusiastic about his world-class stamp collection. He was certainly a naval martinet, equally capable of intimidating visitors and his children. His time as Duke of York was particularly unimpressive; as his official biographer put it, "For seventeen years in fact he did nothing at all but kill animals and stick in stamps."[9] But like others who waited long to become king, George greatly improved when he finally got the job. After his bumpy start, many of his later political interventions were well judged. Following a bad fall from his horse during the Great War, he was often in great pain and his already short temper became shorter still. But he coped well with a changed world in which socialist politicians arrived at Buckingham Palace and the aristocracy was losing its power.

When he first became king before the war, George V loathed having to side with the democratically elected radical Liberal government against the House of Lords. But he bit his tongue and grimly got on with it. He found young Winston Churchill an impudent puppy and never took to cocky Lloyd George, particularly when he began to debase the honors system by selling off titles. But there was no public protest: George sat them both out. Later, after the creation of the Irish Republic, he made a truly important intervention in Northern Ireland; his appeal for conciliation did much to soothe tempers when it seemed to many that a wider war in Ireland was unavoidable.

Later in life, remembering the Great War with horror, he was too soft on the subject of Hitler and too skeptical of Churchill's warnings, but he was hardly alone in that. For this story, what matters most is how King George remade the monarchy itself. How the Queen reigns today, what she does, how she is seen and described—all have their origins in decisions taken by her grandfather when Europe was writhing in blood-soaked turmoil and Britain was facing starvation and defeat at the hands of U-boat captains. This is the first man who matters in Elizabeth's life, the cigar-scented, bearded old naval officer whom she played with as a child and remembers well, George V really was the founder of "the Firm."

Through it all, the King was greatly helped by his wife. In press photographs and formal pictures, Queen Mary looks about as grandly stony-faced as any Royal could be. She is a dominant figure in the story of the House of Windsor, born at Kensington Palace in the zenith of Queen Victoria's reign, surviving both her husband and her son King George VI, and living, just, to see her granddaughter Elizabeth be crowned queen in 1953. Her birth had been communicated to the royals of Europe by letters written in German; she watched her son's funeral on television. Queen Mary's influence on today's British monarchy was considerable, if mostly forgotten. Although she was imposing—she was rather like the frosted prow of some ancient warship—and overenthusiastic about being given presents by those she visited, Mary was a keen social reformer and dedicated good-doer. As her husband reshaped the monarchy, she formed a close alliance with a radical female trade union leader named Mary Macarthur who had led campaigns to raise the wages of the "sweated labor" of Edwardian women sewing blouses, working in jam factories or forging chains. A notorious firebrand, Macarthur was married to the Labour Party chairman Will Anderson. When Macarthur was invited by Queen Mary to Buckingham Palace, she, in Macarthur's own words, "positively lectured the Queen on the inequality of the classes, the injustice of

it." She concluded, rightly or not, that "The Queen does understand and grasp the whole situation from a Trade Union point of
view."[10]

The first "situation" was the profound effect of the war from
its earliest days on trade and business, as large numbers of female
workers lost their jobs. Queen Mary and her aristocratic friends had
encouraged a great surge of knitting and needlework as war work,
which only made life harder for female employees of the clothing
industry. Macarthur begged one friend to do everything in her power
"to stop these women knitting!" Queen Mary got the point and
launched The Queen's Work for Women Fund, which raised money
to subsidize projects for unemployed women. An all-party committee was set up, and though the Queen herself did not join the MPs,
she heckled them from the sidelines and interested herself in the
problem, behavior that was new to royalty. As the war dragged on,
more and more women were recruited to replace fighting men, and
the challenges changed. Queen Mary, like the King, became an
obsessive and relentless visitor to food centers and hospitals, always
insisting on seeing the most seriously wounded. She worked to raise
money for relief funds and Christmas boxes for troops, and was
affectionately described as "a charitable bulldozer." In her paperwork and replies to charitable requests, she was equally relentless.
She was later said to have retorted to a tired princess complaining
about yet another boring hospital visit, "We are the royal family—
and we love hospitals." And she noted in the margin of one biography of her, which claimed that she was easily bored, "As a matter of
fact, The Queen is never bored." It is an attitude, a doggedness, the
current Queen shares.

After the war ended, all this activity became part of the early
Windsors' unending effort to demonstrate royal relevance. There
was plenty of evidence of the need for change. In 1918, Lord Cromer,
a kind of ancient crocodile of public service, warned that "the
Monarchy is not so stable now." That November, George V visited
a rally of thirty-five thousand ex-servicemen in Hyde Park, and

though he and other members of the royal family were duly cheered, afterward the men broke through to press round the King, complaining about their poor pensions, joblessness and lack of decent houses. He was mobbed, not in an entirely friendly way, and nearly pulled off his horse. Protest banners were raised and it was no easy thing for the police to get him safely out of the park. After silently riding back to Buckingham Palace with the Prince of Wales, the King dismounted and said: "Those men were in a funny temper," before shaking his head and striding into the building.

As a consequence of this sort of political pressure, the charitable efforts and public visits by the Royals became the monarchy's most notable aspects, arguably more important than its ceremonial state functions. The future king George VI was made president of the Boys Welfare Association, and the Prince of Wales, later Edward VIII, became patron of the National Council of Social Services. (The latter was sent on visits across the more depressed parts of Britain, during which he demonstrated the charisma he would become famous for.) George V began to compile a map showing the charitable public work being done by the family, almost like a military campaign, with flags to show where they had been; later he produced a chart that showed the productivity of its individual members, which would be brought to him each Christmas at Sandringham. One writer describes "the King poring over his charts like a sea captain over his log books."[11]

Not all the early reform ideas were immediately accepted. Clive Wigram, a former Bengal Lancer who became equerry to George and later his private secretary, argued shortly after the war that it was time to open up Buckingham Palace and its garden to "people of all classes," including schoolteachers and civil servants, "on the lines of the White House receptions." With that idea, Wigram was too early by about eighty years. But in all this we can see what was, effectively, the creation of a new kind of monarchy. The crisis of 1917 produced a "Britishized" royal family that cut itself off from its German origins and its Russian relatives, and made determined efforts to dig itself into the subsoil of British life more snugly than before. Lord Stamfordham, apart from choosing its name, gave the House of Windsor its founding principle when he wrote in the same year, "We must endeavour to induce the thinking working classes, socialist and others, to regard the Crown, not as a mere figurehead and an institution which, as they put it, 'don't count,' but as a living power for good . . . affecting the interests and well-being of all classes." That was the job George set out to do, and which his son and granddaughter then took on. It is the most important sentence a British courtier has ever written, and it remains the most influential.

Even as the House of Windsor changed, the royal family was still extremely rich, attended by aristocratic servants and most of the time physically remote in their castles and palaces. At Buckingham Palace during the 1920s, a brown Windsor silence descended, heavy curtains and country-life routines shutting out the febrile noise of the Jazz Age. After the war, George and Mary stayed in Britain, traveling abroad for just seven weeks during the sixteen years between the Armistice and the King's death. He preferred the company of his immediate family to that of anyone else; living as a pious countryman, his day was run with clockwork precision, attended by a pet parrot and emotionally dependent on a daily phone call to his sister, Princess Victoria. (In one of the many good stories about George, she was once put through to Buckingham Palace and began the conversation: "Hello, you old fool," only to be interrupted by the operator: "Beg pardon, your Royal Highness, His Majesty is not yet on the line."[12]) He was contemptuous of literary types and intellectuals generally, dismissing them as "eyebrows"—until he discovered the correct word was highbrow.

Yet politically, the man Princess Elizabeth came to know as "Grandpa England" had proved himself an astute operator, a master of the strategic retreat who was determined to win over working-class critics, if not eyebrows. When Britain's first, short-lived Labour government arrived in 1924, George speculated privately on what his grandmother Queen Victoria would have made of it (not much), but then went on to do his best to make the new cabinet ministers— described by one as "MacDonald the starveling clerk, Thomas the engine-driver, Henderson the foundry labourer and Clynes the mill-hand"[13] —feel welcome at Buckingham Palace, Windsor and Balmoral. He developed real friendships with several of them. Under George V, the imperial pomp of the nineteenth century and the angry confrontations of Edwardian Britain faded; despite all the dire predictions, the monarchy once again became a symbol of unity, easing itself away from the political fray.

Another monarch might not have pulled it off. Had George's weak, noisy elder brother Eddy, Duke of Clarence, not died of flu in 1892, the story of the British monarchy might have been shorter. King George, who married the woman who had originally been betrothed to Eddy, displayed many traits which reappear in the current Queen's reign. He was quietly pious and emotionally reserved, with an utter belief in duty and family. More than seventy years ago the fervently patriotic historian Sir Arthur Bryant said of George V that he and his Queen represented the secret convictions of every decent English person at a time when other more intellectual leaders of the nation were "preaching the gospel of disintegration and many of its social leaders were making bad manners and loose living a social fashion."[14]

Despite the florid language, Bryant's judgment also applies to Queen Elizabeth. This is hardly surprising: for the first ten years of her life, Grandpa England was part of her life, waving at her from his window in Buckingham Palace, playing with her as he had not with his own children, and delighting in her company. After his death, which moved Elizabeth greatly, his widow, Queen Mary, was heavily involved in her education. If she is her parents' child, she was her grandparents' grandchild too.

When Elizabeth was born in 1926, she was joining not just a

family, but a family campaign. A decade later, however, the campaign—and the House of Windsor—almost completely came apart.

UNCLE DAVID'S CRISIS

The Queen's "Uncle David," as King Edward VIII was known in the family, was the Bad King, the Windsor Who Got It Wrong. He was the vain, self-indulgent celebrity who demonstrated that charisma, while useful in politics or entertainment, is a flimsy material from which to build a constitutional monarch. Bored by duty, King Edward sought pleasure. And when a senior royal behaves truly badly, he (or she) wrecks everything.

The dreadful warning of Edward VIII is one of the foundations of the Queen's worldview. Up until she was nine, she knew him quite well as the engaging, cheerful Uncle David who would romp into her parents' home and play games. Then he stopped romping and vanished into newspaper headlines and exile.

The droll, immaculately dressed, yet always sad-eyed prince had for a long time been the hope of the British Empire. Trained by the navy, he struggled hard during the Great War to be allowed to fight in the trenches, getting near enough to the front line to be shelled. After the war, he had been sent on ritual tours of the Empire, touching that now-vanished world at its grandest moment before it began to crumple, meeting and greeting adoring crowds from the highlands of India to the snowy wastes of Canada. He read out the speeches written for him with fluency and grace. In the 1920s he was, for British newspaper readers, the beau ideal of the modern man. Though a demon rider to hounds, he also sought out the new world of nightclubs and golf links. He was taken at face value by the masses, in Britain and overseas, as an attractive man of energy, advanced views and great charisma. Yet "David" was, before Diana, the prime example of what can happen when a leading member of the royal family starts to behave like a starstruck celebrity. The little people's rules did not apply to him; as well, he was privately contemptuous of the courtly world enclosing him.

Despite his bad behavior, one can sympathize. His autobiography, though self-serving and whiny, provides a convincing account of the stultifying life of George V's interwar court, with its slow dinners, endless protocol and early nights. Edward was also tinged with the progressive ideas of the day. When his father, at the end of the Great War, called upon his eldest son to remember his position and who he was, Edward reflected: "But who exactly was I? The idea that my birth and title should somehow or other set me apart from and above other people struck me as wrong. . . . Without understanding why, I was in unconscious rebellion against my position. That is what comes, perhaps, of sending an impressionable Prince to school and war."[15] But Edward rebelled not by rethinking the role and rhythm of monarchy, or even declaring for its abolition, but by being selfish and wayward. He took married mistresses, then brutally dumped them. He danced into the small hours and infuriated his staff with his petulant demands. Behind the scenes, he caused despair to the people on whom he depended, and no senior member of the royal family can afford to do that. Unlike the rest of us, they are attended on, followed and guided by a small army of their own. And as in any army, if the chief loses the support of the soldiers, everything goes.

"Tommy" Lascelles, the decorated war veteran and intensely patriotic assistant private secretary to the Prince of Wales, was starstruck by Edward when he first met him. A passionate monarchist who later served George VI and, briefly, the present Queen, Lascelles was delighted by his new job. As time went on, though, he grew more and more alarmed by the capriciousness of his "Chief"; in the end, he became thoroughly disillusioned. During their 1927 tour of Canada, he took counsel from the then prime minister, who was part of the British group:

I felt such despair about him [the Prince of Wales] that I sought
a secret colloquy with Stanley Baldwin one evening . . . I told
him directly that, in my considered opinion, the Heir Apparent,
in his unbridled pursuit of wine and women, and whatever selfish whim occupied him at the moment, was rapidly going to the
devil, and unless he mended his ways, would soon become no fit
wearer of the British Crown. I expected to get my head bitten
off; but Baldwin heard me to the end, and, after a pause, said he
agreed with every word I had said. I went on, "You know, sometimes when I sit in York House waiting to get the result of some
point-to-point in which he is riding, I can't help thinking that
the best thing that could happen to him, and to the country, would
be for him to break his neck." "God forgive me," said Stanley
Baldwin, "I have often thought the same."[16]

That is quite a moment: the prime minister and a private secretary to the heir to the throne agreeing it would be better for Britain
if the future king were killed in an accident. Lascelles considered
resignation, but was short of money and long on patriotism.
Encouraged by his wife, he soldiered on. Yet only a year later, writing to her during another tour, this ardent royalist was questioning
whether monarchy was really such a "flawless and indispensable
institution" after all. The thoughtless behavior of the Prince had
made the life of any courtier with the slightest self-respect intoler-
able. Lascelles reflected: "It is like being the right-hand man of a
busy millionaire, when one is not at all certain that capitalism is a
good thing. . . . Why *should* I undo an hour's work just because
another man suddenly decides he wants to play golf at three instead
of five? Why *should* I continually hang about on one foot or the
other because another man can't take the trouble to go and change
his clothes in time?"[17] For an explanation as to why the Queen
places such emphasis on behaving well to her staff (never her "servants"), and expects her family to treat them with similar thought-
fulness and courtesy, look no further than Uncle David.

Lascelles—not the last senior courtier to grind his teeth about a Prince of Wales—finally exploded at Edward during their lion- and elephant-hunting expedition in East Africa in November 1928. When the King fell seriously ill, Baldwin cabled the Prince repeat- edly, begging him to come home at once. Lascelles showed Edward the cables, but the Prince, who was having far too much fun to want to leave Africa, replied that he didn't believe a word. It was, he said, "just some election dodge of old Baldwin's. It doesn't mean a thing." Lascelles recounted that after this "incredibly callous behaviour, he lost his temper with the heir to the British Empire: 'Sir,' I said, 'the King of England is dying; and if that means noth- ing to you, it means a great deal to us.' He looked at me, went out without a word, and spent the remainder of the evening in the suc- cessful seduction of a Mrs. Barnes, wife of the local Commissioner. He told me so himself next morning."[18]

In January 1929, Lascelles wrote the Prince a blunt letter and later gave him a verbal dressing-down. As Lascelles described it, "I paced his room for the best part of an hour, telling him, as I might have told a younger brother, exactly what I thought of him and his whole scheme of life, and foretelling, with an accuracy that might have surprised me at the time, that he would lose the throne of England." To their mutual credit the two men parted relatively affa- bly. Lascelles returned to serve George V shortly before he died, and remained at Buckingham Palace through the next two reigns. He was not surprised by the abdication when it came, but he was appalled by what he saw as a dereliction of duty. Once exiled, the Duke of Windsor referred to Lascelles simply as "the evil snake."

Some argue that the abdication crisis of 1936 was the defining moment of the Windsors; it was certainly their biggest shock. For seventy years, the crisis has been exhaustively described by histori- ans, novelists and journalists: the wild rumors about the sexual hold Wallis Simpson had over the King; the brutal political battle between the King and Stanley Baldwin; the endless arguments about a morganatic marriage (in which he would have been King but Wallis would not have been Queen); and the fight over money and status when the King finally did abdicate. What matters in the Queen's story is that without the abdication, Elizabeth would have led a quiet life, probably as a little-known royal countrywoman, enjoying her dogs and horses and supporting local charities. Her father would surely have lived longer since he would not have had to endure the heavy responsibilities of kingship during the world war to come. Her sister too would have led a happier and more private life. In the event, Elizabeth seems to have observed which paths "David" chose and invariably moved in the opposite direction—as evidenced most especially by her careful negotiation of that other great embarrassment for the Windsor dynasty, Diana's separation from Prince Charles.

During the abdication crisis, the new dynasty looked into the abyss. Had Edward fought to stay on as King and succeeded, it might well have meant the breakup of the British Empire, with very great consequences for the war to follow. As it was, the institution of monarchy was exposed and sniggered at around the world. The House of Windsor felt itself wobble. These things are not forgotten in the family.

Almost as soon as Edward VIII abdicated and became the Duke of Windsor, going abroad to marry without the support of his brother or parents, he was vigorously erased from the story. The monarchy's solid virtues were reinstated, and the British court swiftly reverted to the style of the old king George V. Once again, the royal family embraced the values it had so long embodied: convention, family, duty.

GOOD KING GEORGE

Anyone looking for a way to better understand King George VI's service to his country should not turn first to the recent film about his struggle with his stammer. Good though it is, the movie's unforgettable image is of Colin Firth bellowing four-lettered words.

Look instead at a photograph of "Bertie" when he was Prince of Wales, such as the Philip de László portrait of 1931, and then compare it to a picture of him after the war, such as the official portrait in RAF uniform taken twenty years later. The King experienced health problems as he aged, and, like most of his generation, he was a heavy smoker. Even so, the alteration is shocking. In his mid-thirties, he looked like an adult boy, with a sensitive, carefree face, big dark eyes and full lips. By his mid-fifties, he has the hair of a young man and the face of someone in his seventies; his visage is haggard, lined and sunken, an image of exhausted decay. Even though he worked in Churchill's shadow, being a wartime leader did this to him.

Another measure of the alteration can be found in the fearlessly frank diaries of Harold Nicolson, the politician and writer responsible for the official life of George's father. In 1929 he found the Prince "just a snipe from the Windsor marshes" but by 1940 was writing after meeting him that he was no longer "a foolish loutish boy" but calm and reassuring. Nicolson wrote that he and the Queen were "resolute and sensible. WE SHALL WIN. I know that now."[19]

George VI knew what being King would do to him. He felt he was horribly ill-equipped for the job. On the day "David" finally made it clear to his younger brother that he was abdicating, after having left him hanging in suspense for days, the future King went to see his mother, Queen Mary, "& when I told her what had happened I broke down and sobbed like a child."[20] (She said later that he cried for an hour on her shoulder.) The next day, as he was watching his brother make his final preparations for departure, he told Lord Mountbatten, one of his closest friends, "Dickie, this is absolutely terrible. I never wanted this to happen; I'm quite unprepared for it. David has been trained for this all his life. I've never even seen a State Paper. I'm only a Naval Officer, it's the only thing I know about."[21] For once, Mountbatten's encyclopedic memory for royal anecdotage proved useful: he happened to remember his father telling him that King George V had said just the same when his elder brother died, only to be told: "George, you're wrong. There is no more fitting preparation for a King than to have been trained in the Navy."

Whether that assessment is true or not—and there is a case for it, since the navy puts the trainee monarch alongside all types and classes of men in a confined place, and teaches good timekeeping, practicality and stress management—it was only part of the answer. "Bertie" had been struggling all his life with a severe stammer, perhaps derived from lifelong feelings of inadequacy prompted by comparisons with his glamorous and self-assured brother, whom he once idolized. He spent his early years with his siblings in York Cottage, a crowded home in the grounds of Sandringham, before going to the tough boarding environment of the Royal Naval College on the Isle of Wight, which had once been Queen Victoria's favored southern retreat, Osborne. This must have been a challenging experience for a shy boy who had never mixed well with other children. He was bullied and struggled to make his mark, coming sixty-eighth out of sixty-eight in his final exams.

Bertie nevertheless went on to the next phase of his naval training at Dartmouth, did a year at Oxford and was commissioned as a junior midshipman a year before the beginning of the Great War. As a boy he had had bowlegs and been forced to wear excruciatingly painful leg braces. His digestive system was badly impaired, perhaps partly as a result of neglectful feeding by an early nurse. During the war, he repeatedly spent time away from his ship in hospitals but he did manage to participate in the titanic, if indecisive, Battle of Jutland. Unable to speak well in public because of his famous stammer, untrained in statecraft, physically in poor shape (though a good rider and tennis player), he seemed about as badly suited to become the King-Emperor as a man could be.

Yet he had shown another side to his character, a streak of determination and persistence that would change his reputation. After the war, he fell in love with a glamorous Scottish aristocrat. Elizabeth Bowes Lyon was only twenty when they met for the first time at a dance in 1920. She was besieged by confident and pushy admirers, but Bertie paid court and made his first marriage proposal through an emissary. Though it was rejected, he refused to give up, and in January 1923 his proposal was finally accepted.

This was a side to Bertie his parents had not seen before, and they were delighted. Elizabeth was the first commoner to be ushered into the family since the 1917 Windsor revolution. ("Commoner" in this respect means only "non-royal," since she came from a distinguished Scottish landowning family.) It would be a pivot in his life. As his brother's behavior became progressively more scandalous, his father began to see Bertie in a kinder light. When his second son married, George V wrote that "you have always been so sensible and easy to work with, and you have always been ready to listen to my advice and to agree with my opinions about people and things, that I feel we have always got on very well together (very different from dear David)." Later George was reported to have said he hoped his eldest son would not marry, so that Bertie and then little Elizabeth would succeed instead.

Between the wars Bertie had settled into the quiet life of a private gentleman, while not shirking the royal duties imposed by his father. He was interested in industry and public works, opening a summer camp for boys from very different backgrounds. But his inclinations were profoundly private and quietly conservative, and he reveled in a warm family life, leaning on a wife who was, according to courtiers at the time, even more instinctively conservative than he was. He was deeply suspicious of socialists, liberals and indeed any politicians who were not "sound" Tories of the old school. He loathed public speaking and experienced a deeply embarrassing moment in May 1925 when he struggled to complete a speech at the Empire Exhibition at Wembley. As the authors of a book on the King's speech defect put it, "It would be difficult to overestimate the psychological effect that the speech had both on Bertie and his family, and the problem that his dismal performance threw up for the monarchy. Such speeches were meant to be part of the daily routine of the Duke, who was second in line to the throne, yet he had conspicuously failed to rise to the challenge."[22]

Though he had tried almost every reputable speech therapist in London, in October 1926 Bertie's wife persuaded him to meet Lionel Logue, the Australian whose unorthodox skills would do so much to help him. Speech therapy was still in its infancy, a hit-or-miss affair which oscillated between psychology, physical work on the diaphragm, lungs and tongue, and exercises both useful and bizarre. Logue was not medically trained but was himself a good and self-confident speech maker and performer whose optimism and energy won over his suspicious and pessimistic royal client. The most striking thing about the treatment was the sheer relentlessness and frequency of the sessions. In a little over a year, running through to December 1927, Bertie endured eighty-two sessions with Logue in Harley Street. He practiced day after day at home, breaking engagements and leaving his beloved hunting field early to force himself through tongue twisters, breathing exercises and reading practice. Little by little, the intense effort paid off and audiences who had been expecting a monosyllabic, stuttering performance found themselves listening to relatively fluent speeches. Through-out, his wife was urging him on, sitting beside him, her knuckles white with tension. As the years went on—during foreign visits and while making numerous home speeches and even broadcasts—Bertie got better.

Speech defects do not disappear overnight, and absolute cures are rare. The psychological pressures of his early upbringing could not be simply magicked away; like so many people, the future King lived with the scar tissue of those hard years and learned to cope with the consequences. Once he became king there was vicious gossip about him, even before it was known that he would take his father's name (he might have been the first King Albert). He was, it was said, too nervous and dim to manage the duties of kingship; he would barely make it through his Coronation.

Certainly in his first years as King, George VI had to endure a torrent of loud clubland muttering and drawing-room whispering. He did not visit India for the expected durbar (and, despite being its last emperor, never visited India at all). Unhelpfully, the somewhat cloddish Archbishop of Canterbury of the day openly discussed his stammer. His brother bombarded him with unwanted advice from his Austrian exile. When his first prime minister, Stanley Baldwin, who had been an avuncular source of support, quickly resigned, George VI was forlorn. Yet again he showed the tenacity which had won him his wife and subdued his stammer, applying himself to royal business and duty with a grim vigor Edward VIII had been incapable of. King Edward had horrified the political establishment by ignoring boxes of official papers, sending them back with whisky-glass stains or, worse, showing them around, so that Whitehall officials began to censor what was sent to the Palace.

George read his papers and kept his counsel, and gradually he began to overcome his meager constitutional education. The establishment responded, warily and then with relief. The British press, which had hushed up the Edward and Wallis affair almost until the last moment, returned to its former instincts for loyalty and discretion. In many ways, this proved to be bad for the monarchy. Though it allowed George VI to grow into the role of King, it also made it possible for the royal family to revert to past habits, including a knee-jerk preference for "safe" aristocratic and Conservative politicians, just at the moment when they were to prove wanting. The court was deeply suspicious of Churchill in particular, who had been belligerently pro-Edward. More generally, Lascelles and his colleagues provided a protective crust of tradition and precedence around the four-strong family, which lasted until the 1950s.

Yet in the run-up to World War II, George VI was still an inexperienced monarch, finding his way. When his second prime minister, Neville Chamberlain, embarked on the policy of appeasement, the King backed him so enthusiastically that some MPs believed he was behaving too politically, breaking his constitutional role. George wanted to make personal King-to-Führer appeals himself, and he insisted that Chamberlain join him on the balcony at Buckingham Palace after Chamberlain's now-notorious visit to Munich. The atmosphere is hard to recapture: at the time most British people were also delighted. The King issued a message to the Empire promising "the time of anxiety is past" and thanking God and Mr. Chamberlain for "a new era of friendship and prosperity." This was a family view: his mother, Queen Mary, wrote to him expressing her exasperation with the critics of the Munich Agreement and asking why people couldn't simply be grateful that Chamberlain had come home bringing peace. "It is always so easy for people to criticize when they don't know the ins and outs of the question," she complained. After the war started and Britain's early Norway campaign failed, Chamberlain was forced to resign; when he did, the King was aghast, and angry with the prime minister's critics. (Princess Elizabeth, hearing the news of Chamberlain's resignation, cried.) To replace Chamberlain the King wanted Lord Halifax, another arch-appeaser and a high-Tory aristocrat. Only with great reluctance did he eventually accept the idea that the rogue elephant Winston Churchill was the better choice, and he took quite some time to get used to him.

One eminent royal biographer concluded: "George VI was not a born leader. He could seem shy and harassed, aloof and even morose."[23] He was also famous for his outbursts of temper, his "gnashes," as the family called them. Yet the war made his reputation, as it was to make Churchill's and Mountbatten's. Underneath the thin skin was an intelligent and sensitive man with an iron sense of duty.

The first real evidence that George VI might prove a good King came during his visit to America in June 1939. He was on a long-planned visit to Canada and President Roosevelt invited him south. No reigning British sovereign had ever traveled to the United States, but Roosevelt had seized his moment. According to his wife, he believed "we might all soon be engaged in a life or death struggle, in which Great Britain would be our first line of defence" and wanted "to create a bond of friendship."[24]

The visit was a great success. Both the King and Queen Elizabeth were greeted ecstatically, and they impressed American politicians, newspapers and crowds with their informality and warmth. The Queen wrote to her daughter Elizabeth and described the excitement of dining outside, with all the food jumbled together, including "HOT DOGS!" At his home on the Hudson River, President Roosevelt and George VI talked long into the night about such difficult issues as debts, steel exports, naval bases, the Soviet position and how to win round American opinion from isolationism. Roosevelt went far further than most Americans would have been comfortable with at the time: he promised, according to the King's note, that "If London was bombed USA would come in." All this was meticulously recorded by him the next day and sent back to the British government. (When President Obama visited London in the spring of 2011, he brought as a present for the Queen a bound volume of photographs of this visit: it meant a lot to her father and so meant a lot to her too.)

When war with Germany broke out, the King's most important role was to support the bigger and even more sensitive personality of his prime minister. Thrown into Churchill's giant shadow, he never complained. George VI was privy to the deepest secrets of wartime, including the Enigma intercepts; he also had prior knowledge of the invention and then the use of the atomic bomb. Despite occasional spats, he and the arch-royalist Churchill became close friends. He worked hard, ruthlessly cut back the costs of the court and supported his extraordinary prime minister in every way. He famously refused to leave London during the Blitz—though the royal family spent their nights at Windsor, where Princess Elizabeth was largely sheltered from the privations of wartime. Buckingham Palace was bombed nine times.

During the war, the King thought up the idea of the George Cross and George Medal to honor civilian heroes, building in a smaller way on his father's creation of the OBE. He visited British forces in North Africa, Italy and—most dramatically—heavily bombed Malta. He argued with Churchill over the latter's enthusiasm for going to France after D-day, pointing out that as King he was unable to go and he was therefore being put in an unfair position. (Churchill grumpily stayed at home a little longer.) By the end of the war, the King had become a genuine symbol of British doggedness: shy, devout, and surprisingly humble in an age when so many countries had monsters for their heads of state.

After the war was over, George supported Indian independence and demonstrated his hostility to South African racism during a visit there. Just as Queen Victoria had been horrified by slavery in the United States and had delighted in the close attention of her Indian servants, so George VI gave every indication of being genuinely color-blind, though of course his empire as a whole was not.

The King, however, was no radical and found it hard to accept Churchill's election defeat in 1945. He was always privately dubious about Attlee's socialist administration. Just as his father had had to cope with the first arrival of a Labour government in 1924, so the son had to swallow his instincts and deal with unfamiliar men holding alarming views. He coped but did not enjoy it. In many ways, George VI remained a highly conservative prewar traditionalist; meticulous about dress, honors and court precedence, obsessively keen on shooting, he was a thinner, clean-shaven version of his father. The future Labour leader Hugh Gaitskell said he was "a fairly reactionary person." When he needed an operation on his leg to restore the blood supply choked by arteriosclerosis, he was told he should be operated on in hospital and refused on the odd grounds of court protocol: "I have never heard of a King going to a hospital before." But he worked intensely hard, bit his rebellious tongue, and kept the constitutional monarchy in good repair.

All this was observed and noted by his elder daughter, the serious-minded girl he knew would be Queen. He introduced Elizabeth early into the work and rituals that being the British monarch would entail. In 1955, when the Queen unveiled a memorial to her father, she praised his wartime steadfastness, his "friendliness and simplicity," his "warm and friendly sympathies," his "unassuming humanity" and pointed out that he had sacrificed himself during bouts of serious illness: "his courage in overcoming it endeared him to everybody." After the torment of the first global war, his father, George V, had fervently hoped the monarchy would become associated with precisely these qualities.

The House of Windsor has an unusually direct transmission of ideas and behavior from its origin in 1917 through grandfather, father and daughter. In a radical change carried through by conservative people with a strong sense of duty and purpose, these three have become Britain's new model monarchs. They have been called the welfare monarchy, or the democracy monarchy, or even the suburban monarchy. The essence of this new paradigm is a paradox: the ruler who is servant to her subjects.

When Elizabeth II became queen people talked rather pompously of a "new Elizabethan age" and asked whether the Britain of the mid-twentieth century could surprise the world like the English of the age of Drake, Shakespeare and Bacon. The Queen put them right. In her Christmas broadcast of 1953 she said she did not "feel at all like my great Tudor forebear, who was blessed with neither husband nor children, who ruled as a despot and was never able to leave her native shores." Yet she went on to compare modern Britain, rich in courage and enterprise, with the poor, small but "great in spirit" England of the earlier Elizabeth. It is also true that the Queen and the Windsors shared something else with the Tudors: they, too, reinvented themselves as a dynasty.

GLAMOROUS DICKIE

Except for her husband, the single biggest influence on the Queen was her father. But there are two other major characters without whom we cannot understand the Queen and her reign. One is, obviously, her mother, but first we will consider a less obvious influence, and a more ambiguous one, whose impact was at its height in the mid-twentieth century. Traveling alongside the future Edward VIII on those post-1918 tours had been a besotted admirer who was part of the family. Like the Prince, he had been held in his grandmother Queen Victoria's arms as a baby and given, as one of his names, "Albert," in memory of her husband. Today he is remembered simply as "Mountbatten," the Prince's cousin and one of the most exotic, too-big-to-be-true characters in twentieth-century British history.

"Dickie" Mountbatten was just fifteen when his father, Prince Louis Battenberg, had been forced to resign as First Sea Lord. Prince Battenberg and his son were members of a relatively junior branch of the interwoven tree of European royal dynasties. Even so, the Battenbergs had holidayed with the Romanovs in Russia and felt entitled to meddle in the affairs of kings from Sweden to Greece. Louis Mountbatten, as he became, was a British naval officer in the Great War; between the wars, he rose through the naval ranks, became very close to the future British king, and then married one of the richest women in Britain.

Mountbatten got his great career break during the Second World War despite a series of early embarrassments as a serving captain. His destroyer, HMS *Kelly*, hit mines and once another ship, and it was badly damaged by bombers after he sent nighttime signals that were picked up by the enemy. Yet Mountbatten's sense of theater and his ability to make stirring speeches meant that after he had nursed the wounded ship back home, he became a national hero and the subject of a wartime propaganda film by Noël Coward, *In Which We Serve*. Later in the war, the *Kelly* was bombed and sunk off Crete, where Mountbatten's flotilla of destroyers was trying to hold off the German invasion. He was very lucky to survive; 136 members of his crew did not.

Though the *Kelly* was facing impossible odds and none of these mishaps was explicitly his fault, naval historians and Mountbatten's biographers generally agree that he was a dashing but not particularly good commander of ships. But thanks to Winston Churchill, who recognized a dynamic and publicity-conscious personality rather like his own, Mountbatten was soon raised far above his rank to become Chief of Combined Operations. Later he rose even further and became Supreme Allied Commander for South East Asia. There he would successfully lead the fight to retake Burma and Malaya from the Japanese.

Wars accelerate everything, including promotions, but to go from being the captain of a destroyer mocked for depth-charging a shoal of fish to becoming one of the grand masters of strategy in a global conflict was quite extraordinary. Particularly in the difficult conditions of the early 1940s, Mountbatten's charisma and the surging self-confidence that communicated itself in ever wider circles mattered enormously. He had always milked his connections and shamelessly lobbied for every job he wanted, right back to his appointment accompanying the Prince of Wales on his foreign jaunts. After the abdication, he had quickly switched allegiance to the new King George VI and never forgot to remind all around him about his close royal ties. Long ago Churchill had acquiesced in Mountbatten's father's humiliating removal from the Admiralty; now Churchill was his fervent supporter. Mountbatten, it seemed, had everything. He had the flair for PR and self-promotion that a tired Britain responded to, just like Churchill's favored soldier, Field Marshal Bernard Montgomery. He had good looks, personal courage, charm and the self-possession of a very wealthy man. And he was part of the royal establishment at a time when that counted for a lot. No wonder so many well-placed people hated him with such cold and sparkling intensity.

After the war and Churchill's defeat in the 1945 general election, the new Labour prime minister, Clement Attlee, asked Mountbatten to become the last Viceroy of India and finish the independence negotiations with India and Pakistan. He did so, working to a tight timetable and with energetic ruthlessness. He and his lively wife, Edwina, enjoyed the grand style of the final days of the Indian

Empire. Their vice-regal house put Buckingham Palace to shame; their daughter compared it to the greatest palaces of the Russian Tsar. Beyond the busy but civilized withdrawal of the senior echelons of the Raj, a ragged dissolution began across the subcontinent. Mountbatten worked hard for a total of 125 days to end Britain's Indian Empire, making a number of brutal decisions very quickly. Churchill, for one, was appalled. Nobody had fought for the Empire harder or had loved it more than he had, and he now regarded his former protégé as a traitor.

The partition resulted in terrible bloodshed, the worst slaughter and migration in the history of the subcontinent. This was not Mountbatten's fault, and he and Edwina did their best to organize help. Yet at some level, Britain no longer seemed to care about the agonies of its former colonized people. Mountbatten returned to the navy and continued to prosper until becoming Admiral of the Fleet, Chief of the Defence Staff and at last, in 1955, First Sea Lord—the job his father had been forced from forty-one years before. That final great promotion was given with the reluctant agreement of the elderly prime minister, Winston Churchill. For Mountbatten, this revenge could hardly have been sweeter. He moved back to his father's old office, and on his first day he wrote in his diary, "Thrill to sit under Papa's picture."

Mountbatten was a huge influence on the Windsors during the earlier part of the Queen's reign—if not so directly on her, then on her husband and her son. First and most important, he acted as a kind of semi-guardian to Prince Philip from early 1930 onward. In its most melodramatic version, the story of "Uncle Dickie" and his young charge has Mountbatten shaping Philip in his own image, intriguing to marry him off to Princess Elizabeth and then exulting in a family triumph when she became queen. This is greatly overcooked. It is true that Mountbatten urged Philip to follow a naval career; it is also true that Mountbatten was a keen and dynastic matchmaker. (Years later, he would try to interest Prince Charles in one of his granddaughters.) He also worked hard and successfully to achieve Prince Philip's naturalization as a British citizen rather than a Greek one. (In February 1947, Philip took his mother's anglicized name, Mountbatten, rather than what would have been his paternal family name, the Danish one of Schleswig-Holstein-Sonderburg-Glücksburg, thus making it much easier for him to marry.) Finally, it is true that after Philip and Elizabeth married, Mountbatten campaigned long, hard and unsuccessfully for the replacement of "Windsor" with Mountbatten-Windsor as the royal family name.

But the Duke of Edinburgh has repeatedly made it clear that he thinks Mountbatten overstated his involvement in his upbringing, complaining that his own father and mother were being written out of the picture, and that he had spent more time staying with his grandmother and other relatives. One gets the impression that he resented Uncle Dickie overplaying his hand. It was he, not his uncle, who decided he should marry the future Queen. At the time they were wooing, Philip wrote a terse letter to Mountbatten, humorously but effectively warning him off: "I am not being rude, but it is apparent that you like being General Manager of this little show, and I am rather afraid she might not take to the idea quite as docilely as I do."[25]

Much later, Mountbatten would develop an especially close relationship with Philip's first son, Prince Charles. By then, he had long been a special intimate of the inner royal family, included in holidays and private visits, his self-serving and oft-repeated stories listened to with tolerant amusement, and his vast range of connections admired. Yet for all the affection and warmth there was something held back, at least by the older royals, for Uncle Dickie also provided an unsettling link with Uncle David.

Not long after he and the Prince of Wales returned from their expedition to India, Mountbatten married heiress Edwina Ashley at a glittering society wedding—and the future Edward VIII was his best man. The Mountbattens were key members of the Prince's "set" and remained close friends during his brief reign. Though he disapproved of the abdication, fighting vigorously as a member of the "King's party" alongside Churchill, Mountbatten kept in close touch with the exiled former monarch, offered to be his best man when he married Mrs. Simpson, and later passed messages between him and the court. He was on hand to rescue the pair from France in 1940 as the Germans closed in. He was the middle man in negotiations about titles and money after the war, and he did his best to repair relations. In this he was unsuccessful: Queen Elizabeth, the Queen Mother, never forgave the Duke of Windsor for his dereliction of duty.

Mountbatten had a far greater sense of duty and was much more energetic than Edward, and he always deplored the abdication. But he and Edwina had the same relaxed attitude to infidelity, and like the former king Mountbatten was thought to be a bit "too much." He lived in high style and had an almost endearing streak of vanity. He and Montgomery once counted each other's medals; when Mountbatten found that he had one decoration fewer, he got himself awarded two more. He was inclined to woo the media rather than shun them. After the Duke of Windsor died, Mountbatten claimed, perhaps more kindly than accurately, that he had been "my best friend all my life."[26]

The Queen Mother had spread a strong antipathy to that best friend throughout her family, and it is possible that a certain suspicion of Mountbatten passed to her daughter. It would not be surprising if there was a certain ambiguity about him in the Duke of Edinburgh's mind as well. For the Windsor dynasty, which had come to believe that success was about being comparatively quiet and subdued, Mountbatten's style—which had been tested and found wanting in the 1930s—may well have seemed dangerously flamboyant.

QUEEN ELIZABETH

A gentler flamboyance was a primary characteristic of the young girl who was successfully wooed in the world of the "Bright Young Things" and became an important presence at Queen Elizabeth II's shoulder through most of her reign. Queen Elizabeth as she was properly known—or the Queen Mother, as she was mostly known for the second half of her life—ended up as a much-loved granny figure who lived into the current century. To the Queen she was "Mummy"; to millions of the Queen's subjects she was an idealized doughty old duck, with a twinkle in her eye and a decent-sized drink near at hand.

She seemed to have been always with us. For almost everyone alive by the year 2000 that was literally true. Born in 1900, she lived for slightly more than the twentieth century. She was alive during the reigns of six monarchs: Queen Victoria, Edward VII, her father-in-law George V, Edward VIII, her husband George VI and her daughter Elizabeth II. To Britons old enough to remember, she was above all a living link to World War II and the Blitz in particular. Her comment after Buckingham Palace was bombed, that at last she could "now look the East End in the face," was the most famous thing she ever said. To some she seemed to overshadow her daughter when the two were present together. The Queen's family say she depended heavily on her mother as a sounding board and source of fun.

Queen Elizabeth liked to flirt with men; well into her nineties she enjoyed the company of a male with a raffish twinkle in his eye. She liked anecdotes about "naughty" friends and relatives, and she recommended the stories of Maupassant about love and romance. She possessed natural charisma and shrewd intelligence and could be very funny. The ballet choreographer Sir Frederick Ashton was a favorite dancing partner of the Queen Mother's at Sandringham when balls were held there. She would gesture to him when she wanted to dance, but once, as he went over to take her hand, the Queen herself interposed and suggested he dance with her. Ashton did not refuse his monarch; as they twirled round and passed the Queen Mother's table, she hissed at him: "Social climber!"

For half her life she was a widow, but in general a merry one.

Her role in the inner sanctum of "the Firm" was enormously important. Strongly opinionated and occasionally steely to the point of
cruelty, she was more interesting than her later public image of a
little old lady who liked horses and gin and tonics and big pink hats.
(For the record, her drink of choice was actually gin and Dubonnet,
a dreadful concoction and a taste for which she passed to her daughter.) With those she felt relaxed around, she liked an argument and
liked to win it, just as she liked to win at the card game Racing
Demon—enough, it has to be said, to indulge in some outrageous
cheating. Her husband's official biographer said of her that Queen
Elizabeth had "a small drop of arsenic at the centre of that marsh-
mallow."[27] She was famously vague about money and ran up large
overdrafts. Yet her charisma, which in her day rivaled that of Diana
in hers, and her tough sense of Christian duty—the two were not
alike in every way—kept her out of trouble.

Her strongly conservative views remained mostly private and
she became adept at blocking dangerous questions or simply ignoring "unwise" subjects, strategies she passed down to her daughter.
Nor was her conservatism simply a matter of holding partisan Tory
beliefs. She was, for instance, passionately hostile to the Social
Democratic Party, formed in the 1980s—but not because it was left
of center. She disliked the SDP because it had broken away from
and damaged "the good old Labour Party." For her, loyalty was all.
If Lord Stamfordham was the commoner who, with George V, created the House of Windsor, Queen Elizabeth was the aristocratic
commoner who gave it much of its style and many of its codes.

The youngest daughter of the Earl of Strathmore (whose castle
at Glamis in Angus could have been a setting for Disneyland),
Lady Elizabeth Angela Marguerite Bowes Lyon was a vivacious,
attractive girl who eventually became the first non-Royal to benefit
from George V's rewriting of the family rules in 1917. She may
have been brought up in a privileged family—with its fair share of
bloodthirsty history, cads and romantic martyrs—and in a home
with many ancient royal connections, but when she finally joined

the royal family in 1923 she was looked on as an outsider. The lack of precedent caused a rather pompous official debate about how exactly she would be described as the Duke of York's wife, and whether she would be a Royal Highness (she would). She herself replied to one of her oldest friends who had written asking how to address her: "I really don't know! It might be *anything*—you might try 'All Hail Duchess,' that is an Alice in Wonderland sort of Duchess, or just 'Greetings' or 'What Ho, Duchess' or 'Say, Dutch'—in fact you can please yourself."[28]

Elizabeth had spent most of her girlhood in her family's southern house, St. Paul's Walden Bury in Hertfordshire, with nine older brothers and sisters. The girl called "Buffy" by her family lived the golden Edwardian idyll as it still existed for a few, surrounded by servants and immaculate lawns, completely isolated from the Britain of Suffragette protests, trade union strikes and bitter political argument. It was a childhood of woodland rambles and hideouts, horses and shooting parties, candlelit balls, in-jokes and family sing-alongs. Elizabeth attended school only sporadically; most of her education came from governesses, in particular a young German woman who wrote in amazement about the grandness and extravagance of life at Glamis Castle just before the Great War. This lost world would leave some mark on "Buffy's" daughter, because it put a very secure and self-certain woman at the heart of the Windsor dynasty. She would inspire much more than a love of horses and a fierce belief in family loyalty in the current Queen.

The war brought out the old spirit of noblesse oblige as Glamis and St. Paul's Walden Bury were used for convalescent soldiers, with Lady Strathmore presiding over her hospitals. The teenage Elizabeth knitted endlessly, packaged presents for troops at the front and stuffed sleeping bags. At Glamis, she grew used to mingling with injured, plain-speaking working-class men who were not her servants, an experience that would later help with her "common touch." The Bowes Lyons were strongly religious, none more so than Elizabeth. During the war one brother, in the Black Watch, was killed; another was taken prisoner. Alongside the privilege there was loss, grief and much dependence on Christian prayer and church attendance, all of which was in due course passed on to her elder daughter.

Scottish-British patriotism and a passionate dislike of Germans were rooted in Elizabeth's character long before the rise of Hitler. So was her gusto for life—her enthusiasm for food, music, dancing and parties were all uncorked as soon as the war ended. She was better educated than her own daughter, but conspicuously failed at an open exam, writing afterward, "*DAMN THE EXAM*!! . . . What *was* the use of toiling down to that—er—place Hackney? None, I tell you none. It makes me *boil* with rage to think of that vile stuff, tapioca, eating for—nothing? Oh hell. . . . Yes, I am very disappointed."[29] Given the later criticism of her for failing to give Princess Elizabeth a better and broader education, the tapioca may have a lot to answer for.

Initially Elizabeth was uncertain about Bertie, but when she kept refusing him she may also have been properly nervous about the implications of becoming a "Royal." This was an intensely formal, frock-coated and traditionalist court, presided over by a somewhat forbidding monarch. In a revealing letter to Bertie, she wrote of Frogmore, the house by Windsor Castle where Victoria's mausoleum was built: "Having never seen Frogmore, I imagine it as a large white Tomb full of frogs! I can't think why, but that is the impression it gives me—isn't it silly?"[30] She liked jazz and nightclubs, and ran into trouble with George V when she and Bertie stayed out until three a.m. at a nightclub, the Follies, at London's Metropole Hotel.

William Shawcross, Elizabeth's official biographer, wrote that upon her marriage she was entering "a sort of golden incarceration. The young Duchess could no longer go shopping alone; she could not travel on trains alone, or on buses at all. She was no longer able to see her friends as spontaneously as she loved to do. . . . All in all, the Duchess was isolated and restricted in a way she had never been before."[31] Her situation was, in short, strikingly similar to that of another young aristocratic woman who entered the family in 1981.

Like Diana, Elizabeth proved an early hit with the public. Like Diana, she made a particular success of an early tour of Australia, overshadowing—as Diana did—her husband. Her smile was endlessly discussed. Like her daughter, today's Queen, Elizabeth would grit her teeth and head off on extended royal tours, leaving her own children behind. But by the time the present Queen was born, her mother had already shown herself to be far wilier and shrewder than Diana would ever be. Elizabeth won over her growling father-in-law with apologetic letters, tact and charm. Formidable Queen Mary, pleased with Elizabeth's effect on her son, thawed too. And Elizabeth was quick to take on her new obligations as a cadet Windsor, picking up patronage duty, visiting duty, opening-things duty as if born to it. Above all, despite those initial refusals and perhaps against expectations—and certainly unlike Diana—she was sustained by a very happy marriage.

The Queen Mother's influence on her daughter was perhaps less than that of the current Queen's husband. She did not pass on her flirtatiousness or her enthusiasm for racy gossip. Her daughter is more careful of money and more reserved, and she takes life more seriously. But Queen Elizabeth did pass on a passion for horse racing, a world within a world where the current Queen has been able to lighten up and forget human bloodlines for the even chancier business of equine ones. And her greatest service to her daughter can be measured by her loss: when the Queen Mother died at the ripe age of 101, the Queen lost not only her mother but an extraordinarily close, lifelong companion.

❧

PART TWO

Lilibet

The fusion of the personal and the public makes the history of the royal family particularly significant, and without some understanding of the Queen's older relatives, it is quite impossible to understand her. Almost everything about the Queen's public behavior—from the time she spends with official boxes of paperwork and her attitude toward public engagements and church services, to her annual pilgrimages from Windsor to Sandringham and Balmoral, or her solemnity in public and her suspicion of journalists—thrums with the DNA of Windsor tradition. The two last Georges, their Queens, and the lesser royals of the twentieth century loom large in the London palaces. They hang in paintings, stare back from photographs and leave traces everywhere, in the furnishings and knickknacks they once chose.

Queen Victoria casts a special spell in the rooms and palaces she created. She was the builder, not only in physical terms but also in the way she established a particular atmosphere. Her famous sense of morality, not overwhelmingly evident in British monarchy before, somehow suffuses the institution still, like a background hum. Without this history the Queen would not be the Queen. Without it Britain would be a substantially different place. The Hanoverians and Windsors have distinctive faces but a wide range of temperaments, from dutiful to reckless, careful to carefree, pious to naughty. The Queen has not only learned many lessons from her family but is clearly on the dutiful, careful and pious end of the register. Even in very early photos, she stares back with a calm, unruffled and distinctly Windsor self-assurance.

That confidence and poise was practically a birthright: she was, after all, born into a world of quiet, order and privilege. But outside the walls of 17 Bruton Street, Mayfair, where Elizabeth was delivered by cesarean section at 2:40 a.m. on April 21, 1926, Britain was a riven nation. Days later, on May 3, a general strike would begin, which many thought would be the start of a socialist or communist revolution of the kind that had swept away some of the baby's relatives in Europe nine years before. As it happened, Britain would be spared political upheaval; the conservative, patriotic temperament of the middle classes would be shored up by its monarchy; and Elizabeth, whose birth was greeted by a modest group of well-wishers outside, would become its greatest twentieth-century monarch. One of the shrewdest historians of the period, David Cannadine, says she was a child of two worlds: "She is a child of aristocracy, her mother of course was an aristocrat, not a Royal, and she was a child of empire—her father and her grandfather were emperors of India, and that was part of the apparently eternal order of things in 1926."[1]

Bruton Street today is a small street of expensive art galleries, restaurants and car showrooms between Berkeley Square, where once the nightingales sang, and New Bond Street, where the fashion victims stalk. The Strathmores' house, where the future Queen was born, has been knocked down. In 1926, her parents were staying there after rejecting life in a pretty but unmodernized country house in Richmond Park, which had been offered to them by the King—and which is now the Royal Ballet School, featured in the sneakers-to-fame tale *Billy Elliot*. They had wanted somewhere more central, more convenient, and cozier.

Four physicians of the utmost fame attended the Duchess, and after a difficult labor, Buckingham Palace was told of the birth of a daughter early the following morning. During those tumultuous days leading to the General Strike, the Duke of York was anxiously attending Commons debates. The King had made his feelings of private sympathy for the miners clear to one coal owner: "Try living on their wages before you judge them," he had replied to Lord Durham's outburst against "damned revolutionaries." (The interests of monarchy are not identical to the interests of big money; monarchy needs stability even more than money does.)

George V's government felt it was facing social breakdown and anarchy, and it was mobilizing the middle and upper classes to do their bit against the trade unions' militant eruption. The home secretary, Sir William Joynson-Hicks, a peppery man, was obliged to break off preparations for the political crisis to be present at the princess's birth. This absurd tradition was said to date back to the suspicion that James II's wife smuggled in a male baby after a fake pregnancy, but it probably had more to do with the old habit of courtiers crowding round the Royals at important moments, even into the birthing rooms. Either way, even in 1926 it felt a bit odd. A sense of tradition also means knowing which traditions to quietly drop.

In all this, one might have expected the Queen's birth to be little discussed. Though she was third in line to the throne, her uncle and his brother were both still comparatively young men. If her mother produced a son later on he would, under British laws of succession, have immediately leapfrogged Elizabeth. So it did not seem particularly likely that this golden-haired infant would one day reign. Yet the birth of the Duke of York's daughter did capture the attention of newspapers, perhaps scrabbling around in dark days for some good, light news, and did attract an immediate crowd in the street, which stayed for weeks. One newspaper speculated about the child becoming a future Queen Elizabeth, but the overall tone was one of celebration for another young member of what was, by modern standards, a small royal family, rather short on children.

Elizabeth was christened with water from the River Jordan in Buckingham Palace and cried during the service. She was soon put under the wing of Clara Cooper, or "Alah" Knight, the brisk, lanky daughter of a Hertfordshire farmer who had looked after her mother from when she was one month old. That summer the baby was taken to Glamis Castle, her mother's family's home, then back to London. But by January 1927, when she was nine months old, her parents left her and embarked upon a thirty-thousand-mile, six-month sea voyage to Australia and New Zealand. Her mother was upset to leave the baby, but the Empire called and Elizabeth would stay behind with her nurse and grandparents. Before she could have been conscious of it, the competing demands of royal work and family life were already tugging in opposite directions.

Is this long absence proof of the brutal assessment of one royal librarian, who said that "the House of Hanover, like ducks, produce bad parents; they trample on their young."[2]? Not really: in the 1920s the upper classes saw far less of their children than would be considered normal now. Nurses, nannies and later boarding schools left parents freer to pursue their adult lives. Today, we might think it heartless; then it was ordinary. Beyond that, however, the weight of Crown and Empire rested on the Windsors with a gravity outsiders cannot easily understand. For seventy years, five monarchs—Victoria, Edward VII, George V, Edward VIII and George VI—carried the "I" of Imperator, or Emperor, after the "R" of kingship, and thus "RI" meant a global role. These kings and queens felt that they themselves were History and had the job of carrying the national story through to the next generation. If there were doubts, for instance, about the longer-term loyalty of Australia and New Zealand to the Empire, then it was absolutely the job of the royal family to do their best to mend things. Everyone understood that the yearning of a mother for a baby was a lesser matter.

Even so, Elizabeth was born into a close, physically affectionate family, and she probably had a warmer and more secure upbringing than many of the children of the great aristocratic dynasties of inter-war Britain. We know a lot about that upbringing because of the indiscretion of the Princess's governess, Marion Crawford, who lived with the family for sixteen years, from 1933 to 1949, and who then wrote a book, *The Little Princesses*, in 1950 about her experiences. Crawford, a Scottish teacher who had wanted to work with deprived children, had been recommended to the Yorks by titled relatives and became by all accounts a dedicated and energetic tutor to both Elizabeth and her younger sister, Margaret. Crawford's book contains not a single damning fact or serious embarrassment of any kind, and Elizabeth emerges as very serious and orderly but also sweet-natured, kind and loving. Yet when Crawford's book was published—now more than sixty years ago—the retired governess was brutally cut off from all contact with the royal family. After a short and ignominious career as a magazine journalist she went into effective exile, having long delayed her marriage. When she died, no member of the royal family came to her funeral. Her name is never mentioned.

This guillotine blade of silence is worth dwelling on. After all, "Crawfie"—the nickname was given to her by Elizabeth herself—was someone who knew the future Queen intimately and during her formative years. She was not family, but she was close. Perhaps it was the fact that "Crawfie" felt almost like family that made her behavior seem so hurtful. By today's standards, her crime was a comparatively venial one: her affection, even adoration, for her charges shines through her writing. So why the intense anger? The answer is that she was the first. Before her no intimate of the Windsors had "blabbed."

Royal life is not private in the way most of us understand privacy. Even when they are not on public view the royal family is almost constantly surrounded by valets, maids, butlers, police protection officers, drivers and the like. Royal family members barely draw an unobserved breath. They know there is an insatiable interest in the smallest aspects of their lives and the briefest comment they make. Few of us could bear a life under constant surveillance and commentary; imagine being watched while eating breakfast, brushing your hair, dressing, exercising, finishing a last nighttime drink. So the discreet silence of those around them is not merely convenient. It is basic to living a tolerable life, to having some at least semiprivate space. Inside Buckingham Palace, even senior aides take great care to avoid bumping into the Queen or Duke by accident.

A shield wall surrounds the senior Royals. Inside it, utter loyalty is expected. Crawford did not simply tell a few bland stories about the color of wallpapers, or sweet things little Princess Margaret said. She yanked open the curtain on a sensitive part of Princess Elizabeth's life, her childhood and adolescent years, when the Queen's personality was forming. Having done that, Crawford compounded her sin by continuing to write about the young woman, from presumed knowledge, in the press. Imagine how Elizabeth must have felt, sizing up old and trusted staff in front of whom she needed to be occasionally off guard and relaxed, and wondering always—will your book be the next one?

Back in the 1950s, Elizabeth had no way of knowing how extensively her family's lives would later be exposed, not least by renegade members of the family itself. Marion Crawford may have been silly, even greedy, but she was not wicked or, by her lights, disloyal. But with royalty there are harsher rules. Cross a line and the line re-forms around you. You are never allowed within it again.

Still, anyone truly interested in the Queen owes much to Crawford for the anecdotes and descriptions she provided. The historian A. N. Wilson has gone so far as to say that because she lived so long with the princesses, and because childhood is the most interesting part of life, "Crawfie will remain the most important Royal historian of the twentieth century and her book will deserve to be read when all the constitutional experts and all the spies at the Royal keyholes of the present generation have been forgotten."[3] But by royal standards, if not by Crawfie's, it makes sense to call this disloyalty.

The most important revelation in this unconventional historian's account is that the Queen had a very happy, very secure childhood, underpinned by her mother's sense of fun, her father's attentions and her sister's companionship. Crawford's book offers enough detail of bathtime romps, dressing up, horseplay and laughter to be wholly convincing. George VI, both as Duke of York and King, was a physically active parent, keen on riding lessons and games with his daughters. As others have said, he had a sense of fun rather than a sense of humor, but for small children, the former is much more important. He liked cards and charades and mimicry and playacting, and so did his daughters. In her book, Crawford revealed that the Duchess had written a note for him in case of her death, reminding him "not to ridicule your children or laugh at them. When they say funny things it is usually quite innocent . . . always try & talk very quietly to children. . . . Remember how your father, by shouting at you, & making you feel uncomfortable, lost all your real affection. None of his sons are his friends."[4]

Whether or not George needed this excellent advice, his daughters were his friends. The family lived much of the time in a rather oddly extended Victorian house called Royal Lodge, now occupied by Prince Andrew, the current Duke of York. Standing on the grounds of Windsor Great Park, it is surrounded by huge trees and a chapel and beautiful gardens; once there, one could be a hundred miles from London. It had been rebuilt in the 1840s but by the 1920s was in poor shape and badly in need of the renovation undertaken by George. Later, after the family had left their last private house—a tall building facing Green Park across Piccadilly that was bombed during the war and has now disappeared—the

King would begin to educate Elizabeth in her constitutional role, ensuring that she read newspapers, understood public affairs and had a good grounding in politics. But from her early years, the tight "we four" of the family gave her a sense of security and belonging she has never lost. If hers was an abnormal family in its wealth, role and history, it nevertheless looked a bit like an ideal version of the nuclear "Janet and John" unit emerging in the suburbs of 1930s Britain.

But Crawford's account also makes it clear that the princesses were almost entirely cut off from ordinary life. They had no friends outside a tight circle of relatives and a few high-born families. If the world was gawping through railings at the young girls playing in a private London park, the two sisters were staring back from upstairs windows at the traffic and crowds outside. Their seclusion was only increased by the gift of the Royal Lodge in 1931, by that point a fine mansion lavishly done up by the Duke and Duchess, where the family could spend weekends far away from crowds. In its gardens was "a gift from the people of Wales," a scale model of a thatched and plastered Welsh cottage with fully fitted rooms, where the princesses could play.

Attempts were made to take the girls into the real world of London—a trip on the Underground and to a YWCA, museum visits, a ride on a bus and excursions to swimming pools. Yet unless people had been cleared away in advance, crowds formed as soon as the princesses were spotted, and their shouting made it difficult to continue. Soon, a campaign by the IRA made "security issues," which would dog Elizabeth all her life, another reason to build high that wall. When the princesses moved to Buckingham Palace, a Girl Guide group was established to help them enjoy some relationships with girls their own age. It was a successful experiment but hardly a radical one: the other Guides and Brownies were all the daughters of relatives, noble families and courtiers. Little wonder, then, that the Queen developed an avid curiosity about the lives of her subjects.

By the time she was ten, the likely future course of her life unrolled ahead of her. Fortunately, her emotionally secure start in life allowed her to tramp down that claret-colored carpet uncomplainingly. In the Queen's family story, there was angst, rebellion, psychological damage and transformation. But there was almost none of that in her formative years, and the Queen's character in her eighties is strikingly similar to the character described when she was a toddler and child. Around her, uncles, sisters, sons and in-laws have misbehaved, raged against fate, or made bad personal choices. With only one significant exception, her marriage to Prince Philip, she has done nothing against the grain of what was expected. She has uttered not a single shocking phrase in public. There are no reliable recorded incidents of the Queen losing her temper, using bad language, or refusing to carry out a duty expected of her.

Crawford's portrait of a girl who loved games and horseplay is echoed in the descriptions provided by those who are friends of the Queen's today. People close to her speak of her wry wit, her talent for mimicry and her shrewd intelligence, helped by an extraordinary memory for people and events. Outside a tiny circle, none of this is seen. The public does know that she has a lovely, lightbulb-on, smile. But as if to save electricity, it quickly snaps off (usually because she is concentrating on the next task). Her most often used and most effective tactic is silence. Politicians say she is a mistress of the icy silence, the "you may go now" silence, the "I disagree" silence and the plain "you make the running" silence. Otherwise, she understates by instinct.

These lifelong habits seem odder in a culture which has come to celebrate exhibitionism and even dysfunction, the constant bubble and elbowing of a mobile, restless society, short of attention and endlessly reshuffling itself. From her earliest years, by contrast, the Queen's society was one in which everyone was supposed to know their place. Many have rebelled against that world; others find in it a strange freedom.

Elizabeth was born when the hierarchies of aristocracy, honor and chivalry were taken seriously by the middle classes—professional and business people who were themselves graded like the lines of sediment on a cliff face. Details of title, degree, dress and address still mattered tremendously, and it was a time when newspaper-reading working-class people could generally tell the difference between an earl and a duke, when "respectable" was an accolade that mattered. As scores of novels and plays remind us, however, this worldview was changing. Beyond the Palace gates and the Bruton Street doors, the great handbook of "Society" had begun to thin out, and then fall apart, after the Great War. The aristocratic families had lost disproportionate numbers of the sons who were meant to keep the bloodlines going. Democratic politics, which was only fully established in Britain in the Queen's lifetime—women got the vote on equal terms to men when she was two—would push meritocratic ideas ahead. No longer did birth equal destiny. Money replaced breeding. This cultural revolution would eventually take the British to a point where the only person in the country who seemed to know her place in the old way sat at its lonely apex—the Queen herself.

❦

The dominant event in Elizabeth's young life was the moment in 1936 when her father became king, after which she was next in line to the throne. (She became the Heiress Presumptive, not the Heir Apparent, because being female she was only "presumed" to succeed.) Though the Yorks' home at 145 Piccadilly had been a place of strain and nervous tension as the drama following Edward's abdication unfolded outside, the princesses had been protected from much of what was happening. Apparently it was Crawford who told them that their father would shortly become king: "When I broke the news to Margaret and Lilibet that they were going to live in Buckingham Palace they looked at me in horror. 'What!' Lilibet said. 'You mean for ever?'"

Crawford reports that on the day of the proclamation, Bertie left "looking very grave" and dressed as an Admiral of the Fleet. Then she writes: "I had to explain to them that when Papa came home to lunch at one o'clock he would be King of England and they would have to curtsy to him. The royal children from their earliest years had always curtsied to their grandparents. 'And now you mean we must do it to Papa and Mummie?' Lilibet asked. 'Margaret too?' 'Margaret also,' I told her, 'and try not to topple over.'" When the King returned they curtsied: "I think perhaps nothing that had occurred had brought the change in his condition to him as clearly as this did. He stood for a moment touched and taken aback. Then he stooped and kissed them both warmly."

The move to Buckingham Palace was even more of a shock. The future Queen's mother described it as the worst move of her life, and Crawford found the palace uncomfortable in the extreme, painting a picture of a gloomy dilapidated grandeur, with awkwardly placed electrical fittings, endless corridors and chilly rooms infested with mice. It was not the courtiers or footmen that impressed Crawford but the sinister-sounding figure of the Palace Vermin Man who patrolled with various weapons including the "sticky trap"—a piece of cardboard with a lump of aniseed in the middle, surrounded by a sea of treacle. Eventually the new royal family made Buckingham Palace—that grand hotel and staff headquarters of the British monarchy—rather more comfortable, but Crawford remembered her first night there "with a shudder. . . . The wind moaned in the chimneys like a thousand ghosts, I was homesick as I had not been for a long time."

Another child might have been traumatized not just by the move from a familiar house into a walled institution, but by the prospect of an entirely changed future. Though one account of Elizabeth's childhood claims that she prayed furiously hard for a brother to be born, it smacks of a novel. Later, Princess Margaret said that she had asked Elizabeth whether their father's accession meant she herself would one day be Queen: "She replied, 'Yes, I suppose it does.'"[5] But as far as we know she did not mention the matter again, and she seems to have been, in her tidy, quiet way, relatively calm about it all.

After her father's Coronation on May 12, 1937, Elizabeth wrote her own account of the great event for her parents. Cheerful, literal and very much the product of an eleven-year-old's sensibility, the report pronounces the end of the service as "rather boring as it was all prayers," expresses enthusiasm about the "sandwiches, stuffed rolls, orangeade and lemonade" that followed, and admits exhaustion by the day's end. But Elizabeth was clearly excited rather than intimidated by her initiation into the family business: "I thought it all *very, very* wonderful and I expect the Abbey did, too. The arches and beams at the top were covered with a sort of haze of wonder as Papa was crowned, at least I thought so." These are not the words of a girl horrified at the prospect of being Queen herself one day. In 1937, with a still-young father, that day would have seemed unimaginably distant. But from this moment on, the Princess was treated with even greater warmth and interest by the press, and she soon learned—not least from her grandmother Mary—the solemn public demeanor expected of royalty.

Demeanor aside, what else was she learning? She never went to school, and it has been often said that the Queen is therefore badly educated, having never been exposed to the formal curriculum and structure of a normal classroom. Crawford included examples of the timetable of study hours she had drawn up, and Queen Mary's advice on extra lessons; she also complained about the Duchess's habit of interfering in her daughters' education and taking them away from study for more enjoyable and frivolous times. Neither Crawford nor Queen Mary was much impressed by the Duchess's response to a request for more books—when they arrived, they were all by P. G. Wodehouse. Yet Elizabeth had a good French governess and learned fluent French early on. She did have to endure a long school day, and there was emphasis on dancing, drawing and riding alongside the French, math and history; but overall it was a perfectly respectable curriculum.

By the time Elizabeth was thirteen, she was being taught some history by the Royal Archivist. She was also sent to Eton for lessons in constitutional history given by the school's somewhat eccentric vice-provost Henry Marten, notorious for chewing his hankies and eating lumps of sugar kept in his pockets. Meanwhile the King began to show Elizabeth state papers and gently talk her through the duties she would one day have to take on.

It is not true, then, to say the Queen was badly educated. She was just differently educated. She was, and is, very fast at absorbing information and always had remarkable powers of concentration. From early on, she became shrewd at sizing up people, and good at recalling names and faces. Although going to a proper school might have helped her understand non-royal life, the lack of a formal education did not cripple her intellectually.

A SAILOR PRINCE

Another crucial moment in Elizabeth's early life occurred in July 1939 when, at age thirteen, she clapped eyes on Prince Philip of Greece, a boisterous eighteen-year-old cadet at the Royal Naval College at Dartmouth. She was visiting the Naval College with her parents on a two-day visit from the Royal Yacht, the *Victoria and Albert*. Prince Philip was deputed to look after the girls—by himself, apparently, because of an outbreak of mumps among the other cadets. He played games with them, jumped over tennis nets, wolfed platefuls of food and generally romped, ending by rowing his boat after the departing Royal Yacht until the King had to bellow at him to go back. In a telling photograph—the first to show the two of them in the same frame—Elizabeth is looking intently at whatever is being paraded, solemn and rather alone. In the back of the picture, Philip is guffawing at some joke.

Censorious Crawfie thought Philip showed off rather too much during those two days, but Elizabeth was delighted and never took her eyes off him. She began a correspondence with the Prince, which continued through the war while he served with the navy in the Mediterranean and Far East. She put a photograph of Philip up in her bedroom. When she was chided for giving succor to gossips, she swapped the first photo for one of him wearing a big, bushy beard, which she hoped disguised him. For her it seems to have been love at first sight. (It wasn't quite, because the two had met before, at a royal wedding and at the 1937 Coronation, but those unmemorable encounters between children barely count.) And true love, the classic *"coup de foudre,"* is rare enough to make the Queen a lucky woman.

At the outset, the match was not viewed favorably by everyone at the Palace. Philip was relatively poor and came from a scattered family that was rescued by the Royal Navy after Greek republicans turned on his father, Prince Andrew of Greece, in the wake of a disastrous war against Kemal Ataturk's resurgent nationalist Turks. But Philip was no stranger to the British Royals. His mother had been born at Windsor Castle and he was related to Princess Elizabeth through multiple cousin connections, reaching back to Queen Victoria and Prince Albert, who were great-great-grandparents of them both. His family was Danish, if it was anything, but more to the point it was really one of those royal-hyphenated families, purveyors of monarchs and princess wives to half of monarchical Europe.

The family's involvement with Greece began after the country became independent of the Ottoman Empire in 1830. This event prompted the "protecting powers" of Britain, France and Russia to insist that Greece be headed by an imported monarch, a strategy meant to limit the chance of civil war. In 1862, after the first choice for the Greek throne proved unsuitable, a teenage prince from Copenhagen, Philip's grandfather, was selected as King George I. Though he was both assiduous and popular, assassination and various political revolts made Greek kingship a chancy business. Philip's father, Andrew, was a dedicated soldier who did his best to serve Greece in a catastrophic war against Turkey soon after the end of

World War I. Ultimately, Andrew became one of the scapegoats for Greece's humiliating defeat by Turkey.

Prince Andrew might well have been executed by firing squad; others similarly accused were. But George V intervened, and a British agent fixed things so that in return for accepting exile, Andrew and his family would be allowed to escape. This they duly did from Corfu, where the bulk of the family had been living. Carried away on a British destroyer, the infant Prince Philip slept in an orange box and then went into exile with his parents and four older sisters. The family made their way to Rome, London and eventually to Paris, where they settled at a family-owned home, surrounded by other Greek exiles and Prince Andrew's brothers. During the 1920s Philip's family enjoyed a relatively settled and comfortable family life there, but eventually his parents separated. His mother, Princess Alice, became mentally ill, possibly with bipolar disorder; suffering from a form of religious mania, she was treated by Freudians, forcibly removed from her family and sent to a Swiss clinic. She was therefore effectively separated from her son for much of his childhood, including the crucial years between the ages of ten and fifteen. Later in life, she was a nun in the Greek Orthodox Church; after her recovery she became an intensely spiritual and almost saintly individual who nursed the injured and took great risks to save Jews in Athens during World War II.

Philip is seen as a rough, no-nonsense man, but he has reserves of spiritual interest that may be connected to the example of his unusual and little-known mother. She spent the last part of her life in London living with the rest of the royal family, much loved and admired. His father, meanwhile, wrote a book of war memoirs to defend his reputation and settled down in Cannes with a mistress whose claim to being an aristocrat was not perhaps soundly based. He never returned to his wife, even after her recovery, and he too cut himself off from the son whose company he had once enjoyed. Questioned later in life about this, Philip shrugged it off as something he just had to get on with, but if he has been a defensive and somewhat suspicious adult, it is not unreasonable to point to this disrupted childhood.

Prince Philip found some sense of stability in schools; he was also looked after by his mother's relatives in Britain, starting with his grandmother Victoria—herself a granddaughter of Queen Victoria. As important, however, were his mother's brothers, the Battenbergs, now known as the Milford Havens and the Mountbattens after the 1917 revolution of the names. George, Marquess of Milford Haven, was a particular help. Married to Nada, a wildly exotic Russian, he offered the young Philip a genuine haven during school holidays. After starting his education at an experimental American school in Paris, Philip went to the prep school Cheam, and then to a boarding school at Salem in Germany, owned by relatives—unfortunately, he arrived just as the Nazis were coming to power. He was a multilingual, cosmopolitan boy, fluent in Greek and French as well as English. His royal relatives were scattered all over Europe and he seemed always on the move, from *schloss* to palace, estate to hotel. But it was the close German connections that caused the most heartache later on.

All of Philip's sisters married German princes who remained loyal to their country in the Nazi years. His oldest sister, Margarita, married Friedel Hohenlohe-Langenburg, who joined the Nazi Party and offered to introduce its leaders to British royalty.[6] His sister Sophie married Christoph Hesse, who joined both the party and the SS, serving during the war in the Luftwaffe. His sister Cecile married Don Hesse, another prince, who also joined the Nazis. His sister Theodora married the Margrave of Baden, who was less keen on the Nazis but nevertheless served in Germany through the war. These connections to siblings in Germany divided Philip from most of his close family throughout World War II and explain why British newspapers were so eager to emphasize Philip's "essential Englishness" when he later became betrothed to Elizabeth—the result of a campaign of shameless spinning and elbow grabbing of editors by Mountbatten. They also explain why the groom's side of the aisle was sparse when he married.

Philip's time at the German school in Salem was relatively brief. He watched the steady advance of Nazi ideology in the classrooms and apparently found it all mildly risible. Salem's visionary founder, Kurt Hahn, had already fled Germany; later, he would become a huge influence on Philip when the young prince left Germany for Britain again. Hahn was one of the great educational visionaries of early-twentieth-century Europe. A brilliant Jewish intellectual who had been private secretary to Imperial Germany's last chancellor, Hahn believed Western society had been badly corrupted, most recently by the cruelty and militarism of the Great War. He felt strongly that the next generation had to be better educated in morals and civic duty, and he had devised the school in Salem accordingly. Though initially admiring of Hitler, Hahn quickly became disillusioned. He was briefly imprisoned and eventually had to escape to Britain via Switzerland. Hahn set up another school, Gordonstoun, in the northeast of Scotland, urged on by influential and rich admirers. Arriving in the fall of 1934, Prince Philip was one of the earliest pupils.

Thus one exile molded another. Hahn thought teenagers had an inner sense of right and wrong, but had to be helped to find it; this could best be done by testing them mentally but also through physical exertion and adventures. Gordonstoun's mix of cold baths, early runs, relentless outdoor activity and social work was not so different from that of other progressive boarding schools at the time, but it was undeniably tough. Hahn wrote, "Education must enable young people to effect what they have recognized to be right, despite hardships, despite dangers, despite inner skepticism, despite boredom, and despite mockery from the world." Further, Hahn said, "It is the sin of the soul to force young people into opinions— indoctrination is of the devil—but it is culpable neglect not to impel young people into experiences."

Hahn would go on to found other schools, as well as the Out-ward Bound movement. But his influence is most clearly felt in modern Britain through the Duke of Edinburgh's Award Scheme, which reflects Hahn's belief in the importance of adventure and the toughening effect of a little adversity. Hahn was no kind of surro-gate parent to Philip, but he seems to have had a big influence on him. The Duke of Edinburgh's lack of self-pity, his belief in practi-cality, his defiantly rough edges, his well-hidden spiritual side and his interest in nature can all be traced back not just to his parents and the buffeting of his unusual family life, but also to the Gordon-stoun ethic.

When Philip left the school Hahn gave him a thoughtful final report, noting the young prince's recklessness, sense of service and intelligence. He said he was "often naughty, never nasty." Philip's debt to Hahn has been passed on in areas such as his concern for the plight of inner-city youth and the environment, interests that were in turn passed on to Prince Charles.

Prince Philip's childhood was filled with trauma, and in 1937 another disaster struck when his sister Cecile and her husband the Grand Duke of Hesse were killed in an air crash. The pair had been flying with their two young sons to a wedding in London when the plane went down over Belgium, killing everyone on board, includ-ing the princess's stillborn fourth child. A lone surviving daughter, who had not been on the flight, died two years later of meningitis. Not long after that, George Milford Haven, who had been so kind to the young prince, died of cancer. Philip had already developed a tough protective shell, but the double blows must have hit the adolescent boy very hard.

After Gordonstoun, Philip joined the Royal Navy, going through the same training at Dartford that his uncle Mountbatten and both Georges V and VI had experienced. He experienced some family pressure to join the Greek navy, and later he said that he would have preferred being a fighter pilot in the RAF. But the British navy was an obvious choice, one of nationality as much as of fighting service.

Nobody dreamed she would be
Queen: the baby Elizabeth with
the Duke and Duchess of York.
(*Mary Evans*)

She preferred horses, even then.
(*Corbis*)

Learning the ropes
in the family firm:
Princess Elizabeth in
1932 after a church
service near Balmoral,
with her formidable
grandmother
Queen Mary and
the man she called
"Grandpa England,"
George V. (*Getty*)

A future king, already looking out of place? The Prince of Wales, later Edward VIII (*left*), and the young Louis Mountbatten, in a canvas swimming pool on HMS *Renown* during an imperial trip, 1920. (*Getty*)

Too modern for monarchy: "Uncle David" with his niece Princess Elizabeth, in 1933. (*Getty*)

"We four": a happy and private family before the storm, 1936. (*Getty*)

Thrilled, nevertheless: Princess Elizabeth, royal note-taker, after her father's coronation as George VI, 1937. (*Getty*)

An exuberant Prince Philip of Greece (*seated*) prepares to entertain the young princesses during George VI's visit to Dartmouth Royal Naval College, 1939. (*Getty*)

Early training for public performances: Princesses Elizabeth (*right*) and Margaret in a private pantomime of *Aladdin* at Windsor, 1943. (*Getty*)

Her most important teacher: Princess Elizabeth with her father, 1946. (*Getty*)

There were many rumored suitors: Princess Elizabeth dancing with the son of the Marquess of Abergavenny at her first public ball in 1946. (*Mary Evans*)

A rare escape from Austerity Britain: playing tag with midshipmen aboard HMS *Vanguard* en route to South Africa for the postwar royal visit, 1947. (*Corbis*)

The secret is out: Princess Elizabeth and Prince Philip of Greece together at the wedding of Patricia Mountbatten and Lord Brabourne, 1946. (*Getty*)

Watch your tongue, Daddy: the infant Princess Anne with Prince Philip, Princess Elizabeth, and Prince Charles in 1951. (*Getty*)

The final farewell: King George VI (*center*) waves good-bye to his daughter at London Airport, January 31, 1952.(*Getty*)

Queen Elizabeth II, in black, arrives in what is now her kingdom seven days later. (*Press Association Images*)

Children in the East End get news of a party. (*Corbis*)

The most solemn moment: the Queen's Coronation, June 2, 1953. (*Getty*)

Philip remained a prince of Greece at a time when, however briefly, its royal family seemed to be coming back into favor. In different circumstances, he could have hoped to be a king in Athens, but the family pull in London, and perhaps the lure of a much bigger and more exciting power, was greater. And if there had been any doubt as to the true nationality of this Danish-Greek-German boy who had had a French-American, English and Scottish education, then it was ended by the war, which saw him fight hard for Britain against the forces in which his sisters' husbands served.

Prince Philip had what people used to call "a good war." He was first posted to the Indian Ocean, perhaps to keep him, as a Greek citizen, out of direct action. Only after the summer of 1940, when Greece entered the conflict, did he see real fighting in the Mediterranean on the battleship HMS *Valiant*. At the Battle of Cape Matapan, Philip used his searchlight to pick out Italian cruisers, which were duly sunk; afterward, he was specifically mentioned in dispatches. He was later posted to a destroyer, becoming the youngest first lieutenant in the Royal Navy and serving in the North Sea.

In July 1943 his ship HMS *Wallace* was involved in the invasion of Sicily; thanks to a clever trick devised by Philip—he ordered the creation of a burning fake ship as a decoy—the *Wallace* was saved from a nighttime bomber attack. Later, he served in the Far East as the Pacific war against Japan entered its final stages, and in 1945 he witnessed the Japanese surrender. Philip was clearly a brave and talented sailor but he told his biographer Gyles Brandreth that he did not believe he would have progressed to the top of the service had he made it his full-time career: "Given the way of the British press, I wouldn't have got very far. Every promotion would have been seen as me being treated as a special case."[7]

By the time the war ended, when Philip was seriously considering proposing to Princess Elizabeth, his character was fully formed; at age twenty-four, he was recognizably the same man he is today, aged ninety. Some things have changed, of course: as a young man, he was flirtatious and physically boisterous, with a great enthusiasm for practical jokes and sending up older people. That has gone. But as a naval officer he was considered both ingenious and energetic—and also peppery and abrasive. He was a man's man, prepared to challenge anyone's opinion; unlike his serious and shy future wife, he was an extrovert. He could be startlingly rude, yet he was also guarded, sensitive and thoughtful. In time, he would give his children the close parenting he himself never had. And so in all these ways, he would become the sinewy paradox who has spent sixty years walking in the Queen's shadow, but very much at her side.

WINDSOR IN WARTIME

The war years were not, the Queen has said privately, a time of great privation or danger for her. While the King and Queen kept returning to Buckingham Palace and lived there through the worst of the Blitz, the princesses themselves lived at Windsor Castle, their whereabouts a national secret. This was sensible: the royal family was a prime German target and if the King was killed, Berlin had good reason to hope his exiled brother might be persuaded to return as a puppet monarch. On September 13, 1940, George VI and Queen Elizabeth nearly died when a German bomb hit the Palace. Had the window in the room where they were standing been closed, instead of open, they would have been seriously injured by flying glass; one of the workmen nearby was killed. Showing true self-assurance, a policeman observed to the Queen that it had been "a magnificent piece of bombing, if I may say so, Ma'am." (There was a postwar rumor that the attack had been directed by one of Prince Philip's brothers-in-law, but according to Philip Eade's recent biography of Philip there seems no evidence for it.)

After visiting the East End the following day, Queen Elizabeth wrote to her mother-in-law that "I really felt as if I was walking in a dead city."[8] Her natural ebullience soon reasserted itself, however, emerging clearly at the end of a letter to a cousin: "I am still just as frightened of bombs & guns going off, as I was at the beginning. I turn bright red, and my heart hammers—in fact I'm a beastly coward, but I do believe that a lot of people are, so I don't mind! . . . Tinkety tonk old fruit, & down with the Nazis."[9] She also took up revolver practice in case it should be necessary to make a final stand against German paratroopers, while the King carried a rifle and revolver with him, and practiced with them in the grounds of Buckingham Palace.

For the princesses, life was less interesting. Windsor Castle became the future Queen's home—she thinks of it that way still—but during the war it was a partly packed-up and sandbagged home, protected by troops and antiaircraft guns. Its thousand-plus rooms, staff of hundreds and ancient walls, reinforced during wartime with steel and concrete and barbed wire, provided a refuge but one that was steeped in gloomy history. Crawford commented that it was a fortress, not a home. The princesses could follow the war on the radio and socialize, a little, with officers stationed at Windsor, but it cut them off even further from normal life. Though they were rationed and sometimes had to rush down to an air-raid shelter in the dungeon—Elizabeth protesting initially that she had to dress properly first—they saw little of the reality of the war. The death of the King's youngest brother, the Duke of Kent, in an air crash in 1942 dealt the kind of blow to this family that others all over Britain were having to endure.

One of the Queen's earlier biographers, Robert Lacey, reflected that the war confirmed her already formidable sense of duty: "The atmosphere of 1949 did not encourage whimsicality in anybody. So Princess Elizabeth developed from a serious child into a serious girl with no discernable break in continuity, and any tendency to eccentricity or rebellion was stifled."[10] Assailed by grim national news and surrounded by the castle's stony royal history, Elizabeth had no chance to experience the freer, wilder adolescence that, for instance, her mother had enjoyed in the 1920s. Her somewhat solemn nature and her sense of duty were not created during the war, but those years reinforced that side of her character.

But life during wartime was not all grim. The Windsor enthusiasm for games and dressing up expressed itself in annual Christmas pantomimes, in which both princesses dressed and acted. (Anyone curious about the Queen's youthful legs should see the picture of her costumed as Aladdin.) It was one such performance that caused Prince Philip—invited to stay at Windsor during his leave at the end of 1943—to roar with laughter, and perhaps began to fire his interest in Elizabeth properly. The Queen said later that she thought the pantomimes were her father's way of beginning to prepare the girls for a life of performance. It was, in any case, their first time up on a stage, and although Margaret enjoyed the pantomimes hugely, Elizabeth did not.

The Girl Guiding continued, and there were dances and picnics and childhood games. Philip appeared now and again, blown in on a sea-salted wind. Elizabeth spent much of her time with her sister, who was four years her junior. For most of their childhood the girls dressed alike, but beyond any superficial resemblance they were not alike. There were tales of girlish fights: reportedly, Margaret occasionally bit her sister, who responded with sometimes cutting remarks about Margaret's weight and clumsiness.[11] Soon enough it was clear to Margaret that if her sister was to become Queen, she would be left in a lifelong shadow. She was said to have complained: "I am nothing." Elizabeth, it was asserted, retorted, "Margaret always wants what I want." Later anecdotes have Elizabeth firmly if fondly rebuking Margaret for not paying enough attention to being polite in public and "good."

Temperament is a mysterious ingredient, and Margaret—fifteen by the time the war ended—was her father's cheeky pet. She was funny, clever and musical, and while Elizabeth was being trained for the throne, Margaret was allowed liberties. No doubt Margaret's nature was shaped considerably by her place in the family order, but her talents for biting wit, mimicry and music suggest a woman who would have flourished in other circumstances. World War II, as it happened, also brought an important new figure into her life: in the last two years of the war, Buckingham Palace employed an RAF war hero named Peter Townsend as the King's equerry. Margaret would eventually turn to him.

Elizabeth had obstinately petitioned her father to allow her to do war work more substantial than a radio broadcast or ceremonial function. She finally got her way when she joined the Auxiliary Territorial Service, or ATS, shortly before the end of the war, learning to service trucks and cars, as well as drilling and driving. It was a rare chance for her to mix with others of her age, though she was never quite allowed to forget her position; after training session, she was whisked away and so seldom enjoyed frank conversations with the others. She tried to make friends and hoped to do more, but Hitler fell first. In practical terms her contribution to the war effort was show, rather than practice: a pretty young princess in military uniform, wielding a wrench, made fine propaganda.

When VE day finally came, Elizabeth and Margaret were allowed by their father to mingle with the crowds outside Buckingham Palace. They marched arm in arm in a small party up Piccadilly, into the Ritz and then on to Hyde Park, singing songs and cheering, before standing outside the Palace and joining in the rousing call for the King and Queen to appear. Walking the crowded streets with their caps pulled down, the girls were barely recognized, though a Dutch serviceman noticed them and thoughtfully made no fuss. One of those in Elizabeth's group, the Queen's great racing friend Lord Porchester, then in the Household Cavalry, recalled: "Everyone was very jolly, linking arms in the streets and singing, 'Run, Rabbit, Run,' 'Hang out the Washing on the Siegfried Line,' 'Roll Out the Barrel,' that sort of thing all night."[12] It is poignant that this very rare experience of a fragment of street life remains an important memory for the Queen.

The following day, she and the rest of the royal family drove into the East End and then to south London to visit the worst hit of recent V2 rocket attack sites. The Londoners she came across at the war's end were the people of a different capital, a different country than the London and Britain of today. Overwhelmingly white, they were extraordinarily shabby and poorly washed compared to modern Londoners. Many were in uniform and the rest wore wartime coupon-bought clothing; they were a tea-drinking, cigarette-smoking, wireless-addicted people who had begun turning against the class-bound Britain from before the war. When Japan surrendered on August 14, there was another wild party in the streets and the Princess wrote in her diary: "Out in crowd, Whitehall, Mall, St J [James] St, Piccadilly, Park Lane, Constitution Hill, ran through Ritz. Walked miles, drank in Dorchester, saw parents twice, miles away, so many people."[12]

As committed to the monarchy as ever, the people would shortly kick out the great wartime leader Winston Churchill and usher in a Labour government. George VI, despite his irascible suspicion of socialists, would come to terms with an administration of patriotic, anticommunist reformers, and later the years of socialist reform and the championing of equality. Much sooner than expected, his daughter would have to find ways of reigning effectively in a part-nationalized Britain of the National Health Service and powerful trade unions.

That core of grand London that the Princess and her friends had encountered—with its aristocratic homes, hotels and clubs—continued for a while as a citadel of tradition in a changing world. The imperial pomp of the Victorian monarchy was still visible through the wartime grime. Soon officials in bowlers, striped trousers and rolled umbrellas were again taking tea in the clubs of St. James's. The Household Cavalry and Guards returned in their scarlet uniforms and their gleaming breastplates, while from the palaces behind them, colonial governors with pith helmets and feathers were dispatched by the Court of St. James. And in the drab aftermath of war, when London seemed a blackened and in places toothless old girl, attempts were made to revive the ritual of the "Season" and the High Society of the 1930s.

Accomplishing this was not easy. Old London Society, with the court at its apex, had relied on battle fleets of wealthy aristocratic and landed families, whose sons and daughters would be married off after a round of parties and entertainments. But now Britain was broke. Death duties had been increased to 75 percent on estates of over £1 million and income taxes were at historically high levels. Titled London landowners sold off swaths of their property in the capital; around the country, from Scotland to Devon, land was auctioned at rock-bottom prices. Of London's great private houses, where before the war so many social-season parties were held, hardly one was left intact. Even if they had not been bombed, they were soon knocked down for offices or converted into museums. As for the country homes, four hundred were demolished in the decade after the war; in 1955, says the historian David Cannadine, they were disappearing at the rate of one every five days.

The social world her parents had known vanished before Princess Elizabeth's eyes. Postwar gossips suggested that princesses Elizabeth and Margaret might be won by one of the heirs with map names; young men from the Westmorland, Rutland and Blandford families were proposed as potential suitors. And the two girls did enjoy the company of Guards officers at postwar weekend parties at Sandringham and Windsor. Yet the Windsors were now a social summit without a mountain of wealth and glamour to support them.

The old Season did reappear, after a fashion. Queen Charlotte's Birthday Ball for debutantes, one of the key matrimonial markets of earlier decades, restarted in March 1946. In May 1948 the grandest of the Season events returned when George VI, dressed in his admiral's uniform, mingled with twenty-five hundred guests for the first "presentation" of debutantes since the war. (Though Princess Elizabeth was there, attired in dove-gray silk, she was perhaps skeptical, as she would later abandon these presentations.) But the Season could hardly be the same and soon, with the solitary exception (until 1960) of Londonderry House, all the private palaces had gone. The Royals had Clarence House, Marlborough House and Buckingham Palace, but they were left in lonely splendor.[13]

For the Windsors themselves, life was brighter. The royal calendar, which dated only to the early years of the century, revived in its comforting predictability, a round of Sandringham Christmases, Balmoral summers and Windsor weekends. Horse racing, like football and rugby, was soon as popular as ever. The Ascot Gold Cup, which had been held at Newmarket during the war, returned immediately to home turf in 1945. The Grand National, which had been canceled in 1940, was back again in 1946. The Henley Regatta, canceled during the war, returned as a shortened one-day "peace regatta" in 1945. Yet the message of wartime service was a solemn one. Royal garden parties returned, but the first ones were held in honor of some of the thousands of prisoners of war recently returned from Germany. And for the royal family, rounds of hospital, military and civic openings, as well as parades and speeches, were back with a vengeance.

Princess Elizabeth was being trained in public engagements that were stodgily routine. When she was knocked against a tree by her horse while riding at Windsor in September 1945, the Palace immediately reassured the press that she would be able to inspect the Grenadier Guards, attend a Girl Guides event and hand out diplomas in domestic science in Glasgow. She was sent to open extensions to schools for the deaf and disability centers in the West Country; she visited a children's hospital in east London and the Eisteddfod at Mountain Ash in Wales, where she was proclaimed a Bard—one of the Queen's less likely titles. Her speeches did not sound spontaneous, nor were they meant to. Only in the country did she sometimes escape, efficiently dispatching stags during stalks in the Highlands, and with increasing confidence displaying her family's skill with guns, horses and excitable dogs.

LOVE AND MARRIAGE

All the while, Elizabeth had kept her secret, though not from those nearest to her. On July 9, 1946, the royal family held the first "proper" Buckingham Palace garden party since the war, which *The Times*'s reporter thought a glorious occasion: "The spacious lawns of the Palace grounds are still brilliantly green from earlier rains and beneath yesterday's bright skies were the ideal natural carpet. . . . There was as at Ascot, relaxation of pre-war rules of dress." The prime minister, Clem Attlee, was among seven thousand guests, ranging from foreign royals to farmers. So too was one Prince Philip Mountbatten, back from service in the Far East a few months earlier. His name began to crop up in other newspaper reports of weddings and parties where Princess Elizabeth could also be found. By the end of the year the Greek prince had successfully applied for British citizenship and readers of *The Times* were being reassured: "Non-naval readers of the report that Prince Philip of Greece had applied for naturalization may not recognize under that title the grandson of one very distinguished British admiral and the nephew of another. . . . But for the abnormal conditions arising from a state of war, he would ordinarily have become a British subject on passing out of Dartmouth in 1939 and formally entering the Navy."

This was no ordinary correction to the record, for by then Prince Philip had asked Princess Elizabeth to marry him and she had told her father. The King, worried that she was too young, insisted on a condition: the young couple would have to wait. Imperial business must come first, and the royal family were pledged to visit South Africa. This would be an important and lengthy visit, part of the Princess's training for the life to come. And since the trip would last four months, it would also give her plenty of time to reflect and ask herself whether she was sure about marrying.

After eighteen months of close mutual admiration, Prince Philip's proposal had come at Balmoral. Later, he provided a studiously vague account, saying that "one thing led to another. I suppose I began to think about it seriously, oh, let me think now, when I got back in '46 and went to Balmoral. It was then that we, that it became, you know, that we began to think about it seriously."[14] His "you know" no doubt reflects an embarrassment about public soul baring rather than anything else; like the Queen, he comes from a generation less willing to express emotion than today's. She accepted at once, and then began to work on her father. This was a less complicated wooing than that of George and Elizabeth following the previous war. But it did not go down well with everyone.

The courtiers' case against the Philip connection focused on his German relatives, his bumptiousness, and his lack of deference, all of it tut-tutted about by Queen Elizabeth's family, the Bowes Lyons, and the Palace old guard, later described by Princess Margaret as "the men with moustaches." A mixture of snobbery with a whiff of racism echoed through the cold, grand corridors. But it seems that George VI himself took quickly to the young prince—who, it is said, saw the King wearing his kilt and with a grin promptly curtsied. George's caution was more about his daughter's youth and inexperience: she had met her fiancé, after all, when she was only thirteen. In the meantime there had been serious alternatives put forward. A brace of dukes' sons and the offspring of an earl had been mentioned. They were all beside the point. Princess Elizabeth manifestly believed in duty, but she had a mind and a will of her own. So the couple were engaged, but privately. Any public announcement would wait until the family's return from South Africa, by which point she would have turned twenty-one.

The main purpose of the trip was to try to bind South Africa more tightly back into the Commonwealth. The royal party, steaming toward sunlight and plenty aboard the last of the great British battleships, HMS *Vanguard*, left behind a Britain huddling through an austere, grim winter, among the worst of the century. The King felt badly enough about it to cable Attlee and offer to come back; the prime minister said no, because the mission was important. In 1947, though the real, India-centered Empire was dying, many British people still thought of themselves as an imperial race and looked to "English" sister-nations overseas as a global family. Empire Day was still celebrated; Australia, South Africa, Kenya and New Zealand beckoned as places for ambitious Britons to settle in, and many believed that the idea of a globe-spanning British trade system was eminently sensible. Few politicians expected independence to come soon to the African or Middle Eastern possessions, and the British army maintained massive bases in the Mediterranean. But South Africa—so rich, so large, so strategically placed—was a weak link.

Its rulers divided between the Dutch-speaking Boers and the English settlers, the country had stuck with Britain during the war. Jan Smuts had become the only non-British field marshal at Churchill's side and a hugely popular figure in Britain, but the anti-British Afrikaners were by now reasserting themselves. Among those on the rise were pro-Nazi racists, who would later help create the apartheid system, which locked black Africans, comprising 75 percent of the population, out of power. Wooing South Africa—cheering the pro-British faction, calming the Afrikaner one and making gestures toward the black majority—was a tricky, perhaps impossible, task. Afrikaner newspapers were often hostile and the King found the strain of endless speeches hard; on one occasion Elizabeth had to cajole him into speaking. But the welcome and celebrations in Cape Town were exuberant, the royal party were followed by huge crowds, and on the surface, at least, the trip seemed to be a huge success.

For Elizabeth and Margaret, their first time abroad was very special, a cascade of sensations. Elizabeth learned the absolute importance of timekeeping, prodding her mother forward when she dawdled, and she managed to keep looking interested during long days of official engagements. She also impressed everyone with her radio broadcast on her twenty-first birthday, making what she called a simple dedication: "I declare before you that my whole life, whether it be long or short, shall be devoted to your service and the service of our great Imperial Commonwealth to which we all belong. But I shall not have the strength to carry out this resolution unless you join in it with me." Though the speech had been written by Lascelles, the Princess had contributed her own thoughts and ideas, and it attracted a great deal of comment in the English-speaking world. Listening to it now, there is something eerie, atavistic and mysterious about its phrases and cadences; it is as if we are witnessing a young woman making herself into some kind of living human sacrifice.

At the time, however, many heard it as a call to arms from a Greater Britain. Soon, however, there was no Imperial Commonwealth left: with India's independence six months later, the Empire disappeared. King George VI had been a King-Emperor; his daughter would not be Queen-Empress. And with India gone, South Africa seemed a significant part of the new Commonwealth's importance. But it was not to be, and thirteen years later, after the rise of Afrikaner nationalism, bitter rows and a formal declaration by the Commonwealth in 1960 of its multiracial status, South Africa would leave on its lonely voyage as an apartheid state.

The Princess, after enjoying riding on African beaches, the closeness of the family and the unaccustomed sunlight, returned to Britain as determined as ever to wed Prince Philip. The announcement came on July 10, 1947. Unlike some of the courtiers, the public seem to have welcomed the news enthusiastically, despite a hostile opinion poll eighteen months earlier. The Prince—as he was popularly known, even though naturalization meant that his title was now meaningless and Lieutenant Mountbatten would have been more accurate—became for the first time a public figure. His MG sports car was identified, pointed out and photographed. His picture appeared everywhere. He was given a security detail and a valet, even though he barely had the wardrobe to be brushed.

At a party to celebrate the announcement, other royals noted that Philip was still in his shabby naval uniform. His prospects were now golden but his income was modest. He traveled third class on trains and was from an entirely different world than the still-rich aristocratic Old Etonians the court circles would have preferred. What Philip brought instead was a restless, inquiring energy and great physical glamour. He also had powerful friends and allies. His future title, Duke of Edinburgh, was settled with the help of friendly journalists. The King sketched designs for his coat of arms. Both he and his bride were awarded the Order of the Garter. He would become HRH. Thus is a partial outsider prepared for royal authority.

꒰꒱

What kind of wedding would it be? This was the darkest moment of the austerity years. In 1947 Britain faced a grave financial crisis, a run on the pound, low productivity, feeble exports and recurrent strikes. That year, rations of meat, bacon, ham and fats fell below wartime levels, to their lowest ever; clothes rations were cut; gasoline was in short supply; foreign currency could be purchased only for essential travel. How would people react to a luxurious wedding? Not surprisingly, both court and government trod warily at first. Prince Philip wanted an unostentatious ceremony. His future father-in-law was in a gloomy mood about the very survival of the monarchy, with so many grand houses shutting up and the imposition of communist regimes in eastern Europe.

Hugh Dalton, the chancellor, was preparing a very lean budget with more tax increases. So many Labour MPs, and no doubt many Labour supporters in the country, did not want any sort of extravagant festival of a wedding. The annual clothing allowance for an adult was forty-eight coupons. Following the announcement that Princess Elizabeth would be allocated a hundred clothing coupons for her wedding, with bridesmaids getting twenty-three coupons each and pages ten coupons, the Labour MP Mabel Ridealgh complained: "It is the general impression among the workers that it would not be proper to spend large sums of money on this wedding when we are asking the workers themselves to economize even in the necessities of life."[15]

But Mabel and others had made a misjudgment. Toward the end of 1947 and despite a torrent of reforming social legislation, people were becoming weary of the shortages and red tape Labour was coming to represent. As preparations for the wedding gathered speed, it began to be clear that outside the political platoons of socialism, there was little enthusiasm for a puritanical, frugal event. The country wanted color and it wanted fun. Behind all the constitutional business, providing that is the job of the monarchy. What was the point of royalty if a royal wedding failed to provide a glow in darkling times?

But before the wedding went ahead, the King and his government tussled about how much money Princess Elizabeth and Prince Philip would get. George VI had run a tight and frugal court during the war, saving a substantial sum (around £200,000). But was this money his or the Treasury's? He wanted a generous settlement for the soon-to-be-weds. Dalton and left-leaning Labour MPs wanted a far smaller settlement, symbol of a more "simple, austere and democratic" monarchy. Some MPs wanted no money paid over at all, believing King George should pay for his daughter out of his own funds. The row went on, mostly behind closed doors.

The King stood his ground. Eventually Dalton was forced to resign anyway, having leaked his budget to a journalist. His successor, Stafford Cripps, despite being another upper-class socialist with a reputation for flinty Puritanism, agreed to a more generous compromise. When the Cripps compromise was put to the Commons, Attlee's main argument was geopolitical. A ceremonial monarchy with simple people at its heart was, he argued, a good democratic alternative to fascist or communist symbolism. The job was a real one, Attlee said, and it must be funded. In the end the King agreed to pass over half his wartime savings; meanwhile, the couple would get about two-thirds of what he had hoped for. Even this deal only squeaked through Parliament: 165 Labour MPs voted for a lower payment still. There was some evidence afterward that resentment about the annuities for the Prince and Princess spread beyond the parliamentary Labour Party. How popular was the monarchy really? No one was certain.

In 1947, unlike today, it was not taken for granted that a royal wedding, even one involving the heir to the throne, had to be a grandly public national ceremony. Historically, most royal weddings had been private affairs, with private parties and some waving from balconies or landaus. This time, the choice of Westminster Abbey followed the precedent set only by George VI and Queen Elizabeth, and after all the financial haggling the decision to hold the ceremony in the abbey ensured that the wedding would be the major national event most of the country wanted. The numbers of guests who could be accommodated in the vast and ancient space, and the traditional processional route to it from Buckingham Palace, meant that a grand spectacular was unavoidable.

Elaborate preparations proceeded apace. The event would be extensively covered on the radio, and early on it was agreed that film cameras would be allowed in so that a cinema presentation could later be shown around the world. Wire, painted wood and electrically lit street decorations were built and erected. Presents began to flood in from around the world, ranging from grand confections of precious stones from Indian princes to what Queen Mary thought was Mahatma Gandhi's loincloth, an item she considered very distasteful. (It was, in fact, simply a piece of linen he had woven himself.) There were tins of condensed milk and fruit from American and Australian well-wishers who worried that the British were still starving. (These would later be distributed to some of the Britons who were not quite starving, but were hungry and bored with rationing.) From ordinary Britons came nylons and cigarette cases, humble knitted jerseys and pictures. The presents were laid out in long lines at St. James's Palace, flash and ordinary alike, to be viewed by anyone who bought a ticket.

Princess Elizabeth took a close interest in everything, but her dress above all. It was designed by Norman Hartnell, a man who greatly influenced Queen Elizabeth's image during her early years. The son of a South London pub owner, Hartnell left Cambridge without a degree to become a designer to the rich and fashionable in Jazz Age London, producing clothes for court parties and movie stars alike. He moved to Bruton Street in Mayfair, just down the way from where the Queen herself had been born, and was soon winning royal commissions, including from Elizabeth's mother. Hartnell became Britain's leading promoter of romantic and extravagant clothing, using a famous French seamstress for his showers of sequins and reintroducing the crinoline. Among his clients were Gertrude Lawrence, Marlene Dietrich and Elizabeth Taylor; among the rivals who admired him were Coco Chanel and Christian Dior.

The dress he created for the 1947 wedding was an extraordinary confection of ivory silk and tulle, corn ears in crystal, embroidered stars and orange blossoms. It required, among other things, ten thousand seed pearls. Almost inevitably there was a minor row about extravagance and patriotism: was the silk from Chinese worms? (Yes, but Nationalist worms, not Communist worms, retorted Hartnell.) A dozen enormous cakes were ordered. The presents, the food and the dress were symbols not just of a wedding, or the returning glamour of royalty, but of all those things the British wanted for themselves but could not yet have. No one had the coupons for a Hartnell special. Nobody else could legally acquire the sugar, marzipan and candied fruit for the cakes, or do more than imagine the cornucopia of good things pouring in from abroad. But this seemed to produce anticipation, not jealousy. The wedding was like a giant shop window: a million noses were pressed against it, and "coming soon" or "coming one day" was written overhead.

It was an early premonition, at the darkest economic hour, of the rosy consumerist dawn.

A darker future lay ahead for the once-grand family of European royalty, a large number of whom had also been invited. A dusty, rather moth-eaten horde of current and former monarchs and consorts converged on London with their old jewels and pre-war clothes, reminding everyone that the Windsors were rare, and lucky, survivors. Some were already exiles. Others were soon to be tipped from their thrones. The royal wedding was a reunion of the old clans, but it had to exclude many. For a start, the German relatives did not get invitations, not even Prince Philip's three surviving sisters. Germans in general were very unpopular and some of the in-laws had served the Nazis. British survival and victory had been won at a horrible human and economic cost, but London was the capital of a successful constitutional monarchy; few other countries could now say the same. Patriotism and monarchism had joined arms, and the ceremony would deliver that message when it was shown on screens across devastated Europe and in America too.

Up and down Britain, as Princess Elizabeth pledged to honor and obey her husband, millions of her future subjects held a "good for us" party. The princess was seen as a national symbol of youth, rebirth, and hope. Of course, nobody at the time could have predicted that only five years later Elizabeth would become Queen, and that her wedding would be outshone by the grander ritual of a Coronation. In the winter of 1947, everyone assumed that the newlyweds had a long time ahead of them to enjoy a certain amount of privacy and freedom, and one another.

Prince Philip began his days as a married man with a real sacrifice: to please his new wife, he gave up smoking. And he quickly discovered how radically their lives would now change. On honeymoon, initially at Mountbatten's home Broadlands, they were spied on by snoopers hanging in the trees and pursuing them to church. The King wrote to Princess Elizabeth during the honeymoon to say that as he had handed her over to the Archbishop of Canterbury and married life, "I felt that I had lost something very precious. . . . I can, I know, always count on you, & now Philip, to help us in our work. Your leaving us has left a great blank in our lives but do remember that your old home is still yours."

The young couple wouldn't be living a great distance away: they had been assigned Clarence House, just a few hundred yards east of Buckingham Palace. Later the home of their son, the Prince of Wales, it was then a mess, almost unfit for living in. While the couple waited for renovations to be finished, they found themselves first at Kensington Palace and then back with the in-laws at Buckingham Palace. But they did not return to royal routine in every respect. Prince Philip was able to walk to work at the Admiralty across St. James's Park, unthinkable nowadays. At night, apparently, he disdained pajamas, despite the cold. Three months later, the Princess was pregnant.

It was during this period, from the late 1940s onward, that Prince Philip's association with a cheerfully louche group of men, artists and actors, photographers and aristocrats, began to cause muttering. Baron Nahum, a photographer and friend, hosted what he called his "Thursday Club" above an oyster bar in Soho where loud and sometimes drunken male parties would take place. Prince Philip has always been a moderate drinker but this set allowed him to relax properly in jovial, undeferential company. This took him to the edge of a gamy, even seamy, set which included the defense minister Jack Profumo, later forced to resign from the Commons for lying, as well as the man at the center of the Profumo scandal, Stephen Ward. A few rumors about romances with actresses and society women began circulating, but after a lifetime's worth of nosing and probing, not a shred of hard evidence that Philip has been unfaithful has ever emerged, and it is a subject which irritates the Duke greatly. Because he was already under fire from courtier snobs, who accused him of not being a proper gentleman (by which they meant a landed bore), the gossip was dangerous and hurtful.

The birth of Prince Charles was greeted with cheering crowds outside Buckingham Palace and sonorous columns in the news-papers. *The Times* produced an editorial which shows just how far the mood of the press toward royalty has changed during Charles's lifetime. His birth was, the paper said, "a national and imperial event" and brought an heir to the throne with direct Danish blood, the first time that had happened since 1042. As for the Princess, she had "fully established herself as the visible representative of the whole of the younger generation, the generation upon which rests the heaviest burden of the Empire's recovery." This time around, it was no longer necessary to have a cabinet minister on hand for the birth; by 1948 the silliness of the tradition had become too embar-rassing. Other traditions, though, were maintained: the boy was named HRH Prince Charles Philip Arthur George, covering most of the royal bases. And thanks to his maternal grandmother's blood, he was the most Scottish heir to the throne since the ill-fated Charles I.

The couple of years that followed were perhaps the happiest of the Queen's life. She was fulfilling her duties, as the papers had noted, but they were not nearly as onerous as they would become. She and Prince Philip made a successful visit to Paris, and in London a theatrical and aristocratic set gathered around the couple now gen-erally known as "the Edinburghs." They finally moved into their own home. Prince Philip was soon appointed second in command of a destroyer in the Mediterranean fleet, HMS *Chequers*. The Princess followed him to Malta later in 1949, and there she was able to live a near-normal life as a naval wife, going shopping, visiting the hair-dresser, making friends, eating at local hotels and restaurants. (The infant Charles was often left in London with his grandparents.) Abroad, the Queen began to cine-film her husband, watched him playing polo, and swam and danced. In August 1950 she gave birth to a second child, Anne. Prince Philip rose to command his first ship, the frigate HMS *Magpie*. Practical work and domesticity dom-inated their lives; for now, as Robert Lacey put it: "Inheriting the throne was something for the 1960s or even the 1970s."

Yet quickly there were warning signs. The King was ill; soon he was diagnosed with cancer, presumably caused by his decades of heavy smoking. Londoners who saw him passing in the streets talked about his gray, shrunken face. He underwent a series of operations. Though personally optimistic about his prospects, George VI increasingly needed Princess Elizabeth to carry out engagements he could not manage. It became clear that she had to be in Britain, and since Prince Philip could hardly command a Mediterranean ship from there, he dolefully gave up his much-loved job. He may have expected or hoped to return to full-time naval service; he would never do so. His wife took on more responsibility, greeting foreign dignitaries and riding in the King's place for Trooping the Colour. She presided at the Privy Council just before Parliament was dissolved for the 1951 election, which ended the Labour years and returned Winston Churchill to power. To many it already seemed that the young couple were eclipsing the monarch, much as Prince William and his new bride later seemed to eclipse Prince Charles.

While the election campaign was being fought, Philip and Elizabeth went on a long tour to Canada, mainly by train, and visited President Truman in Washington, where they were feted. Truman, starstruck, commented, "When I was a little boy, I read about a fairy princess, and there she is." Throughout the trip the Princess's new private secretary Martin Charteris had papers for the Accession Council under his bed, just in case the King died.[16] During the winter of 1951–52, however, the King seemed to make a remarkable recovery. He went to Prince Charles's third birthday party, started shooting again and visited the theater. There was a national day of thanksgiving for the King's recovery, celebrated in churches throughout Britain. The King was pleased to have Churchill back as prime minister—he was never keen on Labour.

George could not, however, manage the next long-planned royal tour, which was to East Africa, Australia and New Zealand. The glamorous young ones would go instead. On January 31, 1952, the

King waved them off at the modestly sized and freezing London Airport. His life of meetings was about to end; hers, to begin.

‿✥‿

People were not prepared for the death of George VI, at home or around the world. He was known to be unwell, but he seemed to have carried on well enough after a lung operation. The day before he died, he had been out for a few hours' sunshine at Sandringham, banging away at hares as usual; that evening, he went quietly to bed, and a footman brought him his nighttime cocoa. On the following wet, sleeting morning, February 6, 1952, black-bordered special editions of the newspapers announcing his death appeared on the streets of London at 11:15 a.m., just half an hour after the official announcement from the Palace. Somber and silent crowds spontaneously appeared on street corners, the Mall and at Westminster; in those days, people came together in public, rather than around television sets. Churchill, weeping in bed, thought it "the worst news." Crowds gathered in newly republican India too, as well as in Australia and Canada. Even in the United States many people reacted with shock. One of the best-known figures of the wartime years, the figurehead of a nation still considered one of the world's leaders, had suddenly gone. He was only fifty-six.

His daughter learned the news from her husband on their Kenyan holiday. They had been staying at the Treetops rest house, watching wildlife from a platform in a giant fig tree. On the way there, the royal party had come dangerously close to a large cow elephant protecting two calves; she had not scented them. Prompted by Prince Philip, Elizabeth and the others had gingerly, quietly, carried on to their vantage point. Perhaps in retrospect the danger to the not-yet Queen has been romantically embellished. But later in her reign, health and safety would have kept them far away.

The news that the King had died came first to a senior courtier, Lieutenant General Frederick Browning. He passed it to Martin Charteris via a journalist. Charteris confirmed it and then told Prince

Philip's aide, Mike Parker, who told the Prince. Parker was later quoted as saying that Prince Philip "looked as if the whole world had dropped on him"—as, in a sense, it had. His wife had gone out to order some horses to be prepared for riding. When she returned, Philip told her the news.

Elizabeth began almost immediately to write letters and messages apologizing for canceling the rest of the trip, and making new arrangements. Very much a member of the stoic generation, she showed no immediate distress. Lady Pamela Mountbatten, her cousin, went in to console her: "In her usual extraordinary way . . . she was thinking about what everybody else was having to do. Typically, she said, 'Oh, thank you. But I am so sorry it means we have to go back to England and it's upsetting everybody's plans.' "[17]

The Queen in the World

Sixty years on, her staying power has given the Queen a personal knowledge of global leaders unmatched by any other person alive. She has had, as houseguests, such near-mythic figures as Emperor Haile Selassie, General Charles de Gaulle, Lech Walesa and Nelson Mandela; controversial twentieth-century monarchs such as the Shah of Iran, Emperor Hirohito of Japan and King Faisal of Saudi Arabia; tyrants such as Ceauşescu of Romania and Mugabe of Zimbabwe; key first-generation African leaders such as Tanzania's Julius Nyerere, Kenneth Kaunda of Zambia, Mobutu Sese Seko of Zaire and Daniel arap Moi of Kenya; and central figures in Russian history like Marshal Nikolay Bulganin, Nikita Khrushchev (who took tea with her and found her to his surprise "completely unpretentious") and Vladimir Putin. A short book could be written solely about her relations with U.S. presidents from Truman and Eisenhower, through Kennedy, Nixon and Reagan, to the Obamas today.

"Reader No. 1," as the British government calls her, has seen every significant secret Foreign Office cable or telegram, and much of the MI6 advice, about international crises and problems from the 1950s onward. As head of state of fifteen nations other than the United Kingdom, she has taken her overseas queenships very seriously. As Head of the Commonwealth, she has had a ringside seat during six decades of global change, witnessing everything from the epic drama of the Indian subcontinent to African decolonization and the transformation of Asia.

Though she may occasionally be tempted to pick up her pen for something longer than a sweeping regal signature, the assumption must be, however, that she would not. She keeps a diary, but sadly not, we are assured, in the Pepys or Crossman or Alan Clark way. Most of her intercourse with world leaders has been at the level of the polite and uncontroversial exchange of expressions of goodwill. Her job is to meet, to listen but not to interrogate. She is Britain's Department of Warmth, the Secretary of State for Friendship. The records of her long and frequent visits to other countries contain endless pictures of singing groups of children, cheering crowds, banquets and march-pasts. A gorgeous cavalcade of dresses, often by Norman Hartnell or Hardy Amies, and hats, dresses or bags, shows the care taken to reflect local sensibilities. The presents received— paintings, silver- and goldware, jewelry, strange carved crocodiles and all the rest—would fill a warehouse.

It is a curious business, this endless exchanging of gifts. Around the world, the corridors and studies of presidents, prime ministerial offices, and anterooms of official headquarters are stuffed with glass cases containing ceremonial swords, ugly ceramics or models made of silver. They create grand clutter that always need dusting. Hardly any provide pleasure. There are exceptions: Nelson Mandela gave Prince Philip a hand-painted chess set of African figures which would make anyone smile. Some are particularly ill-considered: who would want a gilt model oil rig on a stand in a glass box from Saskatchewan? But this is to miss the point. Gift giving goes back to the earliest recorded human civilizations. It is a ritual designed to confirm lack of hostility, lack of war. Today the exchange of gifts provides oil to smooth negotiations, balm for disappointing answers or grease to elicit better ones.

The Queen's travels around the world speak directly to her own idea of what she is for. She has never seen herself as just, or even perhaps mainly, the British Queen. Though most of the trips have been tiring but not difficult, with predictable and reliable welcomes awaiting her, some have been tricky. She has been booed by French-Canadian nationalists and emerged from a church service in Dresden, bombed to pieces by the RAF during the war, to confront a sea of silent and not entirely friendly faces. She has waited in the sweltering heat of the desert, while a panicking King of Morocco tore up the preparations for lunch and offered her only cognac. She has overridden the fears of ministers to visit potentially dangerous places in Africa and Asia. She has dealt calmly with inebriated Russians.

From the very beginning, being Head of the Commonwealth was central, and it is a role she owes to the founders of modern India above all. After World War II, many Americans campaigned against the British Empire as the prime example of bankrupt imperialism, not least because it got in the way of their world-dominating commercial ambition. Even inside the British "family of nations" there were serious strains. Burma became the first country to leave the Empire since the loss of the American colonies. On Easter Monday 1949, the Irish Republic went too. South Africa was already engaged in a debate about seceding. During the war the Australians had toyed with creating their own defensive alliance with the United States. And the formation of India and Pakistan as independent nations robbed George VI of his title "Rex-Imperator." All these changes prompted an urgent question: what kind of international arrangement might victorious but financially exhausted Britain make with her former colonies? What would the role of the Crown be?

Meetings in London produced various ideas, including a standing "Commonwealth Conference" of which the King would be not

King, but president. His private secretary Sir Alan Lascelles was derisive, telling King George that kingship was "an ideal for which men are prepared to work, to fight, and to die; but nobody is going to die for a Conference."[1] Under Nehru, however, India seemed keen to stay inside some kind of Commonwealth. So did the Islamic Republic of Pakistan. How could republics be accommodated to a monarch-led institution? With the Labour prime minister Clement Attlee taking the lead, negotiations led to a classic British compromise. India was not prepared to recognize the King as head of state, or have any truck with British royalty in patronage, oaths, honors or policy. But the Republic of India would recognize the King as Head of the Commonwealth. Eight countries—Britain, Canada, Australia, New Zealand, South Africa, India, Pakistan and Ceylon— duly attended a conference in London in April 1949 and proclaimed after it that the King would be retained "as the symbol of the free association of independent member nations" that would be united "as free and equal members of the Commonwealth of Nations, freely cooperating in the pursuit of peace, liberty and progress."

This declaration, which embodied an idea the Irish republicans had first argued for years before, would become the founding document of the modern Commonwealth. It allowed newly independent states to reject the British monarch as head of state and choose republicanism, yet stay inside the old grouping. This essential idea made the expansion of the Commonwealth possible while, of course, limiting its practical power. Of the fifty-four members today, only sixteen retain the Queen as head of state. They are mostly in the Caribbean or are small Pacific island nations, although Canada, Australia and New Zealand remain major examples. The existence of the Commonwealth provides a crucial distinction between the British monarchy and those of Scandinavia or Spain, thus making it more than a tiny geographical remnant. No wonder the Queen's first major act after her Coronation was to embark on an ambitious six-month tour of her wider authority.

The trip of 1953–54 was both the ultimate introduction to the life she would lead and an unrepeatable time of triumph for the Queen and the Duke. Britain's real power might be hollowed out and her Treasury heavily indebted, but her postwar prestige was at its peak. She was the newest member of the atomic club, her fighting services had won great victories, and across the former Empire there was tremendous optimism. South Africa was a problem, but Australia and New Zealand were seen almost as British versions of California, sunlit new lands where graft was rewarded and a new world could be built away from the class distinctions of Britain. In turn both countries had a seemingly unreserved enthusiasm for the British connection unsullied by rising nationalism. The death of George VI had given Britain an unexpectedly young and beautiful head of state who was already a well-established international star (she had first featured on the front of *Time* magazine at age three). The combination of national prestige and personal novelty would never come in quite the same way again.

It was an epic trip. The Queen flew across the Atlantic to visit Bermuda and Jamaica, and then sailed aboard a hired commercial liner, the *Gothic*, because the Royal Yacht was not yet ready. Prince Charles and Princess Anne were left behind, as the Queen and Princess Margaret had been when their father made his prewar overseas tours. On the *Gothic* the royal party passed through the Panama Canal into the Pacific, visiting Fiji and Tonga and arriving in New Zealand for Christmas. Hers was the first visit to New Zealand by the reigning monarch; the welcome was rapturous, described by one writer as "a national delirium." From there she went to Australia, which was the most triumphant but also most exhausting section of the tour.

As in New Zealand, the Queen of Australia was the first reigning monarch to visit. She spent two months traveling twenty-five hundred miles by train, ten thousand miles by airplane, and nine hundred miles by car; she made more than a hundred speeches and listened to twice as many. She heard her national anthem played an estimated 162 times.[2] It has also been calculated that three-quarters of the entire adult population of Australia turned out to see her. The result was a personal triumph that tested her resilience, her ability to keep a fixed smile in place for hours, and her patience. She objected to the boring speeches of local worthies, but she must have finally realized just what a lifelong diet of boring speeches would be like. Meanwhile, the traveling was exhausting, there was little privacy and the Queen did not get much time off, endlessly changing clothes for public display and redoing her makeup surrounded by curious ladies. When she returned to Australia in 2011for what is likely to be her last visit there, she encountered plenty of people who remembered that 1954 tour as a unique moment in their postwar history. They had stood at roadsides, or in squares or beside schools, and waited and cheered and waved.

The Queen and the Duke then went on to Ceylon (now Sri Lanka), the Cocos Islands, Uganda and Aden before arriving in the Mediterranean, where they at last boarded the spanking-new *Britannia* and sailed home again. When they finally sailed up the Thames, 173 days after they had left, there were greeted by ships and great crowds of admirers. The long journey had provided a crash course in stamina and organization for the new Queen; it also must have reassured her greatly about the monarchy's continuing hold over people's imaginations. It provided a template for many other tours to come—the meticulously planned wardrobe, the careful effort to send subtle compliments to different audiences, the grind of long, hot car journeys at slow speeds, the tweaking of similar speeches for local conditions.

Yet in 1954 the press was far easier to handle than it would later become; royal news was still news about what the Royals said and did during public engagements. Patriotic feeling was at its most fervent. The Queen and her party encountered none of the diplomatic dilemmas or local political protests that came later, so apart from the physical strain, this trip had been easy. In the long run, did it change anything? Without it, surely, the Queen would not have been quite as popular in her farther-flung dominions as she remained.

Doing her bit for the monarchy, she strengthened emotional and sentimental connections in a way that could not have been done without her physical presence. And throughout her reign, this has always been true. Even in the age of television and the Internet, if they wish to matter, Queens have to be seen. Woody Allen once said that 80 percent of success is showing up; for monarchy, the percentage is perhaps even higher.

Abu Dhabi, November 25, 2010

On a sweltering patch of grass and sand, with old Arab dhows bobbing offshore, hundreds of Britons in cream suits, sunglasses and hats are waiting for the Queen. Lines of Arabs in traditional dress are here too, waving sticks in a traditional greeting while girls in shocking pink and lemon dresses vigorously swirl their hair.

Out of a gold-colored Range Rover come the Queen and the Duke of Edinburgh, greeted by Sheikh Khalifa bin Zayed al-Nahyan, the ruler of Abu Dhabi. Off they go to view a modernist pavilion, unveil a rather dull-looking plaque and then walk in a circle past the grinning, waving crowds. Bouquets are thrust and accepted. A sophisticated expat teenager screams: "She looked at me! She's looovely." The Queen is nodding, smiling, looking interested, making small talk and keeping a close eye on the time.

She had touched down late at night and been whisked straight to the gigantic Sheikh Zayed mosque to pay her respects at the tomb of the late ruler of the United Arab Emirates and watch children recite the Quran. That had been quite a scene too: the Queen was in stocking soles and wearing a strange headdress that made her look like a Russian boyar's wife—or a beekeeper, thought some of the watching photographers—as she walked across the world's largest hand-woven carpet and under the world's largest chandelier, so big that when it's cleaned they have to lower a man inside it.

After her outdoor walkabout she will change into a gown and attend a state luncheon to meet all the sheikhs of this confederation of emirates. Sheikh Khalifa will give her (and her husband and son) the Order of Zayed, the United Arab Emirates' highest civil decoration. In return she will make him a Knight Grand Cross of the Most Honourable Order of the Bath. There will be an investiture for the vice-chairman of Emirates Airline and a doctor specializing in diabetes. The Duke of Edinburgh will watch a flypast of jets. The Queen will meet children and business delegations.

Then they will be off again, this time to the neighboring state of Oman, whose Sultan Qaboos deposed his father in 1970 and has become the longest-serving ruler in the region. Sultan Qaboos— who studied in England, went to Sandhurst and is a passionate fan of classical music—has the world's only bagpipe-playing camel-mounted soldiers, some of whom can also parachute and play the bagpipes simultaneously. He is a notable religious liberal and has made a concerted effort to preserve his country's old buildings, mainly Portuguese and medieval forts. He seems to be—though nobody quite says so—gay. His country is the same size as Britain with a population of only around 3.5 million. Again, the Queen and the Duke are flung into a round of parades, banqueting, receptions and a horse display to celebrate the fortieth year of the Sultan's reign, moved to accommodate the Queen's schedule. In a land of sharks-tooth peaks, broiling sand and turquoise-topped minarets—and the original source of frankincense to boot—the Queen seems to have found herself in a world somewhere between Narnia and Briga-doon.

What is it all for? What are these trips really about?

These are the eighty-seventh and eighty-eighth overseas state visits the Queen has undergone in her reign. They have taken her from fjords and frozen northern palaces to tiny islands and the world's busiest, dustiest capitals. They have been paid to dictators and elected presidents, old tyrants and courageous reformers, communists and nationalists. They have been made by Royal Yacht, aircraft and train. Though each is very different, each has involved similar rituals, some of them so archaic they go back to the embassies and diplomacies of old Egypt and ancient China: the gifts, the elaborate feasts and the speeches fluffed up with tactful evasions and courteous euphemism. In the old days the monarchies of Europe sometimes spent years preparing for royal visits. These days they have been thrashed out—two a year, normally—by the royal visits committee of the Foreign Office, Buckingham Palace, overseas embassies and host governments. The Queen has no choice at all about where she goes: if "her" government says she should go to Bulgaria or Tanzania, that's where she heads. And she does so because, underneath the gilded icing of twenty-four-gun salutes, exchanged Grand Crosses, and elaborately exchanged compliments, this is a coldhearted, contemporary and wholly serious business.

Take that original scene, with Arab dhows and the stick-waving welcome party. Its real purpose was not extravagant display but the unveiling of the British architect Norman Foster's winning design for a new national museum for the UAE. Featuring five finlike triangles of glass, the museum will be built on an island off Abu Dhabi, part of an ambitious plan to make this corner of the Gulf a world artistic center. There will also be a Guggenheim gallery and a Performing Arts Center by Zaha Hadid, as well as the first overseas branch of the Louvre. Thanks to Lord Foster and the British Museum, whose director, Neil MacGregor, is also present, Britain has a slice of this huge, oil-funded investment. That huge, glittering mosque the Queen visited had brought work to the British consulting engineers Halcrow Group and Hill International, the lighting company Speirs and Major, and the British artist Kevin Dean. The agreement in Abu Dhabi, the world's seventh-largest oil producer, committed both governments to a further massive rise in bilateral trade to £12 billion by 2015.

The oil companies BP and Shell have been in the UAE since its founding, but these days, design and construction are becoming as important. The UAE is currently Britain's largest market in the Middle East, and according to Prince Andrew, the Duke of York, "the rest of the world has woken up to its potential . . . we have to find ways of increasing our penetration of the market." More than four thousand British businesses are working in the UAE, and around one hundred thousand Britons live there. And the tide of money goes both ways: the UAE's investments in Britain include the London Gateway project, a port and "logistics park" in Essex, whose footprint is twice the size of the city of London and which, if it hits its target of thirty-six thousand new jobs, will make it the largest job-creation project in the UK. In addition, everything from London hotels to football clubs, including Manchester City, are owned by businessmen and investors from the UAE.

But energy remains a crucial reason why the Queen and the British government pay close heed to their friends in the Middle East. The Gulf oil states, from Qatar (which will provide much of Britain's imported gas for the next generation) through to Bahrain and Dubai, have become an economic battleground. Britain's oil and gas bonanza in the North Sea is now over, and since it will not be replaced by wind farms or new nuclear plants, the country now depends on imports and rightly fears too great a dependence on Russia. Its very future as an advanced economy is in play.

The military ties matter, too. The UAE and Oman have strong defense links with Britain, and both Arab countries look across the water at Iran and south at Yemen, where al-Qaeda is again organizing. Without them, waging war in Afghanistan and Iraq would have been almost impossible. Without their help, the struggle against Islamist terrorism becomes much more difficult. The Gulf is rich—a source of oil, gas and money—but it is also surrounded by danger and political instability.

For the Queen, then, these are not exotic destinations. Both countries are switch boxes of modern capitalism and post–Cold War geopolitics, and both are monarchies themselves (and in Oman's case an absolute monarchy). In this modern version of the "great game," nations must play the cards they have, and Britain can play the Queen. Few of the country's rivals have a long-serving, internationally famous monarch in whose company sheikhs seem particularly comfortable, talking horseflesh and architecture.

How much does it matter that an eighty-four-year-old lady with her eighty-nine-year-old husband arrives in a desert land by aircraft and does a lot of walking, nodding, smiling and talking? Consider all the contracts, long-term deals, expressions of friendship, media coverage and personal links restored or established in a visit of just a few days' duration. Then remember that, with a couple of such expeditions every year and the same number of state visits to London by foreign leaders, this trip to Abu Dhabi and Oman is only a small part of the endless process of monarchical diplomacy. Remember the similar visits to Malaysia, the Baltic states and the Balkan ones, to the United States and United Nations, to India, Turkey, South Korea. Add it up and ask again if it matters.

We see the Queen in action overseas doing her trademark walkabouts, or standing straight and silent while soldiers march past her, or sitting with other heads of state. These are such familiar images that most of us barely register them. In truth, though, she is operating much more like a door opener, or perhaps a human assault vessel. She goes first, ushered straight to the centers of power wherever she is, and behind her, in an eager V-formation, come the ministers, civil servants, military and salesmen. Of course, it is not always the same. There are plenty of countries less interested in British royal visits, or where less is at stake. But every visit has its agenda. The parades and the dinners look impressive enough. But the story behind the elaborate public displays of friendship and goodwill is the story that counts.

PART THREE

❈

The Queen at Work

The British constitution, like almost all constitutions, is played out as an endless mutter of meetings. So much talk, so carefully recorded—Parliament, cabinet, cabinet committees, and then the endless meetings inside government offices. Outside Westminster are courts, tribunals, city halls, local government, police committees. One way or another, an outside observer might think that the British, when not in bed or watching television, are mostly busy in meetings.

One weekly meeting—which is not recorded, reported, filmed, minuted or even discussed—is an old meeting described by an old word: the "audience" between the Queen and her prime minister. Neither the Queen nor any premier has ever discussed with outsiders what is talked about, except in the most blandly general terms. She has audiences, too, with the most senior military men, and with retiring cabinet ministers and chancellors. These audiences are the last little black box in the middle of Britain's maze of meetings. Their purpose was perhaps best described by Walter Bagehot, the nineteenth-century journalist who audaciously tried to explain the British constitution (and, mirabile dictu, largely succeeded). Bagehot said the Queen had the right to be consulted; to advise; and to warn. True, he was talking about Queen Victoria, but reading Bagehot was part of Queen Elizabeth's training for her job and his little list is so generally accepted that we may assume she agrees with it. Even in relatively recent times British monarchs have used all three rights vigorously.

The Queen's father expected to be consulted about the detail of wartime operations, insisting that Churchill keep him fully informed even during the most frantic and stressful periods of fighting (something Churchill never complained about). George VI is also widely credited with persuading Clement Attlee, the postwar Labour prime minister, to appoint Ernest Bevin foreign secretary, rather than Hugh Dalton, a man detested by the Windsors. If so, it was a good nudge, since Bevin became one of the greatest foreign secretaries Britain has ever had. But it was the Queen's grandfather George V who was the last truly interventionist monarch. His advice, complaints and warnings were familiar to successive prime ministers from Asquith to Baldwin, and they covered everything from the future of the aristocracy and creeping ministerial socialism to the response to the General Strike and the rise of the dictators. George V, founder of the dynasty, was a bridge between the assertive monarchism of his grandmother and the very cautious approach of his granddaughter. He was an obedient constitutional monarch but not a silent or uncomplaining one.

The Queen's role is harder to gauge. Though her first prime minister was Churchill, she grew up during the most vigorous dose of socialism ever administered to the British, and she developed an acute awareness of the need to tread carefully. She has repeatedly been challenged and tested over royal finances and has always been aware of a vocal minority of republicans who would prefer to see the monarchy's role in British life diminished or abolished altogether. Her disposition has been quieter and more cautious. We are not even sure what she really thought of her prime ministers. The least discreet of them, Harold Macmillan and Tony Blair, have revealed almost nothing about their conversations with the Queen. There have been rumors of favoritism; some say she liked Harold Wilson best of all and detested Margaret Thatcher. But this is mere gossip and in the case of Lady Thatcher, at least, wrong. Sadly for writers, the Queen herself has been the soul of discretion.

Even so, the story of her relationships with the eleven men and one woman who served as her prime minister is central to the meaning of her reign, and can be told in surprising detail through public documents, diaries, recollections and the observations of those around them. And some general points can be made about those audiences. First, by general agreement of civil servants and politicians who have worked with her, the Queen has an extraordinary memory and is very sharp. She enjoys political gossip, remembers detailed precedents and, as she has grown older, has acted more and more as a kind of human library upon which younger premiers can draw. She is "the fount of honors" but it may be more important that she is a "fount of memories." We do not know what was said at her audiences, except in a very few and marginal cases. It is known, for instance, that Wilson's got longer and longer as he struggled to hold his Labour governments together, while Blair's were comparatively short.

Piecing together the hints we have, we can safely assume that the most interesting part of the Queen's audiences occurs when prime ministers talk to her about the problems they are having with their own colleagues. The historian David Cannadine argues that "separating out the functions, as it were—a chairman of the board and chief executive—is actually rather a good idea, and that's what we have in this country; whereas in America you have a President who is both chairman of the board and chief executive; and that is actually quite a lot harder."[1] Prime ministers have plenty of people with whom to discuss the awfulness and treachery of the Opposition.

They have Number Ten staff, other ministers, even journalists. There are far fewer people with whom they can discuss the awfulness of their colleagues.

Wilson was most enthused about his royal audiences as he came to feel besieged by ministers from left- and right-wing factions of the Labour Party. Margaret Thatcher had her troubles with liberal Tories: the Queen had a royal-box view of those epic cabinet battles, and reassured Mrs. Thatcher in 1986, after Michael Heseltine walked out from her government over the Westland affair, that there had been worse moments. John Major struggled with Euroskeptic "bastards" and in 1995 undoubtedly talked in some detail with the Queen about his unusual decision to step down as Tory leader, while remaining prime minister, in order to provoke a fight. At a farewell dinner, Tony Blair wryly remarked that the Queen was the only person with whom he could expatiate on the fine personal qualities of his colleagues.

The highest elected office is a lonely place. An experienced, shrewd and above all reliably discreet confidante is one of the advantages of a well-functioning constitutional monarchy, a blessing that other parliamentary systems rarely offer. The audiences are not primarily for the Queen's benefit, however much she might enjoy hearing at first hand what is happening. Her job is to support and get along with her prime ministers. Some, like Alec Douglas-Home, a Scottish landowner, or David Cameron, who went to school with one of her children (Prince Edward), may be more obvious social pairings than others, such as the Presbyterian minister's son Gordon Brown, or the grocer's daughter from Grantham, Margaret Thatcher. But the challenge of learning about and developing relationships with people from less familiar backgrounds is interesting too.

Lord Butler, who was cabinet secretary during the Thatcher and Major periods, says he thinks that first of all, "all prime ministers have felt that they could talk to her in absolute confidence. That it wouldn't go any further. They also felt, I think, that she gave them sympathy because she was a figure in the public eye and had been for so long, and so they could talk about some of the agonies that you get from that. . . . I think a session of therapy is a rather good phrase." Sir Gus O'Donnell, his latest successor, says something similar: "She's seen it all before—the ups and downs, the wars, the recessions, the recoveries, the good times, the bad times—and she's seen the way different governments respond to these events . . . and she gives sound advice, I'm sure." (He had once asked John Major exactly what she said and was quite properly slapped down.) Everyone who works with the Queen, and who has been interviewed for this book, says she has been a good judge of character. Human judgments about the strengths and weaknesses of a premier—liking, admiration, puzzlement—have clearly mattered more than class.

The new Queen was still making her way back to England from Kenya when, on February 6, 1952, Winston Churchill's cabinet was meeting in the House of Commons. Ancient precedents and modern conditions collided. The last time a monarch had been proclaimed while abroad was in 1714, when the German George of Hanover succeeded Queen Anne. It was a different age, but not an entirely alien one. Anne's reign had seen two-party politics properly emerge, as well as the Union of Scotland and England. She had not really had a prime minister, though Churchill's brilliant ancestor the Duke of Marlborough had been a prime mover at court. Then, as in the 1950s, questions regarding the titles, status and political reach of the Queen were much debated. And no wonder: Anne was the first sovereign of a United Kingdom of Britain, but she was also separately Queen of Ireland and, with arcane arrogance and a fine disregard of the facts on the ground, she called herself Queen of France too.

The new Queen, at twenty-five, was in a very different position, but her politicians agonized about titles. The cabinet thought phrases such as "the Crown Imperial" could "cause difficulties"[2] in the postwar world, and substituted "Head of the Commonwealth" into the recital of titles. Among the countries of which she was now head of state, Pakistan and Ceylon were not Christian, still less Protestant, so "Defender of the Faith" seemed wrong for all her realms. That would have to be fudged. Moreover, she was no longer Queen of "Ireland": it would have to be Northern Ireland. As the debate continued, ministers argued hard and passionately, citing historical precedents with vigor. From the very first moments of her reign, then, the Queen's politicians were entangled with difficult and emotive questions of protocol.

All of this may seem arcane, but Britain was a country soaked in her patriotic and monarchical history. In 1952 the war had been over for only seven years and still loomed large. Contemporary British films included *The Wooden Horse*, about an escape from Stalag Luft III; *The Cruel Sea*, about the Battle of the Atlantic; and *Angels One Five*, about the Battle of Britain. Audiences who came to watch them stood at attention for the national anthem. Regimental reunions and British Legion clubhouses were busily attended. The monarch's picture hung everywhere, from town halls to pubs. National Service had almost a decade yet to run. Historical consciousness was stronger, as evidenced by the films about Captain Hornblower, Queen Victoria or the Scarlet Pimpernel and the patriotic histories of H. E. Marshall's *Our Island Story* (serious) and Sellar and Yeatman's *1066 and All That* (considerably less so). British children were still taught the traditional kings-and-queens-and-famous-battles version of history; British comics imagined the British invading space wearing mustaches and RAF-style caps; and theater audiences accepted the censorship of plays by the Queen's Lord Chamberlain.

Monarchy was sewn through almost every aspect of public life, from the words used by hanging judges and the deferential caution of the BBC and newspapers, to every mention of the former King and now the Queen. Monarchy was for most people the holy of holies, a national religion. No British monarch more recent than Queen Victoria was permitted to be impersonated by actors in films or plays. The fierce commander Richard Colville, a former naval officer who regarded the media with contempt and was the Buckingham Palace press secretary, prohibited any filming of the Queen without his express permission. Broadcasters cringed before him. Newspaper editors, muttering about "the abominable no-man," nevertheless ensured that only the most anodyne of references to royalty appeared.

As a moving spirit in world affairs, the British Empire had departed, but its body remained sprawled across the earth. The loss of British India and its partition into two independent states had come as a shock to many in the United Kingdom, and those who understood the country's finances knew Britain could not afford imperial pretensions. But the great retreat from other parts of the world had not yet begun; Empire Day, May 24, was still celebrated with marches and pageants. Much of sub-Saharan Africa was British. So were Cyprus, Malta, Aden, the Gulf states, Somaliland, the West Indies and Hong Kong. British troops sweltered in a vast camp in Egypt; British companies treated Persia as virtually their own property. Many in Britain felt an intense bond with what was known as the White Commonwealth, and the term "the British race" was used without embarrassment or raised eyebrows. Mass immigration had not yet begun to alter the shape of the country, which still looked white and was merely tinged with exotic newcomers at its edges.

The Royal Navy, though already being scuttled and broken up in shallow seas and at shipyards, was still seen by most people as the great steel fist of British power. Many thought a renewed age of British glory, based on new technology and old standards, was just around the corner. Plenty of older people could remember Queen Victoria's reign but still hadn't realized the immensity of the new power of the United States. So it was hardly surprising that questions about the new Queen's titles were debated so seriously by the old men of her first cabinet. Lower down the tree, others were making lesser verbal adjustments—for senior barristers, King's

Counsel, to become QCs; for the words of the national anthem to change; for new stamps, banknotes and coins to be printed and minted; and for freshly cast pillar boxes and new photographic portraits.

Harold Macmillan reflected with a sense of awe that ministers were preparing for the Accession Council, one of the last remnants of the Anglo-Saxon Witan, "this strange and ancient body." The following day Churchill broke into his familiar prose-poetry in a broadcast: "I, whose youth passed in the august, unchallenged, and tranquil glare of the Victorian Era, may well feel a thrill in invoking once more the prayer and anthem, 'God Save the Queen.'" These were men who had lived through two world wars as members of the ruling class and who knew full well that Britain's place in the world was falling. But both were flushed with optimism about the prospects for a different, better country under a fresh, new Queen.

Churchill had encountered her as a girl, and had found time during the grim days in April 1941, when the British army in Greece was desperately evacuating before the German advance, to send her roses for her fifteenth birthday. Now old, ill and barely able to cope with the demands of being prime minister, he still cast a pungent word-spell over the country. The Queen puts him in a different category from any of his successors and recently recalled being gently rebuked by him. When she and Prince Philip returned from their grueling post-Coronation tour of the Commonwealth in May 1954, Sir Winston was invited to join them for the last part of the voyage on the new Royal Yacht *Britannia* from Yarmouth up the Thames. They were greeted by cheering crowds and a forty-one-gun salute from the Tower of London, but the Queen remembers the grim weather and saying to Churchill as they went up the Pool of London, "Look at this awful dirty river." Churchill turned on her with a growl: "This is the silver thread that goes through British history—never forget it."[3]

No later prime minister would have dared to correct her in that way. She complained at times that Churchill failed to listen to her properly—rather as Queen Victoria complained that her great prime minister Gladstone addressed her as if she were a public meeting. As it happened, on that day on the Thames, Churchill was bluffing a bit. According to his doctor, he was chilled to the marrow, had a cold and "had never been up the river before." When he had first come aboard, he later reported, "I did not at once recognize a masculine figure in khaki trousers. It was the Queen, who had taken off her coat."[4] Princess Elizabeth revered Churchill but by the time she came to the throne, the Conservative grandees were already talking about how to ease him out of Downing Street.

Shortly before George VI had died—so the Queen Mother told Anthony Eden—the King had made up his mind to have a talk with Churchill about retiring. George's death meant it never happened.[5] Churchill, though deeply saddened by the King's demise, had seized on the opportunity the new reign offered as another excellent reason for staying put. Churchill's rich blend of romanticism and self-interest made it perfectly obvious to him that the new Queen would need his grand-paternal, guiding hand for some to come.

THE CORONATION: WHAT IT MEANT

Back in 1953, all was optimism and widening horizons. The Queen's Coronation that June was a national carnival but also a religious celebration and a moment of patriotic rebirth. A year of planning went into it, from the invitations and seating plan at Westminster Abbey to who would make the sandwiches at fetes in villages and housing estates. In the main avenues of central London through which the procession would pass, arches were raised with lights, bunting and crowns. In factories in Birmingham and York (and there were factories there, in those days), flags, bicyclists' pennants, savings boxes, chocolates, biscuits, badges and tea caddies were manufactured. In Stoke and the Potteries, mugs, plates, teapots were fired, painted and packed, the first such painted and colored ware since before the war. Decorative plants with red, white and blue flowers were nurtured by market gardeners. Newspaper editors planned lavish special editions. The best-known writers were signed up by magazines well in advance.

The Coronation Headquarters, center of the official planning effort, opened in Berkeley Square in London, a stone's throw from the Queen's birthplace, in October 1952. Prince Philip, already straining for a more substantial public role, was given the job of chairing the preparations. Far away, the people of St. Keverne on the Lizard peninsula in Cornwall began a difficult negotiation with the Ministry of Food. They had roasted a whole ox for the accession of the last monarch and they were jolly well going to do the same for Elizabeth. This was fighting talk: rationing of meat would last more than another year and at first the ministry responded with outrage.

Peter Hennessy, now Lord Hennessy, has been one of the premier constitutional and social historians of the reign, and for him as a small boy, the Coronation was a pivotal moment. He remembers, as do millions of others, the Coronation mugs at school, a Dinky Toy version of the Golden Coach, and going to watch the great event on his family friend's television in Barnet. But the event was about more than the Coronation as a national celebration. As Hennessy put it:

> You had stories of empire which nobody would dare write or read in that way these days, and here [Britain] was, an ancient settled nation, naturally good at ceremony, comes through the heroic 1940s, standing alone, and yet at the same time we would produce the most advanced bits of kit in the world; and it was one of those rare moments of optimism. And the Queen looked terrific. She was beautiful, and she had this dashing consort . . . and it was going to get better.

For Hennessy it was "the zenith . . . a better yesterday." He felt Britain was on a virtuous upward cycle of improvement. For him the Coronation was "a tonic. . . . Wonderful. Life has never been the same since."[6]

Looking back, it is apparent that the Queen has been the monarch of a nation in decline, and many would say her greatest achievement has been to soften and humanize that inevitable process. But at the time of her Coronation, it seemed she might enjoy a very different reign.

As the day of her accession approached, a moon-faced man with a reassuringly familiar voice, deep and rich as after-dinner chocolate, began to assemble a great pile of Coronation facts and figures. Though the Queen was happily married, it was almost as if she had another suitor. Richard Dimbleby, a committed monarchist, was not exactly wooing the Queen, adore her though he did. But he would soon appear on the Thames in a damp Dutch barge he had bought and which would be moored opposite Westminster to allow its proud owner easy access to the ceremony.

Meanwhile, Dimbleby's employer, the British Broadcasting Corporation, was assiduously wooing the monarchy. This would be the first proper television Coronation; in 1937 only three cameras had been allowed in the vicinity of the ceremony, but they were stationed far from the Abbey, at Hyde Park Corner. For the BBC, which was engaged in a losing battle to fend off commercial television, the Coronation was a perfect opportunity to show what it, a cadet member of the establishment family, could do. Like the monarchy, the BBC had done well out of the war. Like George VI, the BBC in the previous era had been instinctively anti-Churchill, but like the King, it had eventually become a supporter of the war leader. Like the House of Windsor, the BBC had helped tie Britons and imperial subjects together through the darkest years.

As a consequence, in the early 1950s the BBC enjoyed a position hard to imagine today. It was not quite the Church of England; as a Scottish Presbyterian, its first director general, Lord Reith, would have regarded that as a bit flashy. But thanks in part to

Reith, a passionate monarchist, the BBC was solidly part of the establishment—powerful, authoritative, clean-shaven and suavely self-certain. Its current director general, Lieutenant General Sir Ian Jacob, had been an assistant to the war cabinet, but the BBC's patriotism was more complicated than that of the court, not least because it had incorporated the voices of radicals, such as George Orwell and J. B. Priestley. Yet it was a national player, and by the time of the Coronation the BBC felt it had special rights, and it harbored vaulting cultural and moral ambitions. Its wireless services, ranging from the popular Light Programme through the meatier Home Service, to the highbrow Third Programme, were meant, in the words of Jacobs's predecessor, to lead the listener "from good to better, by curiosity, liking and a growth of understanding."

The first reaction of the Palace old guard, and of the cabinet, to the BBC's proposal that it televise the Coronation was that television remained a vulgar medium and should not be allowed inside the Abbey—this despite the fact that it broadcast the funeral of the King in February 1952, helping spark the first wave of mass television purchases. That October, the Palace announced a veto, a decision taken on the advice of the Archbishop of Canterbury and the Duke of Norfolk, and backed up by Churchill and the cabinet. But the BBC refused to take no for an answer and began a quiet lobbying campaign, focused first on the Duke and the Archbishop. When the message finally reached Churchill that the Queen herself was in favor of televising her Coronation, he told the diarist Colville that it was, after all, she who was to be crowned, not the cabinet. "She alone must decide." This would turn out to be a good decision, primarily because it made the Coronation the first one ever to be actually witnessed by the people. Even in Saxon times, a firsthand experience of a Coronation had been more hope than practical reality.

Now the BBC went into action, planning the biggest outside broadcast ever, including ninety-five sound commentary positions (mostly for overseas audiences) and an unheard-of twenty-one television cameras, five of them inside the Abbey. The newspapers began an informal beauty contest about who would be given the ultimate job of reporting on the Coronation itself from a glass-sided box high above the altar. One popular choice was John Snagge, then probably the best-known voice on the wireless—for it was still, just, the age of wireless. Richard Dimbleby, however, was the favorite in newspaper polls, and with his bosses. He had been a brave and unorthodox radio reporter during the war, accompanying RAF bombing raids and witnessing the liberation of Belsen. But he had royal form too. In 1939 he had been the first BBC reporter specially assigned, and accepted, to cover a royal tour, when George VI and Queen Elizabeth had visited Canada. During it, Dimbleby had played the piano for the King and had a long late-night discussion with him about Hitler, democracy and world affairs. Dimbleby's written broadcast describing George VI's lying in state is a perfect model of evocative, romantic news prose.

He thought the House of Windsor meant "justice, respect for the rights of the individual, and freedom." Of the new Queen he said: "She has a great sense of humor that lies just below the surface. . . . Photographs rarely do her justice; she is smaller, slimmer, and altogether more lively than they make her. She has a flashing smile . . . and a clear, incisive voice."[7] This was the man the BBC decided should be, for millions, the voice explaining the images never before seen by a mass audience. Obsessive about proper preparation, Dimbleby spent six months preparing his notes on every aspect of the service. When he left his chilly boat on the morning of the great day, he clambered into the commentary box at 5:30 a.m. and stayed there for seventeen hours. He must have rationed the tea.

The Coronation was arguably the most important moment in the Queen's life and certainly the most important official moment. As the day drew nearer, she practiced the complicated ceremony in the Buckingham Palace ballroom, using sheets to mimic her sixty-foot train and wearing the heavy crown to familiarize her neck with its weight. Dukes drilled. Bishops rehearsed. Dray horses were borrowed for the carriages, the original beasts having departed during the war.

A short walk from the Palace was the royal apothecary, Savory & Moore of New Bond Street, where the holy oil was compounded by its head dispenser from a formula which went back to the Stuart times, and possibly further back still. (It is supposed to involve ambergris, musk, orange, jasmine and rose water.) London, meanwhile, began to disappear under scaffolding and resounded to the banging of hammers as porches, arches and seating were prepared. The papers contained quite a lot of sniffy complaints about the vulgarity of some of the street decorations.

Peers ordered their ceremonial garb and were told that, by special dispensation in these difficult economic conditions, rabbit fur would be considered an acceptable alternative to ermine. Thinking ahead to the long day before them, they were also told they could hide sandwiches in their coronets. Churchill later claimed that he vetoed the charging of the three thousand Abbey guests sixteen shillings each for the sandwiches, and ensured that alcoholic drinks would be available to crowds waiting in the Royal Parks.

The announcement that the Coronation would provide the occasion for a general amnesty of remaining wartime deserters still at large was met with a guarded welcome. Though there were theoretically thirteen thousand of them, many were thought to be Irish and outside the reach of the law, and some had certainly died. *The Spectator* reflected approvingly that "several thousand skeletons can now come out of several thousand closets."[8] When that Coronation amnesty was proposed, it was noted that "the Queen was very keen on this," although the armed forces were hostile.

At the BBC, lessons were being learned from the broadcasting of the King's funeral, when it was felt that there had been too many boring studio items and not enough "from the London streets."[9] Meticulous arrangements were made to keep the Commonwealth up to speed. Canada was then the only other Commonwealth country to have regular television broadcasts, and RAF Canberra bombers were commissioned to fly the film over, stopping only for a quick refueling break in Greenland. In the United States, NBC and CBS planned their own race to air. The interests of French speakers were taken more seriously than perhaps they would be today; one of the five commentators inside the Abbey was French, and the Coronation would prove a major hit across the continent.

In the days leading up to the Coronation, monarchs, cavalry detachments, horses, presidents, ministers and journalists arrived from around the world. Every rentable room in London was let, entire hotels booked up, road closures planned, shopfronts bedecked with red, white and blue, as well as countless coronets and profiled pictures of the young Queen. The wise looked at the weather forecasts and worried.

Coronation Day itself—Tuesday, June 2, 1953—did indeed start cold and wet, not just in London but across most of the United Kingdom. Some thirty thousand people are estimated to have slept out overnight on the paving stones and verges of the processional route, with another twenty thousand trying but failing to find a good spot from which to watch. Writers who wandered among them remembered the war and the Blitz of a decade before and were impressed by the communal spirit and unquenchable cheerfulness. The journalist Philip Hope-Wallace, who overheard a parent tell a fractious child, waiting for twenty-eight hours, "sit still, or I'll crown *you*," was impressed by the endurance: "The crowds schooled to sit out the Luftwaffe's visits on hard cold stone were not going to be put off by a drop of rain. Nor by the fantastic coldness."[10] Many had wrapped themselves in newspapers, which had become sodden overnight. They then had the dilemma of whether to use special Coronation editions of the fresh morning papers as keepsakes or insulation. Either way, one hopes that not many ended up unread, because their front pages announced the astonishing news that with perfect patriotic timing, the New Zealander Edmund Hillary and his guide, Sherpa Tenzing, part of a British-led expedition, had become the first climbers to make it to the top of Everest.

As the crowd roused itself, tea was being sold, and jokes made about brandy being more wanted. Overnight there had been some sing-alongs and impromptu dancing, but not much because of the rain. Then, finally, all those who had waited so long were rewarded by one of the most glittering displays of old-fashioned pageantry in Britain's postwar history. It was a long clatter of cavalry horses' hooves and chinking uniforms, a carnival of exotic costumes, foreign potentates and military marching. There were familiar faces: Churchill, who delighted in uniforms, was done up in his Admiral's gear as Warden of the Cinque Ports. Below a cocked hat and a blue-and-gold tunic that would have suited some South American liberator of the previous century, he beamed and waved. There were unfamiliar faces too: Tonga's jovial Queen Salote Tupou III—the "tallest queen of the smallest monarchy," who lived largely on roast suckling pig and traveled in an open carriage despite the rain—was a particular star.

Waiting inside the Abbey, the nobles shivered in their finery. The Countess of Huntingdon told the readers of the *New Statesman* that her prime memory of the day would be the "element of pity and sympathy" felt for the Queen, "for between the inhuman magnificence of the Crown and the glittering of the vestment-like golden robe, the Queen's face was very young, very human, very tense." Beyond that it was, "Oh, the cold!" The peeresses had been confined in what became a sort of wind tunnel: "Our teeth chattered, we quaked inwardly with cold, we wrapped ourselves in our trains and watched our arms turn blue."[11] Richard Dimbleby, by contrast, sat in the relative comfort and warmth of his commentary box, surrounded by his mass of typed and handwritten notes. Later, after it was all over, he would express his amazement at the poor behavior of some of the peerage, who he felt had behaved like litter louts: "Tiers and tiers of stalls in which the peers had been sitting were covered with sandwich wrapping, sandwiches, morning newspapers, fruit peel, sweets and even a few empty bottles."[12] Well, they had been very cold.

Outside London, the rest of the country celebrated and coped with the rain. On the Moray Firth, too far north for television reception, the warship HMS *Welcome* and local fishing fleet skippers collaborated in an impromptu naval review through a force-eight gale. Farther north still, in Stornoway in the Hebrides, a spry ninety-two-year-old minister celebrated an open-air service and told his parishioners about his memories of an equally wet parade in Edinburgh for Queen Victoria. In Belfast, and across loyalist Northern Ireland, decorative arches were erected. The Welsh hills were dotted with beacons, first smoking and then blazing.

Villages across Britain planted Coronation trees, held running races, fancy-dress parades, football matches, teas for everyone in the hall, and beer-fueled Coronation suppers in pubs. In Dorset, there were tug-of-war contests between neighboring hillside villages, and in St. Keverne in Cornwall they triumphantly roasted their ox, providing a glut of hot sandwiches.[13] In London, 350 foreign guests who could not be fitted into the Palace for the formal lunch were treated to a first outing of the day's most famous culinary invention, "*poulet Reine Elizabeth*," or Coronation Chicken as it was quickly renamed. A dish of poached fowl in a sauce including curried onions, red wine, apricot purée and mayonnaise, it was created by Rosemary Hume of the London Cookery School. (Its generally degraded offspring still fill many a lunchtime sandwich all across Britain; made properly, it can be quite pleasant.)

Farther afield still, public holidays had been declared across the Commonwealth, with yet more fetes, parades and parties. Schoolchildren around the world were given the day off. For people outside Britain, and indeed across much of the country itself, the only way to follow the day's events was by radio. In South Africa, 69 percent of the English-speaking population was estimated to have listened in. Later, when television films had been flown in, Germans, French, Italians and many more would watch the ceremony. In the United States, 85 million watched the rival NBC or CBS programs.

For most people in Britain too this was the television Coronation. The collective memory is of people huddled round a small, rented set in someone else's house, or in the pub. The statistics back this up: surveys showed that 53 percent of the adult population, some 19 million people, watched the BBC's *Coronation Special*, and of those the biggest proportion, 10.4 million, watched in friends' houses, while 7.8 million had rented or bought a set to view in their own home. A further 1.5 million watched in public places, such as cinemas, town halls and pubs. Afterward a remarkable 98 percent of those polled declared themselves "completely satisfied" with the coverage, a proportion the BBC has not always achieved since.

At the start of the 1950s, most British people had never seen a television set. TV was not yet available in northern and central England or much of Scotland. Within five years of the Coronation, television ownership had risen sixfold and the country's entertainment habits were being overturned. Historians often credit the change to the Coronation. This is self-evident nonsense. While it is true that the BBC's coverage of the Coronation propelled huge numbers of people to rent television sets, many of whom then bought them, by then nothing short of a national catastrophe could have halted the spread of the new medium. Still, it would be as important a symbolic moment in the dawning age of television, much as the General Strike of 1926 had been in the acknowledgment of radio's power.

On the day itself the coverage focused on the details of the Queen's silken dress, her serious demeanor and the intricate choreography of the ancient ceremony, which goes back to at least 973 when King Edgar was crowned at Bath, as recorded in the *Anglo-Saxon Chronicle*. The presentation by the Archbishop of "Queen Elizabeth your undoubted Queen" and the answering aristocratic cries of "Vivat!" were perhaps the most dramatic moments. For the Queen nothing mattered more than the religious and spiritual heart of the ceremony, still vivid in her mind as an observer from 1937. She was, and is, a devout Christian and would not have dissented from Archbishop of Canterbury Geoffrey Fisher's words in sermons before the Coronation, when he said that she was "God-called" to exert a spiritual power and lead her subjects by her personal example and duty.

The Archbishop also spoke about the necessity that she give herself to her people as a sacrifice, words that echo those she had broadcast from South Africa on her twenty-first birthday. The Queen took those words entirely seriously and has tried to live up to them ever since; unless we understand that we can never understand the Queen. The Coronation was intended to awe and even to intimidate—and not only those watching, but also its subject. At the ceremony's heart was not the procession, or even the firm thrusting of the heavy seven-pound crown onto her head, but the private moment when under a canopy Fisher anointed her with holy oil: "as Solomon was anointed King by Zadok the Priest and Nathan the Prophet, so be thou anointed, blessed and consecrated Queen over the Peoples, whom the Lord thy God hath given thee." This ancient tradition of anointing goes back to biblical times, though by 1953 no other monarch in the world experienced it.

For Fisher, the service was also meant to demonstrate that the Queen would exemplify domestic duty, fidelity, and a united family home. (He had perhaps not studied the alleged origins of the ceremony, for King Edgar the Peaceable had been a notoriously libertine ruler, peaceful neither on the battlefield nor in the bedchamber.) His argument rang out resonantly through 1950s Britain. Family was at the heart of the monarchical project: first the royal family; then the British family, itself composed of traditional families, clustering round that family; then a further family of nations around that. Later, the "family" metaphor for royalty, which seemed so obvious and strong that day, would be brutally challenged. But whoever's fault all this was, it was not hers. The Queen would do her lifelong best to live up to the Archbishop's uncompromising words, whereas her family would repeatedly test the value and validity of the metaphor.

Watching the Queen in the Abbey that day was young Prince Charles in a silk suit. (The three-year-old Princess Anne had been judged too young to come and left at Buckingham Palace.) Prince Philip, in full naval rig, would be the first to pledge his allegiance to the new monarch, kissing her on the left cheek and promising to become "your liege-man of life and limb and of earthly worship; and faith and truth I will bear unto you, to live and die, against all manner of folks"—a sonorous promise he has stuck to.

In the immediate aftermath of the Coronation—a time of parades, services of thanksgiving, a full-scale naval review at Spithead, and Trooping the Colour—writers competed to find profound meaning in the ceremony.[14] The editorial in a highbrow magazine of the day, *Time and Tide*, on June 13 exemplified the mood. The popular historian C. V. Wedgwood declared that no Queen or sovereign "was ever crowned more fully in the presence of the people," which was factually accurate. The magazine's editorial assertion that "Britain has regained in the past few days that spiritual and moral ascendancy in the world which was hers in 1940" was certainly not. In the same magazine, Robert L. Green, writing "As an American," reassured readers that for Britain, "the years of dullness and cold caused by war and recovery were forgotten." There was much in the same vein, and few sour notes anywhere to the right of the Communist Party.

The diarist in the *New Statesman* thought the Coronation would increase the number of people who felt "the whole thing is out of date, antiquated stuff. . . . Working-class Britain was simply forgotten." Its formidable editor, Kingsley Martin, did not agree. He thought Labour's traditional hostility to the monarchy had been silenced by the correct constitutional behavior of George V and George VI and that the Queen was safely outside politics: "The first rule for all monarchs who wish to preserve their crowns in a democracy is that they should unreservedly accept the advice of the Prime Ministers and never under any circumstances become involved in party politics." The Queen is not an avid reader of the

New Statesman but she followed the Editor Martin doctrine as closely as the Archbishop Fisher one. Martin went on to make one of the most thoughtful assessments of the value of monarchy to a democracy, which deserves to be quoted more often: "Constitutional monarchy is a subtle device which enables us, anthropologically speaking, both to adore and kill our Kings; by dividing supreme authority into two, we can lavish adulation upon the Crown and kick out the government when we choose."[15] And so, since 1953, we have.

THE OLD ELEPHANTS AND THE YOUNG QUEEN

The monarch's most important political job is to appoint a new prime minister if the incumbent should resign or die while in office. This responsibility was particularly challenging during the early years of the Queen's reign because of the Conservative habit of not electing a new leader but allowing one to "emerge."

In June 1953, less than a month after the Coronation, Churchill suffered what seemed a devastating stroke. He was quietly hustled out of Downing Street to Chartwell, his home in Kent, to recuperate, though with little hope for a full recovery. During that summer an establishment news blackout, agreed by press tycoons strolling on the Chartwell lawn, meant that most British people had no idea that their prime minister was incapacitated. The Queen knew more than her subjects, though she wrote him a handwritten letter to say she hoped his stroke was "not too serious and that you will be quite recovered in a very short time." It was serious, but by an extraordinary act of will, Churchill did recover enough to carry on, monitoring his ability to feel his own stubble, to tie his bow tie, and so on, until he was able to accept an invitation from the Queen to go to the St. Leger at Doncaster races, and to Balmoral. At both places, large crowds gathered to cheer—whether more for the Queen or for Churchill it was hard to tell. He was able to speak to the Tory conference in Margate that October, and did not finally stand down as prime minister until April 1955.

For understandable reasons, including pride and worry about his successor, Churchill risked entangling the new Queen in a political crisis. During the quiet, slow summer of the prime minister's illness, Harold Macmillan realized that Churchill would use the excuse of the post-Coronation tour to delay his retirement again. Though the Queen could dissolve Parliament by telegram, if there was a deadlock in the Conservative Party about his successor she would not be able to intervene, Macmillan noted, "in one of those rare crises where the Crown still has a role to play."[16] Senior Tories were alarmed enough to debate whether four of five of them should go to the Queen in a group and ask her to put pressure on Churchill. Lord Moran, Churchill's devoted doctor, thought "there is only one person . . . who can get him to do this and it is the Queen." Lascelles was consulted, but reckoned it would not work: "If she said her part, he would say charmingly, 'It's very good of you, Ma'am, to think of it'—and then he would very politely brush it aside. . . . The King might have done it . . . but he is gone."[17]

The Queen would have been put in a horrible position had she been asked, in effect, to terminate the career of the country's greatest wartime leader. He was the oldest and greatest of what we might call her elephant-premiers—the grand old men with vast experience, clearly senior to her, who had a fatherly relationship with the young Queen. (Churchill, Eden and Macmillan fall into this category—Alec Douglas-Home had a different relationship—and the real break did not come for another decade, with Harold Wilson in 1964.) Undoubtedly it would have been better for the country had Churchill retired a couple of years earlier: he was no longer up to the job, and Eden would have been more seasoned in office. But Churchill loomed so large in postwar Britain that it was difficult to imagine life without him. It is possible, however, that the Queen felt otherwise. Later, when someone remarked to her how marvelous it must have been to have Sir Winston as her first prime minister, she replied: "Not at all. I found him most obstinate."

In any event, she put no pressure on Churchill to step down.

His audiences with her, for which he dressed up in morning coat and top hat, grew longer and longer. He said they mostly talked about racing and polo and expressed great anger at any suggestion that the Queen's status be diminished. A *Daily Mirror* headline in November 1953 asking "Why Not Open the Palace to the People?" aroused his particular fury. The previous February, Lord Moran had recorded a conversation during which he complained to Churchill about the possible abolition of the upper chamber and got little sympathy from the prime minister: "The House of Lords means nothing to him," Lord Moran reported. "The history of England, its romance and changing fortunes, is for Winston embodied in the Royal House. He looked at a new photograph of the Queen. She was in white, with long white gloves, smiling and radiant. 'Lovely,' he murmured. 'She's a pet. I fear they may ask her to do too much. She's doing so well.' "[18] Churchill was entranced, and tremendously pleased to be made a Knight of the Garter by her in June 1954.

⌘

The prime minister's enchantment with the Queen did not extend to her husband. It may well have been worsened by an old man's jealous crush, but Churchill was already hostile to Prince Philip's family. He blamed Lord Mountbatten personally for the loss of British India, a ludicrous charge, reminding us that Churchill's sense of history had significant blind spots. He thought Mountbatten was in general too far to the left in politics, which was not a ludicrous charge. According to his doctor, Churchill said he did not like or trust Prince Philip, and merely hoped he would do the country no harm. This mistrust crystallized when Churchill strongly opposed Philip on the sensitive question of the family name.

The problem went back to the terms of George V's creation of the Windsor dynasty. In 1917 he had simply not thought through the possibility of the Crown passing to another Queen and her children, and therefore the fate of the new Windsor surname. Before the start of the Queen's reign, the best legal advice had suggested that, as with any other family, the children in the royal family should take their father's surname. Prince Philip was not particularly attached to the name Mountbatten, itself a modern invention, and suggested Edinburgh, or even Edinburgh-Windsor, as possibilities. Either way, he wanted to be recognized for himself. Then, at a dinner party in his home on the eve of George VI's funeral, Lord Mountbatten really stirred things up. He boasted that "the House of Mountbatten" now reigned. This comment was heard by an ardent royal traditionalist, Prince August of Hanover, who passed it back to George V's widow, Queen Mary. She was outraged and protested to the prime minister. Churchill immediately took her side.

After a discussion of the issue at a cabinet meeting in March 1952, Harold Macmillan noted that "poor Churchill, who wants to adopt a paternal and fatherly attitude to the Queen, was clearly much distressed himself, and a little alarmed for the future."[19] Macmillan thought Queen Mary was behind it all, favoring Windsor "and all the emphasis on the truly British and native character of the Royal Family. It is also clear that the Duke has the normal attitude of many men towards a mother-in-law of strong character, accentuated by the peculiar circumstances of his position. . . . It is more than likely that he has been told that we are suspicious of him on political grounds."

They were. Deeper currents ran underneath the apparently banal question of the royal name. Tory ministers feared that Philip and his uncle Mountbatten hoped to mount a gentle constitutional coup, influencing the Queen toward some kind of joint—and more liberal—monarchy. There was no evidence for that, but after the war Philip was perceived as more open to Labour than the traditional royals. By April, Churchill was reporting back that the Queen had accepted that her children would be Windsors. Her private secretary Lascelles described standing over her like one of the barons at Runnymede. Nastily, Macmillan wrote in his diary that although "this has been a painful episode . . . it is a very good thing that the influence of the Consort and his family should have had an early rebuff."

It was unfortunate that the cabal of men in charge paid so little heed to Prince Philip's feelings, and the hurt seems to have rankled for a long time. Philip's very identity in his new family was being questioned; famously, he complained that he felt "like a bloody amoeba." The Queen, who is said to have been hurt too, may have felt she had no option but to side with her father's memory and her ministers' views against her husband, but it was a badly handled episode. She later tried to make it up to him, provoking another cabinet debate in February 1955 about whether he could be called "Prince of the Commonwealth," but Canada and South Africa were not keen. Scottish members of the cabinet likewise vetoed Churchill's notion of "Prince of England." Macmillan noted that the Queen "still hankers after some distinctive title for the Duke of Edinburgh" but it was reckoned that simply calling him "the Prince" was "too Machiavelli."

There the matter rested, not happily. The Queen continued to treat Churchill with deference; when he finally left office, she and the Duke of Edinburgh joined him for a farewell dinner party at Number Ten, an honor not repeated until Wilson left office in 1976. Later, as reports came in of his failing health, she initiated the idea that when Churchill died, he should lie in state in Westminster Hall. He would be the unique commoner, in death as in life.

Beyond the matter of Prince Philip's title, it was a rough time for him generally. The Queen wanted him to take over from her as Colonel of the Grenadier Guards, a role she had had since her teenage years and one she particularly valued. But a particularly savage lieutenant colonel led a revolt against giving the role to "some bloody Greek" and Prince Philip quietly retreated, becoming Colonel of the Welsh Guards instead. Later, when his son grew to the age when as Prince of Wales that job was appropriate for him, it was suggested that Philip go to the Grenadiers after all. A lesser man might have turned them down, but Prince Philip accepted, becoming a very engaged and committed figurehead for the Grenadiers, and he remains so today. Though the family name continued to cause arguments, perhaps the final word about Prince Philip's status did not come until 2011 when, at age ninety, he was made Lord High Admiral, a title the Queen herself had carried till then.

Showing great restraint, Prince Philip ignored his early humiliations and began the most vigorously successful years of his life as consort. Regularly voted the most popular member of the royal family, he seemed quite likely to turn his role into a much bigger one. He threw himself into promoting the cause of efficiency in business, or scientific management. He was president of the British Association for the Advancement of Science, and in a series of speeches through the 1950s and into the 1960s, he criticized the stodginess of British industry and mocked the dead hand of trade union conservatism. In 1961, when Prince Philip was asked why British industry was in decline, he suggested it was a national defeat "comparable to any lost military campaign."

This analysis was widely shared by worried economic observers. Nearly a decade before, one of the founders of the Institute for Economic Affairs, Oliver Smedley, had warned that Britain could not survive "in an intensely competitive world if our energies, enterprise and adaptability continue to be fettered by the outmoded trappings and controls of the centrally planned economy."[20] Popular criticism of inefficient trade union practices and restrictive cartels had been a rising issue through the decade. In the press, in thoughtful magazines and among free-market academics, the need for a brisker, more aggressive attitude to wealth making was discussed again and again.

Prince Philip's speeches led to a popular conviction that he was an innovative thinker and a modern man, and he was. His unhappiness over the loss of the Mountbatten surname did not make him shy about testing the old verities of the Palace, and he relished outsiders' challenges about the point and purpose of monarchy. It is safe to speculate that these matters did not trouble his wife, who was more instinctively conservative and held a much clearer public position. But what Prince Philip lacked was a mechanism, a powerful lever or organization of his own that could have given his energy some kind of wider influence. He was condemned by the job he had taken on to be forever a commentator, a speech maker, and occasionally a chairman—but never an executive. It is a dilemma his oldest son has wrestled with too.

Prince Philip's speeches of the later 1950s and 1960s convey a sense of a battle joined. It was not obvious then that Britain would continue her industrial slither downward. The giant Unilever was successfully importing American industrial and commercial techniques; ICI was spending more on research and development by the end of the 1950s than all the British universities put together; ruthless tycoons like Hugh Fraser and Jack Cotton were cutting a swath through commercial property and retail; both the steel and car industries had formed major alliances on the "bigger is better" principle. The City, though stuffy, had begun to reassert an international role that would soon result in the Eurobond market. From Alec Issigonis's radical Mini of 1959 to Christopher Cockerell's hovercraft, Britain had not lost her inventiveness.

Still, Prince Philip became a representative voice for rising concern and anger about the poor industrial and scientific performance of Britain generally, something apparently forgotten in the later dustups about some of his tactless remarks. Even Harold Wilson's Labour Party seized the fashionable enthusiasm for efficiency and better management as a major theme. Prince Philip, in his first two decades as consort, was relevant, pungent and popular.

༄

Not all critics of fustiness, however, nor all modernizers, were welcome. Two figures, one the relatively obscure John Grigg, later Lord Altrincham, and the other the wrinkled celebrity Malcolm Muggeridge, both took potshots at the monarchy during this period. In an article published in an obscure journal that was picked up by the mainstream press, Grigg attacked the Queen's speech-making abilities, complaining that she sounded like "a priggish schoolgirl, captain of the hockey team." Muggeridge attacked the royal "soap opera" in an American magazine in 1957, just ahead of the Queen and Duke's visit, complaining about the dreary and conservative aristocrats surrounding them. His thrust was more an assault on the knee-jerk and sugary monarchism of the British media than the royal family itself, but since it was published under a headline questioning the need for a Queen, the self-same media quickly whipped up the story. What is remarkable, looking back, is not what the men said but the fury of public reaction. Grigg and Muggeridge were threatened, abused, screamed at, and pilloried. To criticize the Queen was still beyond the pale.

Yet the country was changing. Old habits of deference and respect were fraying—a social shift that was accelerated by the disastrous premiership of the Queen's second prime minister. Anthony Eden, who had fought gallantly in World War I, as well as acting as Churchill's anti-appeasement lieutenant and wartime foreign secretary, was well known to the royal family. He had first met the Queen, then aged seven, in 1934, when he was appointed Lord Privy Seal. George V was at his most choleric; in particular, he was in a fury about the antimonarchist comments by the socialist Stafford Cripps, who claimed his attack on "Buckingham Palace influence" was not meant to refer to the King himself. The King confided in Eden, who was a good royalist: "What does he mean by saying, Buckingham Palace is not me? Who else is there, I should like to know? Does he mean the footmen? D'you see the fellow says there is going to be a general election in August? Who is he to decide that? Damned cheek, I call it."[21] Later, in 1947, during the worst of the austerity years, Eden had been a vocal supporter of the monarchy in the Commons against those calling for a slimmed-down Scandinavian style.

By 1955, he had become another of the elephant-premiers,

though a younger, more dashing iteration than Winston. His succession was so widely accepted that there was little danger of the Queen being drawn into this handover. He had been at the top of government throughout the war, and was greatly admired in the country. Though his brief and unsuccessful premiership would draw the Queen into the most potentially dangerous political situation of her entire reign, as he entered Downing Street there was no reason for Elizabeth not to view him with respect and affection. In private Churchill and other Tories had worried about his frail health. Moreover, had the Queen taken widespread soundings in the Conservative Party she might have found a surprisingly strong groundswell of support for another candidate, Rab Butler.

Eden was quickly embroiled in the Suez affair, which had its roots in the decision by Egypt's new ruler, Colonel Gamal Abdel Nasser, to nationalize the Suez Canal, through which much of Europe's oil and other commodities traveled. The British government, unhappy with this abrupt change, connived with the French and Israelis to provide an excuse to evade international law and invade Egypt. Eden's ruse—concocted at a cloak-and-dagger meeting in a villa on the outskirts of Paris between French, British and Israeli ministers—was an Israeli attack against Egypt, which would provide an excuse for Britain and France to intervene to "separate the combatants." Crucially, the United States was kept out of the loop; in the event, they would prove a ferocious and deadly critic of the British.

Eden justified his actions by asserting that Nasser was a lesser, Arab version of Hitler, a demagogue who must be confronted. In Egypt and across the Arab world Nasser was seen as a visionary and liberator, but in Britain, at least to begin with, Eden's case was overwhelmingly accepted. He was the anti-appeaser, after all, a voice much of the country instinctively trusted. Yet soon hard questions were being asked: was this not an act of outdated imperialism? Shouldn't such conflicts be left to the world's new policeman, the United Nations? Was the government telling the whole truth? Was this not, in fact, a British act of aggression? These questions began to bubble from liberal newspapers and the Labour benches in the Commons, fomenting mass demonstrations in the streets. Britain was divided.

Many suspected Eden's account of Britain's role in the invasion. To maintain the ruse, he had to lie to Parliament and conceal the truth even from some of his own ministers. The Queen quickly found herself in a dangerous position. Presumably she saw, and carefully read, the private papers from Number Ten, the Foreign Office and the secret services. Did they reveal what was happening? Perhaps; perhaps not. Senior members of MI6, many cabinet ministers and most of Whitehall had been carefully kept out of the loop. Most historians think that with the help of his officials Eden concealed the truth from the Queen in his audiences with her, of which there were two in the crucial month. If so, Eden's behavior was an outrageous violation of the principles of constitutional monarchy, one that cannot be justified as an effort to protect the Queen. Alternatively, she was one of the select few to know the dangerous truth, and was silently drawn into his lie.

The Queen's own private office was split about Suez. Her private secretary, Michael Adeane, a traditional conservative in the mold of his grandfather Lord Stamfordham, was pro-Eden and pro-Suez. But the two assistant private secretaries, Martin Charteris and Edward Ford, who had both served in the Middle East during the Second World War, were anti. Over the years, there have been persistent rumors that the Queen and Prince Philip were also hostile to the invasion. These surfaced in their clearest form in a book by the historian Robert Lacey for the Queen's Silver Jubilee in 1977. Lacey, a *Sunday Times* writer, had excellent access, eased by Lord Mountbatten, who wanted such a book to be published, and who in deepest privacy gave Lacey a lot of help. Lacey wrote: "Elizabeth II appeared to friends and relatives genuinely surprised by what had been carried out in her name in October and November 1956." Either she "went along with the strategic deception of the rest of the world—including the United States [and of course Parliament]—or else she was taken in by it, like everyone else."

When the manuscript began to circulate not long before the book's publication and Eden discovered that Lacey had concluded the Queen did not know the truth about Suez, he was furious, fully understanding the gravity of the accusation that he had deceived his monarch. Eden concluded that Lacey must have been told this by Mountbatten or by Prince Philip, and he insisted to Lacey that the Queen "understood what we were doing very well."[22] Ill with cancer, the former prime minister confronted Mountbatten, a man he now described as "gaga" and "a congenital liar." Mountbatten said in his diary, "I didn't attempt to deny it [that he was Lacey's source]. . . . It was the author himself who had put the question and I thought I had answered it sufficiently tactfully not to produce the particular statement that had appeared."[23] Lacey came under heavy pressure from Eden to change the story; he did not. It can now be said that Mountbatten was indeed Lacey's source and had told him clearly that the Queen did not know about the deception involving Britain, France and Israel on which the Suez attack had depended. But did Mountbatten really know this? Had the Queen or the Duke told him?

A significant factor not known at the time was that during the Suez affair Mountbatten tried to resign as First Sea Lord and was ordered by the politician in charge of the Admiralty, Lord Hailsham, to stay at his post. This was news that the Queen surely would have known, and it gives strong credence to the belief that she knew about Eden's plot, or at least that something very strange was going on. It is also worth pointing out that when Eden, stricken by illness, went to Sandringham in January 1957 to tell the Queen that he was resigning, she expressed deep personal sadness and offered him an Earldom. She wrote to him almost immediately afterward:

My Dear Anthony,

You know already how deeply I felt your resignation last week, and how much I sympathize in the tragic turn of fate which laid you low at the moment our country is beginning to see the possibility of a brightening in the international sky . . . much has been said and written in the past week about your record in the House of Commons and as a Statesman; I am only anxious that you should realise that that record, which has indeed been won in tempestuous times, is highly valued and will never be forgotten by your Sovereign.

He replied in emotional terms:

It is the bare truth to say that I looked forward to my weekly audience, knowing that I should receive from Your Majesty a wise and impartial reaction to events, which was quite simply the voice of our land. Years ago Baldwin told me that the post of Prime Minister was the most lonely in the world . . . that I have not found it so is due to Your Majesty's unfailing sympathy and understanding.

These are not the words of a Queen outraged about being kept in the dark, or a statesman embarrassed about keeping her there. The two had had longer than average audiences while Eden was prime minister; after his resignation, the Queen accepted the Edens' private hospitality, a most unusual gesture.

After a thorough review of the record, my own belief is that the Queen knew the essential story but that Eden deliberately held back the most embarrassing part of his plan from her, precisely in order to prevent her from being contaminated if it went wrong, as it certainly did. Further, though she said nothing directly, it is reasonable to conclude that the Queen appreciated Eden's discretion in his dealings with her regarding the affair.

The Suez crisis shows how easily a monarch can be drawn into disastrous plans hatched by a prime minister. It also implies that, at least during the earlier years of her reign, the audiences with her prime ministers were more about the Queen listening to and sympathizing with them than about her actively questioning or warning them. Whatever Eden did or did not tell her, such a response would certainly fit with her cautious character.

⚘

The Queen's political education by her early prime ministers was next tested by the succession to Eden. Under other circumstances, the Queen would as a matter of course appoint the Tory she was advised the party would most rally behind, and thus the politician with the best chance of parliamentary success. But in 1957 who could say whom the party really wanted? The newspapers, including those well connected to Conservative circles, assumed the prize would go to Rab Butler, but Harold Macmillan was also considered to be a sound candidate. The issue quickly became extremely complex: Suez had left deep wounds in Parliament and the country. The Tory Party was divided, embarrassed and angry about how things had turned out, with many blaming—variously—the Americans, the media, Eden himself or anti-Suez voices, which had included Butler's. This time, Buckingham Palace could not simply stand aside and wait.

Two men played critical roles during this dramatic moment. One was Sir Michael Adeane, the Queen's private secretary. The other was Robert Gascoyne-Cecil, the fifth Marquess of Salisbury, Leader of the Lords. A friend of the royal family's, the grandson of Queen Victoria's last premier, Gascoyne-Cecil was himself a long-serving Conservative minister who had resigned over appeasement in 1938 and later served under Churchill. The Cecils are one of the ancient political dynasties of England, and no grandee was grander than he.

Adeane, who had been working at the Palace since 1936, was also old-school in his instincts. He was wry, recessive and loyal.

Before serving George VI he had been aide-de-camp to Lord Tweedsmuir, the former novelist John Buchan in Canada (and his son later became private secretary to Prince Charles). Now Adeane called Salisbury, who had just been shooting with the royal family for three days at Sandringham, and asked him to take soundings. Salisbury in turn consulted Lord Kilmuir, the Lord Chancellor. Between them they decided the neatest solution would be to ask members of the cabinet one by one which man, Butler or Macmillan, they favored. This poll would then be supplemented by advice about the mood of the Tory backbenchers, delivered by the then chief whip, a young man called Ted Heath; and about the feelings of the party's grass roots, conveyed through its chairman, Oliver Poole. In the end, however, Kilmuir told Salisbury that the Queen could take any advice she liked "and that she did not have to wait—indeed, ought not to wait—for the result of a Party meeting and election."[24]

This maneuver led to one of the most famous vignettes in Britain's postwar parliamentary history. Cabinet members were led in, one by one, to see Salisbury in an anteroom at the Privy Council Office, whereupon Salisbury asked them, in his lisping voice, which it was to be, "Wab or Hawold?" With only two or perhaps three exceptions, they voted for Harold Macmillan. Macmillan was also the favored candidate of Heath, speaking for the backbenchers, and of Poole, speaking for the party members. Meanwhile the Queen had decided to consult Churchill. Despite his fondness for Butler, when the Grand Old Man arrived with Salisbury at Buckingham Palace, a Union flag rug draped over his knees, he too plumped for Macmillan. The whole process took remarkably little time. On Tuesday, January 8, 1957, Eden traveled to Sandringham to tell the Queen he was resigning. By lunchtime two days later, Macmillan had been to Buckingham Palace and was prime minister.

Almost everyone who has studied the party breakdown after Eden's resignation has concluded that, despite the surprise of the newspapers and Eden's own preference for Rab, Macmillan was the obvious choice. Butler had been an appeaser during the war, and in the mid-1950s that still mattered. More important, he was seen as indecisive, excessively wily and not entirely loyal during the Suez crisis. Ultimately, more Tories, in both Parliament and the country, seemed to be dead set against Butler than were opposed to Macmillan—who would quickly bind the bleeding wounds and stage an impressive Conservative comeback. Even so, it was an unseemly and old-fashioned way of switching prime ministers, and it would sow seeds of doubt in many people's minds about how Britain was really run.

DEMOCRACY AND BIG MAC

Some fifteen months earlier, a disheveled and rather brilliant journalist on the *Spectator* named Henry Fairlie had written a column about the well-connected traitors Burgess and Maclean, in which he coined the term "the establishment" to describe the social exercise of power in England. The handling of the Tory succession suggested that a magic circle of grandees was indeed still shuffling society's cards and pulling Westminster's strings. In fact, this familiar characterization of the establishment—which had always had more than an element of the truth—was becoming increasingly less accurate. The spirit of leveling democracy was militant and marching.

True, debs were still presented at court. At Ascot and royal garden parties, the top hats, tails and uniforms were as ubiquitous as ever. As the 1950s waned, a startling number of the cabinet members were interrelated Old Etonians. Macmillan and his aristocratic friends went shooting at Balmoral and Sandringham, and the prime minister was mildly surprised at a flurry of media hostility when the Queen proposed to go tiger shooting on a visit to India. In the City, bowler hats and rolled umbrellas remained "the thing," and Whitehall followed a near-military system of ranking and caste. The only long-haired people at the BBC were female typists.

Yet the establishment's instincts and solidarity were coming apart—not that they had been quite that strong anyway. Even apparently tight social circles and families fell out, as they have always done. Salisbury himself had been among the old-school aristocrats who were most suspicious of Prince Philip. Now he intervened in another highly sensitive Windsor dilemma.

The trouble had begun on the day of the Coronation when journalists, already in the know, had noticed a gently intimate stroking by Princess Margaret of Group Captain Peter Townsend's lapel. Discretion still held, barely, in the British press, but in New York the story about a possible further marriage, this time of the Queen's sister, was swiftly published. That article was followed, twelve days after the Coronation, by a British Sunday paper, the raucous *People*. Hypocritically, *People* told the story only to denounce it as obviously untrue, since "it is quite unthinkable that a royal princess, third in line of succession to the throne, should even contemplate marriage with a man who has been through the divorce courts." Mischievous though it was, the newspaper had put its inky finger on a real problem. Divorce remained a serious social and moral stigma. Furthermore, under the archaic Royal Marriages Act, Princess Margaret needed her sister's permission to get married until the summer of 1955, when she would be twenty-five, a full two years away. The Queen, observing constitutional propriety, would in turn need the assent of her government. What would she do? What would Whitehall do?

Townsend, the decorated RAF war hero who had become equerry to the King in 1944, had had an unhappy wartime marriage that had recently ended in divorce. He had been spotted by the young Margaret during the South African trip of 1947, and though he was nearly sixteen years older than the Princess, they had fallen in love soon afterward. He had declared his love at the beginning of Coronation year and then informed "Tommy" Lascelles, the Queen's private secretary. A horrified Lascelles barked at Townsend that he was either bad or mad. Churchill agreed, and

Townsend was rather brutally sent off to an RAF desk job in Belgium to get him out of the way of the vivacious and determined princess. There he bided his time, assuming that once the deadline passed and Margaret was twenty-five, he would be free to marry her.

It didn't work out that way. In October 1955, the matter was brought to a boil when Salisbury, a leading High Anglican, told his cabinet colleagues that he could not accept that the Queen's sister could ever marry a divorced man—despite the fact that Townsend had been the innocent party in his divorce. Since the cabinet had to approve the marriage, and would have been riven if Salisbury chose to make a public issue of this by resigning, the peer had effectively destroyed Princess Margaret's hopes.

The debate about whether the Princess ought to be able to marry the divorced RAF man quickly went public. Which counted more: old ways or new, religion or love? The press was divided, with the more popular papers, and those on the left, backing the Princess's right to marry. Attitudes were changing; divorce was gradually becoming more socially acceptable. But Margaret would be judged by a different standard: Eden broke the news to her that, if she went ahead, she would lose both her position in the line of succession and her expanded Civil List allowance. She would also have to live abroad.

The story, having been ignited by a popular newspaper, was now concluded by the highbrow *Times*, which argued in its editorial for October 24 that the Queen was society's "universal representative in whom her people see their better selves ideally reflected; and since part of their ideal is family life, the Queen's family has its own part in the reflection." The proposed marriage would make it inevitable "that this reflection becomes distorted."

Ultimately, Princess Margaret bowed to the pressure and announced that she had decided not to marry Townsend, "mindful of the Church's teaching that Christian marriage is indissoluble, and conscious of my duty to the Commonwealth." It seems to have been a devastating blow to her. She told friends later that she particularly blamed Lascelles and Churchill for what she had been put through and never completely recovered her balance. Although no one can ever know how a marriage that did not happen might have worked out, this warthog-like assertion of the old order seems in retrospect both cruel and faintly silly.

Inevitably, there was much speculation about how the Queen responded. Earlier biographers who knew those involved believe she stood aside from her sister's dilemma, refusing to discuss it and deliberately avoiding taking a position. From a modern perspective this might seem odd. After all, Townsend knew the Queen and Prince Philip. They seem to have liked him, and wished both him and Princess Margaret well. So why was she less than assertive in her sister's cause?

Elizabeth decided to react as Queen first and sister second. Only two years before, in her Coronation Oath, she had promised the church and the world that she would uphold the highest values of Christian family life—and she meant it. Furthermore, she could not ignore her bishops or ministers. If she was pulled by natural affection, she was also tugged by duty, and time and again in her life duty's pull has proved stronger. Still, this episode was an ominous early signal of the problems ahead for the "ideal family" version of modern monarchy. Real families are untidy. Emotions cannot always be conveniently bottled up. Public moralizing and press prurience make it harder still to conceal the messier aspects of private life.

For the press, wartime patriotism and censorship had made discretion a habit, but now all that was coming loose. Prince Philip's decision to tour a swath of the Commonwealth without his wife for six months during the winter of 1956–57 prompted newspaper speculation about the state of the Queen's marriage, leading to an official statement from the Palace: "It is quite untrue that there is any rift between the Queen and the Duke of Edinburgh." Well-meant but ham-fisted, the statement only inflamed the story.

In this period too, Prince Philip became infuriated by the press coverage, complaining bitterly to friends about it. He became increasingly cynical about journalists, and gradually an outgoing, optimistic man keen to explain himself began to turn into a more suspicious one who expected to be misunderstood. This was a significant loss for the British monarchy, but there was probably no help for it. The press was not going to defer or self-censor for long. Papers were fighting cutthroat battles for a large and lucrative market; increasingly worried about television swiping their profits, they were in no mood to hold back on good stories.

Sensibly, the press began to question the implied promise that Royals would never again misbehave or love unwisely. After all, the "family monarchy" of George V and George VI, following the uxorious Victoria, was not the whole story of kings and queens in Britain or anywhere else; historians, for one, have always plundered royalty for its scandals. But if the world was changing around her, the Queen was not about to use her popularity during this period to reconsider family values and personal morality as the central building block of modern monarchy. In her own life, she was a happy and contented mother and wife, one who willingly deferred to Prince Philip in domestic matters. And after the Townsend episode, there seemed to be no family problems ahead. These were years of innocence.

Not in politics, however: there are no innocent times there. A fierce imperialist, Salisbury would fall out with Macmillan over decolonization and emerge as the first president of the right-wing Monday Club. Indeed by the spring of 1957, Salisbury had resigned over Cyprus, believing Macmillan had not been tough enough with the rebel leader Archbishop Makarios, and leading Macmillan to reflect that throughout history "the Cecils, when any friend or colleague has been in real trouble, have stabbed him in the back." When the Macmillans went to Balmoral for their first August visit, perhaps tactlessly, Salisbury was among the party.

That visit did not go smoothly, with Macmillan tending to

lecture the Queen and being unimpressed by Prince Philip: "He is *against* us being a nuclear power. I don't altogether like the tone of his talk. It is too like that of a clever undergraduate, who has just discovered Socialism." This was an absurd judgment on Macmillan's part: the grand premier had clearly had his tweeds ruffled by Prince Philip, who though studiously non-party always sounded more like a radical of the free market—more pro-business right than anti-business left.

Macmillan went on to become a pivotal prime minister in the Queen's reign, in part because, after the ups and downs of the Churchill and Eden administrations, she had time to develop a longer and somewhat more equal relationship with him. He was in a sense her first "normal" prime minister. As foreign secretary in 1955 he had been impressed, and somewhat chastened, to discover how hard she worked to understand political issues, in this case over Iraq: "I did my best to explain the position to her, without boring her. She showed (as her father used to) an uncanny knowledge of details and personalities. She must read the telegrams very carefully."

As prime minister, he may have bored her from time to time— once, when gloomily mentioning his possible resignation, he was rather hurt at her "lack of consternation"—but in general, whatever her private feelings, the relationship seemed to blossom. He sent her long dispatches and often referred to her close reading of papers and sympathetic understanding of his problems. Adeane encouraged him to stay for a drink after his weekly audience, and Macmillan did his best to please her in small ways, as when he tried to help in the vexed question of Prince Philip's title and the family surname. Together, they formed a better, closer partnership.

⚜

Abroad, gusting winds of change swept through much of Britain's former Empire, especially the African territory. With her newly purchased nuclear weaponry, the country still aspired to global reach, and she initially stood proudly aloof from the experimental European Economic Community. But from 1959 on, the Secretary for the Colonies, Iain Macleod, was charged with what was, in effect, a fire sale of the remaining parts of the British Empire.

On this issue the Queen began to assert herself directly, showing a new steeliness during a row in 1961 over whether she should visit Ghana. In 1957 Ghana, under Kwame Nkrumah, had been the first black Commonwealth country to win independence. Because of the Queen's third pregnancy, the visit had already been delayed, greatly to Nkrumah's personal distress. By now, however, he had established a dictatorial rule, which led to deep questions about the purpose of the Commonwealth. Ought it to be an organization of democratic nations under the Queen, or was it a family that would continue to embrace its members, more or less however they behaved? Many British politicians, putting democracy before the brotherhood of the Commonwealth, wanted the Queen to cancel. Macmillan worried that if the matter came up in the Commons he might be defeated.

But the Queen was determined to go. According to Macmillan, she told him she "means to be a Queen and not a puppet" and, if ordered not to do what she thought was her duty, she "did not know how she could carry on." The biographer Lady Longford records the Queen arguing that canceling might push Ghana toward the Soviet Union: "How silly should I look, if I was scared to visit Ghana and then Khrushchev went and had a good reception?"[25] In the runup to her visit, Nkrumah had arrested a number of dissidents, after which a terrorist bomb went off in Accra, the country's capital. Apart from the political dilemma, then, there was a clear risk to the Queen's safety.

Undeterred, the Queen made the trip anyway. While there, she made a speech stating that the Commonwealth family could include a wide amount of disagreement, danced with Nkrumah at a banquet, and was hailed locally as "the greatest socialist monarch in the world." In the banquet hall, many of the seats were empty, having been prepared for opposition leaders now in jail.

Though the Queen demonstrated a cool unconcern for her own safety—a trait repeated later—as well as a gritty determination that the Commonwealth should come first, she did not resolve the central dilemma. Instead, she responded to it in a way that has often seemed very unsatisfactory ever since. "Family" was to be treated with kid gloves, at the national as at the personal level. The Commonwealth, an organization of high ideals, pragmatically accepted some brutal and undemocratic regimes, rather than lose members. The excuse usually offered—that it is better to stay close and try to influence those who are behaving badly—is what parents say about off-the-rails teenagers. But what is tough love, and what is merely fluffy appeasement? Macmillan's withdrawal from empire, essential as it was, would involve the Queen in more morally difficult choices. As she worked hard to create a substantial role for herself as head of a fractious Commonwealth, some of its members were looking more to communist Moscow than to London.

Macmillan's great trick was to keep up a good front, while paddling desperately below the water as he tried to adapt to radically different circumstances. This impersonator of an unflappable aristocrat must in private have brought his Queen much bad and dramatic news. There were the embarrassing deals that needed to be done with the United States to maintain a British nuclear capacity that worked; the loss of South Africa from the Commonwealth in 1961; the terrifying standoffs between the United States and the U.S.S.R.; the startling decline of British manufacturing and recurrent problems with trade balances and inflation; the consequent plea for membership in the Common Market and President de Gaulle's humiliating "non"; the sexual and spying scandals at home. For the Queen, all this must have added up to one of the most difficult periods of her reign. That frothy post-Coronation enthusiasm for a new Elizabethan Age was crashing like spume against a comfortless, rocky shore.

⁂

To safely sustain the monarchy, the Queen would have to change it. She was greatly helped by Prince Philip, who, after the attacks on the stuffiness of the monarchy by Lord Altrincham and Malcolm Muggeridge, seems to have been emboldened in his reformist ideas. He was enthusiastic about opening up the Palace for lunch and supper parties, which allowed the Queen to meet a wider range of people. Characteristic guest lists from 1957 included the pianist Myra Hess, the Labour MP (and future prime minister) Jim Callaghan, the runner Chris Brasher, the Ealing film producer Michael Balcon, the editor of *The Economist*, Donald Tyerman, the poet John Betjeman, and the actress Joyce Grenfell. If these were modest steps toward a more informed and informal style, they seemed radical to those used to her father's court.

Then came a more dramatic change: the Queen, on her own initiative, finally abolished the aristocratic flummery of the Season. The presentation of debutantes at Buckingham Palace, waiting on gilt chairs in their white silk dresses until summoned by the Lord Chamberlain to curtsy to the Queen, sitting on her throne below a red canopy, had continued until 1958. In that year, fourteen hundred girls were paraded over three days. The presentations became a likely target for reform partly because the bloodstock market aspect of it was embarrassingly class-conscious. But it had also become a subject for jokes: in the tart words of the Queen's tart sister, "every tart in London was getting in."

Another significant reform was the Queen's agreement (given reluctantly) to appear once a year on television. Prince Philip supported a longtime ambition of the BBC by persuading his wife to give her traditional Christmas Day broadcast on camera rather than on the radio. It was clearly a risk: if the radio microphone had been an instrument of torture for her father, the Queen felt uncomfortable talking to a television camera. She lacks the glib touch the medium requires. Yet the gamble paid off, and by the early 1960s nearly half the entire population was watching the message. The Christmas messages became an important way for the Queen to communicate directly with the public, and although most of what she said was unsurprising, she occasionally made headlines. Even when she did not, millions made the address a ritual part of a British Christmas Day, many standing to attention in front of their television sets to watch it.

These were modest reforms at a time when the country was changing very fast. Perhaps the Queen and her advisers could have done more: in criticizing the tweedy and unimaginative atmosphere of the old court, Altrincham and Muggeridge had made a valid point. No one could ever expect the Palace to be ahead of the times, but during the postwar years it had fallen a long way behind the changing atmosphere of the country, and, despite Prince Philip, would stay well behind. The key courtiers were by now old, very cautious, and too distanced from the Queen's generation. Her instinct, meanwhile, was usually to wait for advice and consider it, rather than to initiate change herself. Year by year, she was moving into a country where the ghosts of George V and George VI were no longer sufficient guides. Nor were the cabinet ministers or the prime minister himself. Macmillan needed her as part of his controversial balancing act and he enjoyed playing the elderly uncle, but ultimately she would need to move beyond him, too.

His eventual departure was even messier than Eden's, though at least quicker than Churchill's. By the summer of 1963, Macmillan's government was struggling under the embarrassing blow of the Profumo spying, lying and sex scandal. The prime minister was facing a growing rebellion inside the party he had led with guile and brutality. Then, in October, he was diagnosed with a benign tumor of the prostate and informed that an operation was essential. He took the gloomiest possible medical view of his condition and determined that because of the risk that he might have cancer, he must immediately resign.

This time round, however, there was a real choice of successors. They included, yet again, Rab Butler; the popular Lord Hailsham; three new stars, Reggie Maudling, Edward Heath and Iain Macleod; and a man who seemed the outsider, Lord Home. Since Macmillan's illness coincided with the Conservatives' annual conference at Blackpool, some kind of contest in front of the party faithful was inevitable. Macmillan wanted to stop Butler, who was probably the favorite choice of the cabinet. Lying in the King Edward VII Hospital for Sick Officers, he called Lord Home to his bedside to persuade him that he might have to stand, and then used him as his messenger to the Tory conference, carrying news of his resignation. Hailsham, meanwhile, made something of an ass of himself with what Conservative grandees thought vulgar self-promotion. Home, strengthened by his status as Macmillan's man, began to mobilize support. This left the problem of stopping Butler. And at this point, Macmillan's maneuvering drew in the Queen.

Soundings were taken of the party; they showed a surprising surge on all sides for Lord Home. He too had been at one time tarred as a member of the appeasement camp, but by now was known as a likable moderate. Macmillan, through Adeane, arranged to have the Queen visit the prime minister at his bedside—passing in front of television cameras and the world's press—so that he could tender his resignation in person and offer her advice about his successor. That advice, read to her from his bed, was that she should summon Home to Buckingham Palace and ask him whether he could form a government. This was a clear and obvious "bounce," which gave Home a royal stamp of approval before full or systematic advice had been taken from the party.

When they heard what was happening, some of the most talented Tory ministers, including Enoch Powell and Iain Macleod, were inclined to rebel on Butler's behalf and refuse to serve under

Home. But Butler, seeing the prize snatched from his hands for a second time, flinched and perhaps too loyally declined to join the protests. Macmillan had fixed the succession, rather more successfully than Eden had. And of course the Queen had only taken her prime minister's advice. But had she allowed herself to be used? It's worth remembering that she was a still a young woman, trained to receive the advice of older men—men her father's age. According to Ben Pimlott, a later biographer, "When she got the advice to call Alec she thought, 'Thank God.' She loved Alec—he was an old friend. They talked about dogs and shooting together. They were both Scottish landowners, the same sort of people, like old school friends."[26]

Alec Douglas-Home, who now had to renounce his title and stand as an MP for the Commons, had thought he would be the unity candidate. Instead, he discovered that he had to persuade many puzzled and angry colleagues—and in some cases he could not. By the 1960s it was no longer obvious that a straightforward, benign but clearly aristocratic Scottish laird, who loved his salmon fishing and grouse moors, was an electoral asset. Douglas-Home was a close friend of the royal family—particularly of the Queen Mother's family, the Bowes Lyons—and courtiers too would have seen him as "one of us." The Queen herself was not at the time blamed directly for her part in this controversial choice, but much of the Tory Party and many in the country as a whole responded to the fix with fury. In the end, the choice of Douglas-Home in 1963 may well have made possible Harold Wilson's very close election victory the following year.

The most cogent critique of the succession came from Iain Macleod, who attacked Macmillan in the *Spectator* for presiding over an Old Etonian "Magic Circle" that had plotted to deny Butler the premiership. The episode soon came to symbolize all that was wrong and fusty about British political life. Macmillan, wilier than the Queen, had used her ruthlessly as cover to achieve his ends. Thanks to his maneuver, Douglas-Home had been summoned under the unquestionable authority of the Queen's Prerogative, which was endlessly invoked by Macmillan before and afterward in his explanation of these events. Meanwhile, any possibility of Butler refusing to accept what was going on was dashed by her involvement.

In truth, of course, the Queen had nothing personally to do with the succession. Neither she, nor Adeane, nor anyone at Buckingham Palace, took personal soundings or engaged in personal debates about the possible candidates. They too were presented with a fait accompli masquerading as obsequious advice. Here was the final example of a still relatively young Queen being used by her politicians rather than protected by them. The storm, if short, was violent, and fortunately nothing quite like it ever happened again. In the future, parties would choose their leaders by more conventional means. Politicians would display more genuine care for the monarch's reputation. And the Queen would grow wilier.

⊂━━━✦━━⊃

Britannia and the Waves

I t is April 16, 1953. Sir Winston Churchill is still in Downing Street, Stalin has recently died, the first James Bond novel has been published, Crick and Watson have announced the double helix structure of DNA . . . and the Queen is at John Brown's Shipyard on the Clyde in a downpour. She is armed with a bottle of something unpleasant-sounding called "empire wine" to name a new ship, *Britannia*. The vessel will be the eighty-third Royal Yacht, going back in an unbroken line to the reign of Charles II, a family tree of wooden Dutch-style boats, gorgeously decorated miniature warships, paddle steamers and steel-clad ships.

This new one looks nothing like most people's idea of a yacht. It is more like a child's drawing of a ship, with simple lines, a single big funnel, and three masts. As the rain falls, the Queen tells thirty thousand Scottish shipyard workers, their families and their bosses how much the building of the ship had meant to her father: "He felt most strongly, as I do, that a yacht was a necessity and not a luxury for the head of our great British Commonwealth, between whose countries the sea is no barrier but the natural and indestructible highway." Whack goes the wine, hooray go the crowds, and up into the murk wafts the national anthem.

From the very first, then, *Britannia*'s fate and the Common-wealth's were said to be closely interlinked. As Prince Philip later pointed out, she was the first Royal Yacht to be genuinely oceango-ing. The need for a new vessel to replace the last of three *Victoria and Albert*s had been discussed before the war, and was revived by George VI in 1951. By then Britain was under two shadows: post-war austerity and the intensifying Cold War. As a consequence, the original pre-1939 plans were trimmed—the King himself asked for a smaller ship—and the new Royal Yacht was designed so that it could be converted into a floating hospital in any future war. At nearly six thousand tons, with two steam turbine engines providing 12,000 horsepower, she was relatively underpowered. Despite post-war shortages, *Britannia*'s construction was rushed forward partly because it was hoped that the sick King might be helped by sea voy-ages, such as his visit on a battleship to South Africa after the war. He died long before *Britannia* was ready.

For anyone interested in the Queen's personal taste, *Britannia*, now moored at Leith docks in Edinburgh and open to the public, is well worth a visit. In her palaces and castles the Queen inherited the furnishings; these she chose, with the Duke's enthusiastic assis-tance. What they preferred will be familiar to millions of middle-class people of the 1950s: *Britannia* sports a clean-lined, light, unfussy Scandinavian style of decoration with comfortable, simple chairs and beds. The heavier, more ornate styles of the previous generations are nowhere in sight: there is no dark red, no gilding, no heavy oak or strong patterns. The Queen's working desk, lit by a simple lamp, is small and businesslike. The Duke's bedroom has the male simplicity of a naval officer's taste.

By the time the yacht ended her long service more than four decades later, she was also filled with gifts and oddities picked up along the way, from whalebones lifted from a beach by Prince Philip and presentation swords from Arabia, to spears from the South Seas and carved sticks from everywhere. But the effect is of comfort and calm, not of monarchical splendor. There are flashes of grandness—including a special bay for the royal Bentley, which was unloaded by crane, and the almost Venetian elegance of the Royal Barge—but this version of the Royal Yacht feels more like a large Home Counties detached house loaded onto a ship than a floating palace. One politician who traveled aboard her felt "there was a homeliness about *Britannia* which fits in with the Queen's personality. It's not a grand place. It's not a place for thinking grand thoughts."

The Royal Yacht would play a significant role in the story of the Queen's reign—most of it, anyway—and from *Britannia*'s first day we will fast-forward to its last. It is now December 11, 1997. Not Glasgow, this time, but Portsmouth. And no downpour today, for the weather is cold and clear. Tony Blair is Labour prime minister, and after a decision taken by the former Conservative government *Britannia* is being decommissioned. A dozen members of the royal family are here, and the Queen is the last of them to leave the ship she has called home for forty-four years.

Britannia still looks good, with her deep blue hull, her fluttering flags, her gleaming brass. The Royal Marines Band plays "A Life on the Ocean Wave." The Queen seems to be in tears. The ship has taken her and other members of her family on 968 official voyages across the globe. A staggering range of presidents, prime ministers and other notables have been entertained on board. Since that rainy day in 1953, she has traveled a total of 1,087,623 nautical miles, calling at over six hundred ports in 135 countries.

On *Britannia* the Queen has scampered around barefoot, gossiped late at night after visits, mimicked foreign guests, and held intimate dinners for bickering Commonwealth leaders. For those traveling with her, the last hour of the day aboard ship was often particularly fascinating. As one visitor said: "She would kick her shoes off, have a whisky, and it was 'Did you see? Did you see? That chap was looking a bit wobbly.' " In this close atmosphere, the Queen would go ashore on remote islands for long private walks. If she turned around during the first minute or two, it meant she would like company and someone would join her for a privileged, frank gossip; otherwise she went on alone.

Britannia was indeed an oceangoing refuge. The Queen has said that while Buckingham Palace is for work, Windsor Castle for weekends and some state visits, Balmoral and Sandringham for holidays (albeit interrupted with a lot of work and entertaining), the Royal Yacht was where she could fully relax. One royal servant recalls her claiming that it was her only true break of the year and reports her saying: "I walk on at the end of a long summer season, I am absolutely exhausted and you won't see me for a couple of days . . . and at the end of a fortnight I can get off at Aberdeen with a spring in my heels, ready for another year."

The atmosphere on board reflected this more relaxed spirit. The crew were naval recruits who had volunteered to become Yachtsmen and quickly learned a new routine, including the importance of moving around in sneakers while the royal family were aboard, so as not to disturb them. They learned how to keep their eyes off the Queen as they worked; she, in turn, came to know almost all of them by their first names and took a keen interest in their welfare and families. She would become alarmed if any took unnecessary risks. Asked who was accepted to serve on the yacht's crew, one officer says, "There were only two questions: have you got a prison record; and have you got a sense of humor? And if they laughed at the first, there wasn't any need for the second."

Her children honeymooned on board, and she and her husband used the yacht to range through some of the most remote areas on the planet, visiting tiny island members of the Commonwealth otherwise inaccessible for state visits. "Wherever you went," says one senior officer, "everybody came out to look at her and the national dailies were full of it, and the TV news too. There was just an extraordinary aura she carried."

Because of the importance of getting the ship neatly at rest before the morning winds, the state visits would typically start at eight a.m. The Royals would disembark at ten o'clock for a round of official visits, lunches, teas, dances, speeches and openings, returning to the yacht at five p.m. to prepare for a formal dinner on *Britannia* two hours later. Fifty-eight guests would be seated, the Queen presiding at an elevated oval table with two long tables named Victoria and Albert below her. Then at nine p.m. another 250 people would arrive for the reception; each guest would be greeted individually, and the party would continue until the Marines Band beat the retreat at ten-thirty p.m. At five to eleven, the president or local leader would go ashore, and at eleven p.m. the commanding vice admiral would signal down the old voice-pipe for the engines to take her slow ahead. This routine made it possible to visit a remarkable number of countries in a short time: once, for instance, Prince Philip managed eight state visits in the Caribbean in eleven days.

The official side of the Royal Yacht's work produced plenty of memorable cameos. No one who was present has forgotten the banquet the Queen threw aboard *Britannia* for President Yeltsin of Russia in St. Petersburg. Yeltsin was not the first to notice that the wine served at such dinners, though generally excellent, is poured into dispiritingly small glasses. During the banquet, he was notably insistent on plenty of refills, and at one point he began to harangue the Queen for an answer to the question of whether he should stand for reelection. Normally, she is meticulous about avoiding political comment, but on this evening she finally turned and looked hard at him: "Mr. President, from what you have been saying, you will certainly stand again." He roared with delighted laughter.

By tradition there are no speeches at such banquets, but Yeltsin seemed indifferent to protocol. Later in the evening, diners spun round in shock after hearing what sounded like a grenade going off. A huge bang was followed by a splinter of glass—it was Yeltsin's fist slamming onto the table before he rose to his feet to deliver a long speech in Russian. In response, the Queen was eloquently expressionless. After the last guests had staggered into the night, *Britannia* made her way two miles downriver, past sunken submarines and cargo ships. There was no proper illumination, except for what was described by the Russians as a "firework display," in which the explosions were provided by out-of-date howitzer shells. This tricky exit to the open sea was not helped by the fact that the chain-smoking Russian pilot was unsure whether "port" or "starboard" meant left or right.

On the other side of the political divide, the Queen once hosted a banquet on *Britannia* for all the living U.S. presidents. Ronald Reagan caused surprise by saying loudly as he arrived that he had an announcement to make: he now had AIDS. He then tapped each large ear—"one for each." Other *Britannia* evenings included ribald and rivalrous conclaves of Commonwealth leaders who had gathered for the meeting among heads of government off Cyprus, and riotously successful visits to the Caribbean. On one of these, Prince Philip was solemnly shaking hands and making polite inquiries of hundreds of guests coming aboard from Antigua. One was a giant local man who was accompanied by his short but sturdy wife. "What do you do on the island?" asked the Duke. Looming over the Duke, the man eyed him coldly: "Cocaine." Prince Philip, though rarely lost for words, was taken aback and asked his aides how it could have happened that a drug dealer had been invited on board. The man's wife overheard him: "No, no, Dook. Not cocaine. Cookin'. We got a restaurant."

Now that the *Britannia* is gone, many smaller members of the Commonwealth may never see another major royal visit again. That fact is not likely to impress the hard-faced money men of the Treasury, particularly in difficult times. Before her retirement, *Britannia*—with her crew of 260 sailors, 178 of them permanent, and her twenty-six bandsmen—became a mild embarrassment to the navy. When she was launched in 1953, the Royal Navy was the world's third-largest surface fleet; by the time she was decommissioned, it had only around thirty ships. The Royal Yacht became conspicuous, not least because it would inevitably cost more to keep her going. Yet her cost-benefit ratio was easy to work out, even if you put all the Commonwealth and other political roles completely to one side. From 1990 to 1995, *Britannia* was used more and more aggressively to promote British trade; during that period, she under-took about sixty such missions a year. From the Middle East to the United States, CEOs and company presidents were invited on board for presentations by groups of British companies, often those in electronics, engineering and finance.

"We'd go twenty miles off the coast, so their mobile phones wouldn't work, and we'd got them," recalls an officer. Though many companies had good reason to know the effectiveness of the missions, it is hard to put a cash value on them. But one careful estimate found that during a three-year period, deals worth £2.3 billion for British companies were signed. Overall, it was estimated that tax revenues from *Britannia*-related deals earned the Treasury about £700 million a year. Given that the yacht was costing the government around £100 million a year, this would seem to be a good deal.

Even so, many felt that keeping *Britannia* afloat no longer made sense. One official says that although the ship was a wonderful refuge, "my personal view was that it had to go, and you can get the same benefits from hiring a ship for a week or two. It was a very expensive operation, with red boxes being helicoptered out every day from London, containing quite routine stuff; and the Marine Band and so forth." The same source adds, however, that the Queen's need for occasional privacy was poignantly clear even aboard: "Until you're there, you don't realize the lack of her human rights in being in that job: even on *Britannia* there was a certain amount of nervousness that another boat was going to come alongside." In the end, filled with photographs of the royal children and childhood memories, "it was like anybody else's holiday cottage . . . except that it was a ship."

During the outbreak of the Falklands War in April 1982, Vice Admiral Sir Paul Greening, then commanding *Britannia*, argued strongly that she should be sent to the conflict as a casualty evacuation ship. He was overruled, partly because of the unusual type of fuel oil she burned and partly in case she was too tempting an Argentine target. This decision undermined part of the historic case for the Royal Yacht, and a decade later the vultures were hovering. By the 1990s, she was too old to be fully modernized and strengthened. One senior former courtier says that by then she was "on her last legs, full of asbestos, with old turbines; it was like trying to run a [Rolls-Royce] Silver Ghost in today's world. It was lovely, it was beautiful but it was basically over." The navy offered John Major's government a deal: they would pay for half of the yacht's costs, the £5 million needed for the crew's pay, if the two most relevant departments, the Foreign Office and the Board of Trade, shouldered the rest. The ministers of these departments, Douglas Hurd and Michael Heseltine, declined.

Heseltine came aboard at Helsinki just after the Yeltsin visit in October 1994. By one account, he asked Rear Admiral Sir Robert Woodard, commander of *Britannia*, how long it would take the two of them to walk to their rendezvous with the Queen. One and a half minutes, Woodard replied. All right then, said Heseltine, you have one and a half minutes to justify the Royal Yacht. Woodard said there was no point, since the cabinet had obviously already decided to get rid of her, but he could not resist adding that she was a goose laying golden eggs, and if you had such a creature, it did seem stupid to argue about who was paying to feed it. "That's rather clever," replied Heseltine, but he did not save *Britannia*.

Lengthy discussions about a possible replacement for the old ship were held in Whitehall and Buckingham Palace. Some argued in favor of a "national yacht" able to combine business promotion with royal tours—"a perfectly sensible piece of kit we could have produced," according to one of those involved—but the idea did not attract enough support from potential private sector sponsors. Furthermore, "the Queen and Prince Philip's hearts weren't really in it for a replacement," says an official who was there at the time. They loved the old ship, but did not have the appetite for a fight with government ministers for a new one. Prince Philip has said bluntly the decision to decommission the Royal Yacht was wrong: she was "sound as a bell," he said, and he believed that with new engines she could have gone on for half a century.[1] But in the end he bowed to political necessity.

So, good-bye, *Britannia*. The goose still looks good, but it is all clever taxidermy. She is a gleaming, motionless museum, tethered at Edinburgh's port Leith—and she is almost as popular with foreigners as when she was alive.

PART FOUR

Off with Her Head!
The Queen in the Sixties

Harold Wilson was not quite an unknown quantity when he arrived in Downing Street in 1964. As a rising minister in Clement Attlee's government, he had been known to the King. In 1948, while visiting Russia for trade talks, he had refused the offer to stay on to dine with Stalin by explaining that he was due at Buckingham Palace to meet Princess Elizabeth and her fiancé.[1] When he became prime minister, the Queen already knew him as Opposition leader. Despite the faint strands of republicanism evident in Labour in the mid-1960s, he was said to be a keen monarchist. Richard Crossman, the acidic Labour minister and diarist, noted that Wilson was "devoted to the Queen and is very proud that she likes his visits to her."[2] Wilson made a small point early on by refusing to go to kiss hands wearing a tailcoat; instead he wore a regular black jacket (oddly, he compromised with formal striped trousers).

Later this would be described as a "modernizing" gesture. But on all the real issues, from the Queen's interests as Head of the Commonwealth to the royal finances, Wilson backed her strongly.

His Tuesday audiences became steadily more important to him—or so his staff felt—in both his 1964–70 and 1974–76 governments. They crept up in length from twenty minutes, to half an hour, to an hour; at least once, his audience lasted two hours, with the Queen offering him drinks afterward. His staff described him as being "euphoric" after audiences; they also thought she had changed his views on some subjects and worried that he was too besotted.[3] He later said he enjoyed the audiences because they were the only times when he could have a serious conversation, which would not leak, with somebody who wasn't after his job.

By now the Queen's technique was being described as "Socratic." She would not venture opinions herself, but by careful and gently persistent questioning, she could get a prime minister to reflect again and more deeply on the issues of the week. When Wilson resigned, the Queen gave him a photograph of the two of them in the rain together. He kept the picture nearby for the rest of his life.

If this sounds insufferably cozy, then what was talked about during those audiences cannot have been. Like Macmillan and Douglas-Home before him, Wilson was governing in a world perched on the edge of nuclear annihilation. Some of the grimmest messages any monarch has ever had to read were the secret protocols for Britain's slide toward nuclear war with the Soviet Union, which were presented to her during Wilson's first full year in office, 1965. The grisly planning for a possible Armageddon had commenced long before, but it was only during Wilson's first administration that it became clear that Buckingham Palace possessed no copy of GWB, or the War Book. The historian Peter Hennessy, who uncovered the story, wrote: "The Queen did not fully know either the drill that, should the stage of a nuclear exchange be reached, would leave her kingdom largely a smoking and irradiated ruin or the plans for carrying on her government in its aftermath."[4]

Having decided that she did not need the full, detailed picture, Whitehall planners sent her a summary of the stages to war. These included, for example, "Military Vigilance" or "Orange" for an expected enemy attack within one or more hours, and "State Scarlet" for "an enemy attack within a few minutes." The plans also employed Shakespearean code words to stand in for the preparations to mobilize the armed forces and the removal of key members of the government to a village-sized nuclear bunker outside Bath (which, it later turned out, the Russians had known about for ages, and would have quickly obliterated). As for the Queen herself, just as with her father ahead of a likely Nazi invasion, the planners had discussed the possibility of evacuating the royal family to Canada. But although no final decision had been made about exactly how to respond to a Soviet threat, the summary did call for her to board *Britannia* early on in any crisis. Then the plan seems to have been for the Royal Yacht to be sent to a Scottish sea loch, where she would be partly protected from Soviet naval attacks.

Once on board the ship, the Queen would be joined by the home secretary, who in 1965 was Roy Jenkins. Jenkins had to be there because since Prince Philip and the Queen's private secretary— who would also be on board—are both members of her Privy Council, she would then have enough of a quorum to appoint a new prime minister in the event that the previous one had been killed. Peter Hennessy says the Royal Yacht's wartime purpose as a hospital ship was always a cover story: "It was her floating nuclear bunker . . . it would lurk in the sea lochs on the north-west coast of Scotland; the mountains would shield it from the Soviet radar and at night it would go quietly from one sea loch to another." Ashore, her kingdom would be broken down into a dozen mini-kingdoms. But from the ship, Hennessy says, she would be able to create new governments, "so the British constitution was taken care of, even unto Armageddon, and that's what the Royal Yacht was for . . . with that little group of Privy Councillors, ready to do the business."[5]

The Queen may have been unaware of the government's plans for responding to a Soviet attack, but she did know all about the risk of nuclear war. Released official files show that Churchill briefed her in 1954 about the decision to go from atomic bombs to the far more powerful hydrogen bomb, and throughout the Cold War she was the number one reader of secret intelligence, the so-called "Red Book, copy number one." So the world of the 1960s, remembered now as the decade of social revolt, looser morals and "liberation," was for those at the top of the power structure a deadly serious and frightening place.

⚜

The sixties was also the decade when the royal family seemed to give up trying to change with the times, sticking firmly with the hats, tweed jackets, polished brogues and cut-glass accents of the immediate postwar era. The Queen had tried. In 1962, for instance, she went to see *Beyond the Fringe* and had been much amused by its acidly satiric portrait of Macmillan. But she was also withdrawing more toward family life, with the birth of Prince Andrew in 1960 and Prince Edward in 1964. Both boys spent more time with her than had their older siblings. By then perhaps it was becoming apparent that the tougher upbringing of the heir to the throne had not been an unqualified success.

Prince Philip was an active and hardworking parent. His children recall his frequent reading of bedtime stories, his enthusiasm for chasing and running games, and his steady presence. He was genuinely the head of the family, away from the public gaze, and he was largely responsible for running the complex royal estates. Yet no one could say that his relationship with his oldest son had been free of difficulty. He had wanted Charles to be a man's man, in his own image, but the two were very different. Charles had been sent to his father's school, Gordonstoun; he had loathed it, and perhaps by now Philip had realized that his son's temperament was simply not suited to the rough-and-tumble of an institution designed to produce athletes and extroverts. By contrast, Charles had enjoyed himself more in the remote setting of an Australian outback school, Timbertop, which he attended in 1966. And two years later, Prince Charles would go to Cambridge and get a degree in history, a first for any member of the royal family. Even there, however, his image was as a rather nervous "square" young man, a person who was instinctively out of sympathy with the rebellious and exhibitionist times.

Meanwhile, as the decade went on, the Queen began to seem slightly bewildered. No doubt every generation reaches a moment when the changes of style and attitude among younger people become mystifying; for Elizabeth, this occurred during Wilson's premiership, with the advent of student protests and a collapse of the old deference. ("The Sixties" has become a phrase rather than a decade: in fact it was in 1972, during a visit to Stirling University, that the Queen herself encountered bottle-swigging, fist-clenching republican student protestors.) By the later 1960s, the monarchy was confronted by left-wing dissent unlike anything George VI had faced. And because Wilson stood atop a party that had many republicans in it, his royalist instincts helped strike a useful balance during those years.

Labour's left-wing factions—influenced by communist-dominated trade unions but not nearly as extreme as the Trotskyists who infiltrated the party later on—contained strong antimonarchists. Cromwell, the Levellers, Tom Paine and the Victorian radical Charles Bradlaugh, who had refused to take the Oath of Allegiance when elected an MP in 1880, were among the heroes of those on the party's left wing. But these sentiments were heavily diluted by the mainstream, pro-monarchy beliefs of the vast majority of Labour voters and MPs, and at no point did Labour pose a serious threat to the institution. Still, it is possible to imagine an alternative leader to Wilson who would have been less sympathetic to the Queen and whose government might have clipped and reduced the monarchy, beginning a trend. As it was, Labour republicanism expressed itself only in irritated asides in politicians' diaries and the smallest of symbolic protests. Of these, the case of Anthony Wedgwood Benn—as he then was—and the Queen's head was the most memorable.

Well ahead of the 1964 election, Benn had been planning to change the design of British postage stamps as part of a cultural campaign against the older order. He told the Oxford Labour club in May 1963 that a new Labour government should introduce "mood changing measures . . . like no dinner jackets for Labour Ministers at Buckingham Palace, mini-cars for official business and postage stamps without the Queen's head on them." Benn added in his diary that "this last suggestion was the most popular thing in the speech. Republicanism is on the increase."[6] At this stage, Benn's soft republicanism included plans to abolish the honors system, removing from the Crown all traditional lists, and substituting a system under which people would be "thanked" by the House of Commons, after which they might be invited to a reception in Parliament and given green ribbons to wear, with the title "PC" (standing for "Parliamentary Citation"). He planned "certain grades of gratitude: 'high commendation,' 'special thanks,' and so on down to 'general thanks,'" thus mirroring the OBEs, MBEs and knighthoods. Thus republicanism was creeping ahead stealthily, closely connected to left-wing resentment at the class-bound, Lords-influenced tradition of the British state. At the time, hereditary power was a big issue for Benn; in fact, he was in the middle of renouncing his peerage. His nine-year-old son Hilary, later himself a Labour cabinet minister, whipped up a storm by telling American broadcasters that Britain should have an elected president, not a Queen.

When Benn arrived to take the oath of admission to the Privy Council after Labour's victory, he found it "terribly degrading" and made a point of chatting during the rehearsals: "We then went up to the Queen one after another, kneeling and picking up her hand and kissing it, and then bowing. I made the most miniature bow ever seen. . . . I left the Palace boiling with indignation and feeling that this was an attempt to impose tribal magic and personal loyalty on people whose real duty was only to their electors."[7] As postmaster general, Benn then set to work to remove the Queen's head from commemorative stamps. He wanted more modern, well-

Her first, rather
overwhelming, prime
minister: the Queen and
Sir Winston Churchill, 1953.
(*Getty*)

A triumphant, if exhausting, tour:
the Queen was the first reigning
monarch to visit Australia, 1954.
(*Getty*)

Her first U.S. President: the Queen
and Prince Philip with President
Eisenhower in Washington. (*Corbis*)

The Empire is dead, long
live the Commonwealth:
the Queen in the streets
of Karachi, Pakistan, 1961.
(*Getty*)

Not quite a royal carriage:
the Queen travels on the
London Underground's
just-opened Victoria Line,
1969. (*Getty*))

The cars would get bigger: Prince Charles drives Prince Edward in a go-cart, photographed by the Queen, who is a keen taker of snapshots. (*Getty*)

Reinventing tradition: Prince Charles's 1969 investiture as Prince of Wales, at Caernarvon Castle. (*Press Association Images*)

A 1970s family: the Queen and the Duke of Edinburgh celebrate their silver wedding anniversary. (*Getty*)

One of her best advisers: Sir Martin Charteris, the Queen's private secretary, pores over paperwork with her aboard *Britannia* in 1972. (*Getty*)

Where she was most relaxed: the Queen at dinner on the Royal Yacht. (*Getty*)

Labour's leading monarchist: Harold Wilson and the Queen in Downing Street for his farewell dinner in 1976—an honor not given to all prime ministers. (*Press Association Images*)

The glamour of royalty does not excite everyone: the Labour defense secretary Fred Mulley at an RAF review during the 1977 Silver Jubilee. (*Press Association Images*)

But royalty does bring out British eccentricity: a congratulatory postcard too big even for the Buckingham Palace mantelpieces is delivered in 1977. (*Getty*)

The Silver Jubilee was a much-needed tonic during a bleak period for Britain. (*Corbis*)

Always keeping her balance: the Queen comforts her horse Burmese, after blank shots were fired at her during the 1981 Trooping the Colour. At the time, she must have thought she had narrowly escaped assassination. (*Press Association Images*)

drawn pictures of today's world, and he felt the original portrait of the Queen, by the artist Dorothy Wilding, was too fussy.

Unlike the stamps of almost every other nation in the world, those of the UK nowhere mention the country's name. The Queen's head is enough. After working with the famous designer and artist David Gentleman to create a new design, Benn eventually got permission to put the issue to the Queen directly, which he did on March 10, 1965. Shrewdly, Benn had chosen to redesign commemorative stamps for the Battle of Britain, about as patriotic and unquestionable a project as it could be imagined. If the Palace accepted that the Queen's portrait would spoil the excellent drawings he had prepared for these stamps, Benn reasoned, he would then have opened up a gap through which he could push through his wider plan. Queenless stamps might then lead to many other Queenless initiatives. Dust down those scarlet banners!

Benn's diary account of his encounter with the Queen is a drawing-room comedy of misunderstanding and circumlocution. Arriving at the Palace with a box of new designs, Benn proceeded to put his Battle of Britain argument directly to the monarch. She alternately smiled, frowned, seemed embarrassed, denied she had any personal feelings about her head being on all stamps, and later allowed Benn to spread out a range of Gentleman's designs on the floor. For forty minutes or so, Benn seems to have done almost all the talking, and he left the Palace believing that the Queen agreed with him, or at least would not confront him. He was now "convinced that if you went to the Queen to get her consent to abolish the honours list altogether she would nod and say she'd never been keen on it herself and felt sure the time had come to put an end to it. Of course when you do that you have to be terribly charming and nice."[8]

Before and since, many people have mistaken the Queen's cautious politeness for agreement. In this case, any smiles or nods were tactical. The Queen had not agreed. As Benn did his utmost to commission and publicize headless stamps, the Queen's private office went quietly to work on Harold Wilson and the civil service. Benn's own civil servants, meanwhile, more or less ignored his plans. In July the Queen's private secretary, Sir Michael Adeane, told Benn that she was "not too happy" about a set of six Battle of Britain stamps with her head missing from five of them. Benn then made a small tactical retreat, "in view of the bad press I'm getting and the delicate political situation." The loyalist press celebrated a Buckingham Palace victory.

But Benn was not finished. The delicate verbal fencing went on. Benn congratulated himself on charming Palace officials and mused, "I'm sure the Palace is a lot more frightened of me than they have reason to be." As time went on, he developed a better relationship with Adeane, but eventually he realized that Wilson was never going to back him because "he finds the Queen a very useful tool . . . in the long run his attitude simply strengthens the reactionary elements in our society."

After Number Ten ordered Benn to stop commissioning headless stamps, he tried a final line of attack, proposing to write to the Queen and get her verdict on the record. Either she would be shown to be rejecting, personally, the advice of one of her ministers— himself, the country's postmaster general—or the subterfuges of her private office would be exposed. Benn's own private secretary was aghast and told him that this was going too far, that it would bring the Queen into public controversy. By this point, Benn did not have the support of his prime minister, of the Stamp Advisory Committee, or his own civil servants. He was finally forced to back down. The Queen's head stayed. Conceding defeat, Benn wrote that he was putting his "palace vendetta . . . on ice."

For the Royal Mail, the main outcome of Benn's effort was the commissioning of a new portrait of the Queen by the artist Arnold Machin. A conscientious objector who had been imprisoned during the war, Machin was from the Potteries town of Stoke on Trent, where he had trained in ceramic sculpture. In 1964, he had produced the semi-sculpted silhouette of the Queen that would be used on the new decimal coins first circulated in the mid-1960s; now he did something similar for stamps. His portrait was clear and small enough to sit at the edge of commemorative stamps, but large enough to fill the regular ones, allowing a much wider range of designs. Originally Machin wanted the Queen's image to be cut off at the neck. She, perhaps understandably sensitive, did not wish to be cut off at the neck. Instead, a rather fuller dress neckline was proposed, and soon thereafter a modest design classic appeared—the same portrait still seen on every British stamp nearly half a century later.

When Benn left his post as postmaster general, the Queen said she was sure he would miss his stamps. During a final encounter with her, Benn thanked her for being supportive: "She gave me a rather puzzled smile and I bowed and went out backwards." Much later, by which time Benn had become the snow-headed grandfather of British socialism, the Queen was urged to invite him to the Palace to reminisce. She paused: "No. He doesn't like us."

The stamps saga may seem trivial, but it was not meaningless and it remains telling. A clever politician trying to take on the fuddy-duddy Palace found it subtle and at least as clever in its response. The Queen clearly had a strong objection to Benn's proposal, and it's not difficult to see why. Once her image begins to be removed from stamps, it could equally well go from coins and public buildings, and thus the iconography of monarchy starts to wither away. This was not a small matter for her: she understands that symbols matter. Benn understood that too, which was why he persisted so long. As his diaries make clear, he did have a republican agenda, if not a full-throttle one. An admirer of American democracy, he had seen stamps as a probing line of attack that might have led to other things, beginning with the honors system.

Typically, the Queen showed no sign of having a view during her encounter with Benn—indeed, she denied that she even had one. Mindful of her constitutional role, she refused to be backed into a corner or held publicly accountable for any decision. Instead, the well-oiled, rarely heard cogs of the British state revolved on her behalf. The private secretaries at Buckingham Palace, Number Ten and in Benn's own office—connected in turn to the Stamp Advisory Committee and lowlier civil servants in the Postmaster General's Office—blocked Benn so effectively that ultimately he came to understand that he was knocking his head against a brick wall. Trying his best to be charming, and using all his skills of media handling and irrefutable-sounding logic, Benn was simply outplayed. Meanwhile, other Labour ministers with republican instincts kept their comments for their diaries and displayed only the tiniest signs of rebellion, such as small bows and curtsies, or brief delays for meetings. The Queen notices a lot, so she surely noticed these minor discourtesies. But on the issues that really mattered, she more than held her own.

⤜⊹⤛

Of all the cabinet ministers privately offended by the duties required by the Palace, none was more outspoken in his diary, published after his death a decade later to much tut-tutting, than Richard Crossman, the irreverent intellectual. He reported more about the Queen than anyone else of that era. His own journey was from near apoplexy about the flummery of court ritual (noticeably more formal in the 1960s than it is today) to growing admiration for the Queen and her deft use of silences and confidences. Along the way, however, he proved himself a shrewd observer of the uneasy relationship between the Queen and her first socialist ministers. In October 1964 he expressed outrage about the ritual of kissing hands to become members of the Privy Council: "I don't suppose anything more dull, pretentious, or plain silly has ever been invented. There we were, sixteen grown men. For over an hour we were taught how to stand up, how to kneel on one knee on a cushion, how to raise the right hand with the Bible in it, how to advance three paces towards the Queen, how to take the hand and kiss it."

At the actual ceremony, Crossman found "this little woman

with the beautiful waist" who had to go through "this rigmarole" for forty minutes: "We were uneasy, she was uneasy."[9] At that stage Crossman was housing minister, but from August 1966 until 1968 he was leader of the Commons and Lord President of the Council. In this latter role he was the prime link between Parliament and the Queen, expected to attend all Privy Council meetings and present a large number of decisions for royal approval. Crossman had a long and deep interest in the British constitution but found these duties onerous and irrelevant.

On September 20, 1966, he traveled to Balmoral, noting that the Grampian Mountains were not as beautiful as the Scottish west coast, and finding the building "a typical Scottish baronial house, looking as though it had been built yesterday, with a nice conventional rose garden and by the little church, a golf course, which nobody plays on except the staff." His ill temper and mild contempt were not diluted by the formal meeting with the Queen, during which "I read aloud the 50 or 60 titles of the Orders in Council, pausing after every half dozen for the Queen to say, 'agreed.'" It was, he felt, two and a half minutes "of the purest mumbo-jumbo" which had required four ministers, "all busy men, to take a night and day off to travel to Scotland." Once the official business was over, however, Crossman's irritation evaporated and his diarist's eye took over:

> I noticed this time even more than last how shy she can be. . . . If one waits for her to begin the conversation, nothing happens. One has to start the talk and then suddenly the conversation falters because both are feeling, "Oh dear, are we boring each other?" She has a lovely laugh. She laughs with her whole face and she cannot just assume a mere smile because she's really a very spontaneous person . . . she finds it difficult to suppress her emotion. When she is deeply moved and tries to control it, she looks like an angry thunder-cloud. So, very often when she has been deeply touched by the plaudits of the crowd she merely looks terribly bad-tempered.[10]

Sir Godfrey Agnew, the long-serving clerk of the Privy Council, told him a story about an earlier meeting that had gone badly wrong because the four ministers, coached by the then cabinet secretary Sir Edward Bridges, had been kneeling on the wrong side of the room; when they crawled around they knocked a book off a table, which the Queen picked up, looking "blackly furious." Later, Bridges had gone back to apologize, and the Queen told him, "You know, I nearly laughed." He realized then that "when she looked terribly angry it was mainly because she was trying to stop herself laughing." This is a truth about the Queen too few journalists and photographers have understood.

Later on the Queen became genuinely cross with Crossman when he missed a Privy Council at Balmoral because of the Labour conference. Crossman reported: "I made a little explanation and a half-apology about the misunderstandings between the Party and the Court. . . . She didn't relent, she just listened and I thought that was that."[11] Soon Crossman was complaining again about the absurdity of having to travel north. At a dinner with Jeremy Thorpe and the writer Kenneth Rose, Crossman grumbled that a proposed Privy Council date had been judged unacceptable by the Palace because the Queen was out for lunch that day and so could not entertain her ministers; Crossman claimed that he told the Palace that he would eat instead in the servants' hall. "Not very agreeable for the servants, perhaps," said Rose, drily.

By now, however, Crossman felt that he himself was getting on better with the Queen, because "every time you see her, she tends to like you better simply because she's got more used to you." He once asked Agnew whether she preferred the Tories to Labour "because they were our social superiors and he said, 'I don't think so. The Queen doesn't make fine distinctions between politicians of different parties. They all roughly belong to the same social category in her view.' I think that's true." This is an observation that has been repeated by later civil servants and politicians—and of course it does not mean that she regards the politicians' social category as a particularly exciting or elevated one.

The following year, in February 1967, Crossman again came across the Queen's harder edge. A fairly obscure Labour backbencher, Emrys Hughes, who represented famously radical South Ayrshire, had introduced a bill into the Commons called "The Abolition of Titles Bill." As a private member's bill without government backing, it had zero chance of success. Like the home secretary Roy Jenkins, Crossman regarded Hughes as "a jester" but thought any attempt to stop his bill from being debated would look foolish. The Queen clearly disagreed. She was worried about this apparent assault on her prerogative. Adeane approached Wilson, who in turn contacted the Lord Chancellor and chief whip to quash the bill. Crossman recorded: "Ha, ha, there it is. I shall have to arrange it. This is a good example of the Queen and the PM hobnobbing together, the kind of stuffiness I don't take seriously."[12]

Later Crossman and Jenkins did stand up to Wilson and insist that no action should be taken to stop Hughes's bill. When it was finally debated on a Friday in March, the bill attracted just three or four other MPs into the chamber. It was the dampest of damp squibs, emitting no spark or sputter. Afterward, Crossman visited the Palace, where "The Queen said that she'd looked through all the papers on Saturday and found nothing there." Crossman corrected her: there had been reports in the *Guardian* and *The Times*, which had both called it a flop. He could not resist gloating that he and Roy Jenkins had been right to take no action: "It was a mistake to say this, since she didn't reply."

Like the story of Benn and the stamps, the Hughes incident throws a rare light on the Queen's behavior behind the scenes as she moves to protect her role, responds with excessive nervousness about a political fleabite, and puts down an uppity minister merely by staying silent. This latter technique is famous among those who have said something inappropriate, or made a statement with which she disagrees, or out of nervousness burbled on too long in front of her. "She never argues, she just looks at the person very blankly. The corners of her mouth don't turn down. It's not a hostile look. It's just a complete blank—and it's devastating," says one who has watched it happen.

Crossman never stopped pushing the boundaries of correctness. On a later Balmoral visit, when the Queen was late for the Privy Council by twelve minutes, she explained that at the farthest part of her ride, her horse had got a stone in his shoe—"one carries one of those pen-knives, doesn't one, as an instrument for taking out stones, but today was the one day I didn't have it."[13] (The horse had been given to the Queen by the Soviet Communist minister Bulganin, and she found "those Russian horses are very obstinate.") That evening, perhaps inspired by the Soviet theme, Crossman asked the Queen if she had followed the unfolding saga of the traitor Kim Philby and was briskly put in his place: she did not read about such matters, and clearly would not dream of talking about them.

Crossman also had another falling-out with the Palace over his dislike of grand public events. This time, he was trying to get out of attending the State Opening of Parliament in October 1967, pleading a "diplomatic illness." The Duke of Norfolk, in charge of the ceremony, appealed to Harold Wilson, whose office replied that Crossman "suffers from a phobia about public occasions of this sort which make him unable to attend." The Duke was not put off, but wrote to Crossman, saying that he was alarmed and disturbed, and that only the Queen could allow him not to go. Wilson was by now "flustered" and so Crossman went to see Adeane, who said he could have cleared it with the Queen, and could still do so. He then added: "Of course, the Queen has as strong a feeling of dislike of public ceremonies as you do. I don't disguise from you the fact that it will certainly occur to her to ask herself why you should be excused when she has to go, since you're both officials."[14]

Yielding to the inevitable, Crossman attended the ceremony,

though the experience inflamed his republicanism. He thought the State Opening was "like the *Prisoner of Zenda* but not nearly as smart or well done as it would be in Hollywood . . . far more comic, more untidy, more homely, less grand." The Queen's speech, for which he was responsible himself, was "appalling." It's doubtful that the Queen really dislikes ceremonial occasions—it would make her life a long torture, and there is plenty of counterevidence of the great interest and attention to detail she displays. Yet Crossman, grand man that he was, was instantly disarmed by Adeane's implied comparison of two simple state workhorses trudging together in harness.

Though he agitated for change, Crossman was self-aware enough to understand that real republicans inside the Labour government were a small minority of middle-class intellectuals while "working-class socialists . . . are by and large staunchly monarchist. The nearer the Queen they get the more the working-class members of the Cabinet love her and she loves them."[15] There is a wider truth here, which is that in the 1960s, radical republicanism was growing stronger on the fringes of politics but was nowhere near the center of power. But there were issues that could create an impermanent coalition of newspapers, backbench MPs and many voters—and one of the most contentious concerned the Queen's finances.

꧁

Toward the end of the first Wilson government, in 1969, the royal finances had been catapulted into the headlines by none other than Prince Philip, who used an American television interview on November 9 to complain that "the Firm" would "go into the red" the following year because the Civil List allowance was inadequate. He told NBC that the royal family might have to move into smaller premises and give up playing polo. As the predictable media storm blew in, Wilson proposed that the whole matter be investigated by a parliamentary select committee, but only after the 1970 election.

Wilson got his wish; ironically, he went on to lose the election and then played the starring role in the effort to defend the Queen. The Select Committee on the Civil List, to give Wilson's proposed committee its full title, was one of the most important investigations into the monarchy during the Queen's reign. Chaired by the new Tory chancellor, Tony Barber, the committee's membership included Tory grandees such as Norman St. John-Stevas, but also Wilson, the former home secretary Roy Jenkins, and the working-class Labour republican Willie Hamilton. Crossman, no longer in the Commons but editing the then-influential *New Statesman*, kept up a barrage from outside.

The underlying problem was inflation, which had roared ahead since the money agreed for the Queen's public role had been settled at the time of her accession in 1952. The wage bills in particular had far outstripped her budgets. In this age of militancy, the Civil Service Union proudly told the committee that it had managed to get average wages for Royal Household staff up by 200 percent since 1953, compared to 126 percent for the country as a whole. Even so, the union claimed recruiting staff was problematic since "the long and irregular hours are often regarded as outweighing the 'glamour' of the background of the job." This meant that "foreigners" were now being recruited into the kitchens and housemaids' department, which, suggested the union, might pose problems of security.

The monarchy, meanwhile, had been dipping deeply into its reserve funds, and these were about to run out. Something had to be done. But looming over the entire issue was the great mystery of the Queen's private wealth. "Rich lists" had just begun to appear in British papers, and the Queen regularly appeared close to the top. By guessing the capital value of the royal family's historic accumulation of buildings, land and goods, it wasn't difficult to make a partial estimate of the monarch's wealth—but the size of her personal fortune was much harder to determine. She might live in gorgeously decorated rooms, but they belonged to the continuing institution of the monarchy, not to her. She could not sell the furniture, buildings or paintings and spend the proceeds on something else. And her personal tastes, which were consistently modest, revealed little. All her life she has preferred simple food to fancy, and the odd Dubonnet and gin to fine wine. Her wardrobe was statecraft, not pleasure. She traveled for duty, not fun, and apart from horses, she had few indulgences outside the ritual of the royal year.

So what of the wealth was hers? How much ought to be taxed? These appeared as new and interesting questions, and the committee proved a tough investigator. A figure of £100 million, fabulous in those days, was widely touted. Lord Mountbatten, realizing that an exaggerated view of the Queen's wealth could do real damage to her, urged Prince Philip to help sweep away some of the traditional secrecy. Eventually Jock Colville, the former courtier who was now a senior member of Coutts, the royal bankers, suggested that £12 million was more accurate.

The committee was not particularly impressed by the Palace's response. A draft report, which it rejected, even described the Palace request for a review of its allowance as "the most insensitive and brazen pay claim made in the last two hundred years," while one of the committee's Labour members, Douglas Houghton, suggested that the Royal Household should simply become a government department, answerable directly to Parliament. This change would have removed the direct connection between Palace staff and the Queen, and would have been completely unacceptable to her, said Lord Cobbold, then the Lord Chamberlain: "It is almost an item of principle that the Queen regards these people as her own servants and they regard themselves as her servants." Other ideas included removing Prince Philip's separate household and radically cutting back those members of the royal family getting state money. Princess Margaret, it was suggested, should be content with free accommodation, while the Duke of Gloucester, being "very remote from the throne," should have his payments abolished.

The Court Party fought back. The payments to Royals were not simply fees for public duties. They were an acknowledgment that because of their birth, the members of the royal family were mostly people who could not simply go out and earn their living in the ordinary way. In essence, the committee's argument was between radicals who wanted the monarchy brought firmly under the thumb of the Commons on a year-by-year basis, and the monarchists who thought a strong measure of independence was essential for the Queen. Not surprisingly, the monarchists won. The radicals were in the minority, and did not include Wilson: the inclusion of Houghton and Hamilton, the monarchy's most unrelenting foe at the time, now looks like a classic piece of establishment window dressing.

The committee did its best to itemize the Queen's work, from the ceremonial duties, the reading of state papers and the endless visiting, to her private meetings with ministers and ambassadors and her work managing the palaces. Of course, she did not report on her activities to her own Parliament; that job was taken by Adeane, who emphasized in a long and detailed presentation how hard she worked, how many foreign trips she made, and how much of a strain being constantly on display really was.

With Wilson playing a leading role in protecting her role, the committee eventually recommended more than doubling the Queen's state income, from £475,000 a year to £980,000. These were difficult times for the British economy, and many Labour and Liberal MPs thought the proposals far too generous. But most Labour MPs abstained and in the Tory-dominated Commons of the early 1970s, the settlement passed easily. Yet a significant number of MPs voted against it, and some made eloquent speeches in favor of forcing the Queen to pay taxes on her private income and reducing the size of the monarchy. Princess Margaret in particular came in for some sharp criticism for her lack of involvement in official duties.

Overall, it was a Pyrrhic victory for the Queen's forces. First, the legislation created a system of parliamentary review of the Civil List allowance. Admittedly, this was only envisaged as happening every decade, but it meant the Queen would in effect have to explain and justify royal housekeeping to the Commons for the rest of her reign. Second, the row over taxation and her unknown private wealth would not go away. Barely mentioned during the previous two decades, now it was referred to again and again in the press, and by critical MPs. Not until 2010, forty years on, did the Palace win back this ground and reestablish financial independence.

After serving on the select committee, Willie Hamilton became the public face of antimonarchism in the 1970s and 1980s. Unlike Crossman, he was no middle-class intellectual. The child of a Durham miner, Hamilton had grown up "in spitting distance of the pit" and in appalling poverty; his was a life of cockroaches, unsanitary outdoor toilets, grime and anger. Born in 1917 when George V was creating the House of Windsor, Hamilton vividly remembered that he had been lined up outside the school gates at age ten to wave at "some royal personage" who was to go past in a car. It was cold. The wait was long. The car flashed past. "That day, a little revolutionary was born."[16] After wartime army service and a job as a schoolteacher, Hamilton fought Communists in Fife and became a Labour MP in 1950.

In some ways, he was a dangerous enemy. He was dogged, hardworking, incorruptible and entirely fearless. After his experience on the select committee, he went on to write a controversial, bestselling book called *My Queen and I*, which lambasted the institution, the Queen herself and her family. He saw the monarchy as the ermine coat covering a rotten system. He focused particularly on the cost, the tax question, the large number of "minor royals," and the absence of any real political role for the Queen.

Yet Hamilton was in other ways the Queen's ideal foe. He was a vinegary and vituperative man who took delight in the number of chips on each of his shoulders. He did not shrink from making personal attacks on the monarch, describing the Queen as a clockwork doll. A flavor of the Hamilton style comes from a Commons debate at the time when he mocked those who liked the Queen Mother for her pleasant smile—"My God, if my wife got that pay, she would never stop laughing"—and said of Princess Margaret, "Why, oh why, are we giving this expensive kept woman [£35,000] for doing what she does?"[17] His outspoken manner made it easy for the newspapers to caricature him and for some of his colleagues to dismiss him. Unfashionably dressed, pinched-looking and often angry, he was soon among the most unpopular politicians in the lounge bars and Conservative clubs of Middle Britain.

THE ROGUE ROYALISTS OF AFRICA

During his second term as prime minister, Wilson was reluctant to engage with Labour republicanism, in part because he had more urgent issues to confront and needed the Queen's help as he took them on. None was more dangerous for the Commonwealth or more embarrassing to London than the defiance of the white minority rulers of Rhodesia. With just one sixteenth of the total population, they had been aggressively fending off any move toward majority rule and were close to breaking with the rest of the Commonwealth. And because hardly anyone was more fervently royalist than the treason-plotting whites of Rhodesia, the authority of the Queen was a central part of the dispute. The Rhodesian story is tangled, and it became truly tragic after Robert Mugabe took over as ruler of the country and turned Africa's breadbasket into an economic wilderness of thuggery, theft and malnutrition. But the story is worth examining in some detail because it throws up hard questions about Britain's role in Africa, the decolonization project, and the Queen's own position as Head of the Commonwealth.

In the 1890s, a huge area north of South Africa had been invaded and colonized by white British settlers. What was then called Southern Rhodesia (it is now Zimbabwe) became a self-governing colony, and it was the richest and most British-dominated part of the northward push. To the colony's north was a protectorate, Northern Rhodesia, with far fewer whites but large mineral deposits.

Alongside it was a smaller protectorate, Nyasaland, with sparse, mainly Scottish settlements.

In 1953 London brokered a deal to join these three entities into a single Central African Federation, a "federal realm of the British Crown." For ten years this unlikely union—with the Queen's head on its coins and postage stamps, and its flag incorporating the Union Jack—survived. But the CAF awkwardly stitched together the self-consciously white-colonial south with territories likely to become black-ruled much more quickly, and deep divisions about the future of colonial Africa ran through Whitehall— not about the eventual end of white rule, regarded as inevitable, but about the timescale and conditions. London's overriding policy was that no former dominion or colony could be granted independence without majority rule. For the CAF, the hope had been to find some middle way between white-supremacist South Africa and the emerging Marxist black independent states. But the independence movements of what became Malawi and Zambia forced the pace. When they triumphed, the whites of Southern Rhodesia opted to go it alone and to reject any early steps toward majority rule.

The Rhodesian whites were led by Ian Smith, a pugnacious farmer. During the war he had been an RAF Hurricane and Spitfire pilot; after being shot down over Italy, he had helped Italian partisans fight the Germans. Rugby- and cricket-playing, blond and intensely patriotic, he thought of himself as a "Britisher" and was about as passionate a monarchist as any Home Counties Conservative could imagine. A most unlikely rebel, he had much of Tory Britain, including many newspapers, rooting for him.

In his discussions with Wilson, Smith essentially asked him to accept his word that Rhodesia would eventually move to majority rule—but only after a long period of education and the final defeat of any communist guerrillas and rebels. Wilson and his advisers did not believe Smith; they were convinced that his plan was to continue white minority rule forever. Trust quickly broke down, and some of the behavior on each side was petulant and petty. When

Churchill died in 1965, for instance, Smith was invited to the state funeral but somehow his invitation for lunch with the rest of the leaders and the Queen went missing.

Recalling the incident, Smith wrote that he was eating with the South African ambassador when "a gentleman in a splendid uniform came up to our table. He informed me that he was the Queen's equerry, and as the Queen had noticed that I was not present at the lunch, she had asked him to make enquiries. . . . The Queen was concerned, the equerry said, and had sent him post-haste to the hotel to express apologies and ask me to accompany him." Smith left for Buckingham Palace where the Queen left her group and immediately went over to express her sorrow that his invitation had not arrived. Prince Philip joined her. Smith remembered: "I was touched by the genuine interest they showed in Rhodesia, and also by how well informed they were. I was impressed too by the amount of time they devoted to talking with me, and by their sincere hope that our problem would be solved amicably."[18]

It was not. Smith's break with Britain, his Unilateral Declaration of Independence, ended with the flourish "God Save the Queen." As a barbed reminder of Rhodesia's role in two world wars, he ensured that his declaration arrived at exactly eleven a.m. London time on November 11, 1965, the moment of wartime remembrance. The UDI proclaimed Elizabeth II "Queen of Rhodesia," a title she never acknowledged.

In the early years of UDI, at least, many of the trappings of monarchy remained. Rhodesian soldiers and airmen kept the uniforms and traditions of the British. The "Royal Rhodesian Air Force," with RAF-like roundels on its aircraft, continued until 1970, and the country's flag incorporated the Union flag until 1969. The Queen's portrait stayed in government buildings. She was on Rhodesian banknotes and coins, and indeed on the un-Bennish stamps of the country rebelling against her.

To many in the old country, the notion that Britain could potentially declare war on Rhodesians, many of whom had fought for her during 1939–45, was fantastic. When the RAF was sent to Zambia, ostensibly to protect its power supplies against a possible Rhodesian attack, RAF officers were soon fraternizing in Rhodesian messes. When, in 1966, Wilson invited Smith aboard the cruiser HMS *Tiger* for further talks, the ship's petty officers invited the rebel Rhodesian leader for drinks, toasted him, and promised the ship's company were entirely on his side. And by such slight indications as her insistence that Smith join a lunch, the Queen suggested that she was at least unhappy about Wilson's attitude toward him. With his sporting record, down-to-earth interests and service background, Smith seemed like just the kind of man who in other circumstances would be a welcome figure for a Windsor dine-and-sleep.

Still, Smith had become a pest. The conflict between traditional "kith and kin" patriotism and the Queen's legal position was expressed most starkly in the figure of Sir Humphrey Gibbs, the governor of Southern Rhodesia. Though a farmer and friend of Ian Smith's, his loyalty to the Queen prompted him to refuse to accept UDI and formally dismiss Smith and his cabinet. Flying the flag from the government house in Salisbury (later Harare), Gibbs obstinately hung on, surrounded and isolated, until 1969, when a referendum finally declared the country a republic. The Queen made her views clear regarding Gibbs's defiance by making him a GCVO—a Knight Grand Cross of the Royal Victorian Order—a personal order that confers a considerably greater honor than he might have otherwise received

Wilson was well aware that military and personal loyalty to the Queen had been one of the few cards he could play with Smith. At one point he flew to Balmoral to suggest to the Queen that Mountbatten might be used as a go-between. That never happened, but Wilson's thinking was shrewd. The Rhodesian whites found the idea of rebelling against their monarch almost—though not quite—as painful as contemplating black rule. They wanted to keep as much of the form of their British origins and loyalties as possible. Yet for the Queen to acquiesce to any of Rhodesia's demands would have outraged the black-majority members of the Commonwealth and, in all probability, have split or even ended the institution. When push came to shove, the scale and inclusiveness of the Commonwealth mattered more than the painful rebellion of people who had stood by Britain and considered themselves to be British.

For their part, Smith and many Rhodesians felt bewildered and betrayed by their monarch, who seemed to be siding with Marxist despots and left-leaning United Nations politicians against their own. As Smith and his allies lost most of their remaining supporters, even ingenious sanctions-busting actions and a ferocious "bush war" against black nationalists failed to hold back the tide of change. But the game was not up for some time: not until 1979, after Margaret Thatcher came to power, did negotiations finally lead to the creation of Zimbabwe. The horror of what followed, for blacks as well as whites, sheds an unsettling light on the simple 1960s faith in progress and democracy. The story also shows that when it comes to protecting its position as the linchpin of a worldwide Commonwealth, the "family firm" is hardheaded and unsentimental.

Sometimes the royal family has been myopic and even sentimental about Commonwealth attachments, as the grim history of Britain's entanglement with the bloody regime of Idi Amin in Uganda shows. Amin ousted the Ugandan leader, Dr. Milton Obote, in 1971, while Obote was at the Commonwealth conference in Singapore. The official British reaction was approval, since Obote had been a threatening and "unhelpful" figure. When the then prime minister Edward Heath was told about it by his private secretary, he said he was "not wholly displeased." The Foreign Office knew little about Amin, but a Ministry of Defence official had remembered him from his days in the King's African Rifles and had found him "the best sergeant he ever had."[19] Other officials described him simply as "a splendid type."

Amin flattered British susceptibilities. He had fought against the Mau-Mau in Kenya, had risen through the native, British-officered

KAR, and was an accomplished rugby player. Better still, he made an early request to come to London and meet the Queen. Heath duly arranged this, a visit that took place on July 12, 1971. At Downing Street they were impressed by his smart, military appearance, though when Amin left, the foreign secretary, Alec Douglas-Home, suggested the new leader might be mad: he had told him Uganda was about to be invaded by the Chinese navy and wanted military support.

Amin went on to supervise a murderous tyranny that is estimated to have killed one hundred thousand Ugandans and included the expulsion of Uganda's Asian population, around thirty thousand of whom came to Britain. Revulsion spread as stories of his cannibalism and torture squads emerged, but he remained the leader of a Commonwealth country and successfully played on his British connections in an increasingly mad mix of menace and humor. When Amin was not invited to the 1973 Commonwealth meeting in Ottawa, he wrote to the Queen's private secretary, asking her to send a Boeing 747 to Kampala to ferry the president and his party to Canada, and to arrange a band of Scottish pipers to greet him. The Queen's staff consulted Heath, who decided it would be too extravagant, and declined.

As Amin murdered former political foes and friends—churchmen, bank and business leaders, playwrights, and journalists—their bodies were dumped in crocodile-infested rivers. Amin awarded himself the Victoria Cross, declared himself King of Scotland, and apparently wrote to the Queen in 1975: "I would like you to arrange for me to visit Scotland, Ireland and Wales to meet the heads of revolutionary movements fighting against your imperialist oppression." He also sent her a Telex inviting her to come to Kampala if she wanted to meet a real man.

This produced much tittering in the British press, but Amin was the very worst of bad jokes. His taunting and inversion of what the Commonwealth was meant to stand for, combined with the reluctance of that organization to antagonize its black members, damaged both it and the Queen. Amin suggested that the former Empire had no clothes; it has plenty, but the sad story of the African rebellions does point to its lack of muscle. Countries are occasionally suspended—Pakistan after a military coup, for instance—and some countries leave, as Fiji and Zimbabwe did. But the Commonwealth is in effect a club, and it has few real sanctions to impose.

Today, with fifty-four members, the Commonwealth comprises around a third of the world's population, but the vast majority of that figure, about 94 percent, is in Asia and Africa; India by herself accounts for more than half. As a consequence, the Commonwealth straddles some of the world's richest and the world's poorest countries. On trade talks, attitudes to regional politics, and much else, they are often at loggerheads. The Commonwealth boasts some proud examples of successful democracy among the "old Commonwealth" countries, including India and Britain herself. But it also includes, and always has included, corrupt and despotic regimes, despite the high and principled language of its founding documents and successive secretaries general. And although it gives Britain extra heft when the Commonwealth is speaking as one voice to other international bodies, most Britons—sadly and wrongly, perhaps—barely notice its existence.

ENTER THE FILMMAKERS . . .

Buffeted by inquisitive MPs over their finances and with the Commonwealth no longer easy to handle, the royal family and its advisers began trying to project a fresher image in the late 1960s. Since the Coronation, the fortunes of the Windsors and the influence of television had become intertwined in ways neither the Queen nor the BBC could have predicted. On the one hand, the advent of television meant that for the first time the Queen would often be entertained privately in much the same way as her subjects. She has never been big on Wagner operas or Pinter plays; she likes the same middle-brow comedies, soap operas and sports coverage enjoyed by most of her fellow Britons. For better or worse, television has democratized taste and given the Queen a window on her country earlier monarchs did not have.

On the other hand, however, television cameras have intruded into her life and made it much more difficult for her to police her privacy. The Queen must wrestle with the obvious problems of access or eavesdropping, but she also has to be aware of the medium's effect on her image. Television, after all, flattens everything. In person, most British people would feel some sense of awe in the presence of the Queen; distanced by the TV lens, they feel none. We want to see more and know more; since television creates the illusion of intimacy, we want close-ups and private moments. Monarchy must respond to changing public tastes, but it unquestionably depends on an aura of mystery and personal distance, Bagehot's "magic." How is it possible to reconcile familiarity and magic? Throughout her reign, the Queen has struggled to answer that question.

The earliest years had presented no serious problems. Richard Dimbleby's encyclopedic knowledge of royal and constitutional history, and the fixed cameras needed for state occasions, established a style of slow-marching, hushed reporting. The Palace simply refused to allow cameras anywhere near private family moments; even filming the outside of palaces was frowned upon. The BBC hierarchy rarely pushed requests for more access; broadcasters dressed formally and waited with shiny shoes for formal announcements.

In 1966, Prince Philip—who had made several scientific programs and so had some experience with television—was a key figure in giving the go-ahead for *Royal Palaces of Britain*, a documentary by Kenneth Clark (who later made the series *Civilisation*) about six royal palaces. This was the first time most people had seen inside the walls and gardens of Windsor Castle, Buckingham Palace, the Palace of Holyroodhouse, Kensington Palace, St. James's Palace and Hampton Court—the paintings, the decor, the flowers, the grand ballrooms. It was a safe subject, in safe hands, safely produced as a joint venture by the BBC and its upstart commercial rival ITV. Broadcast by both channels on Christmas Day 1966, the documentary was a substantial success. If the Coronation cameras had shed daylight on the ancient ritual, Clark had pulled back the curtain on the country's once-mysterious royal residences.

The most startling royal attempt to change with the times came two years later, when the Queen decided to allow television cameras to follow her and her immediate family for a second television documentary. By allowing a spotlight to play over the Queen, the Duke and their children, *Royal Family* went a giant step further than *Royal Palaces*. The documentary followed some of the ritual and pomp of the royal year and tried to explain the Queen's job, but its punch came from the fact that it answered, at least partly, the question, "What are they *like*?" The show allowed anyone with a television a view of the Windsors that was apparently so intimate that only a handful of courtiers and friends of the family had been privy to it before. As in 1966, Prince Philip was crucial to the project: he chaired an advisory committee to oversee the experiment.

For seventy-five days a film crew of eight, again working jointly for the BBC and ITV, were allowed remarkable access to the royal family. The film's producer was the head of BBC documentaries, Richard Cawston, a tall and debonair former army signals officer whose career at the Corporation had made him a master of camera-work, sound, the cutting room and the dubbing theater. Cawston knew he could hardly ask the Queen for a second take, so everything would be at least partly spontaneous "cinema verité." The camera team became so familiar to the family that they almost forgot the crew was there.

The Queen, according to Cawston, became quite an expert about problems of lighting and sound recording. Forty-three hours of film were edited to produce the 105-minute final program. Most viewers today would be struck by the upper-class 1950s accents and old-fashioned clothing, but the informal shots of a family barbecue at Balmoral—as well as those of the Queen driving her car, walking with dogs, and chatting with the young children—are still fresh and interesting. The Queen smiles and sometimes laughs as she goes about the serious business of reigning. Prince Andrew and Prince Edward, who had previously barely been seen by the public, seem to be normal, cheerful boys.

The shrewd script by Sir Antony Jay, later of *Yes Minister* fame, was respectful but lightened with gentle jokes. Of the royal Rolls-Royces he noted, "no cars in the world can have been driven so far, so slowly." Jay says now that he thought the film had emerged "because in the 1960s there couldn't have been a decade that was more anti-monarchy. . . . It was about classlessness. It was about equality. It was about being popular. And all the things that the royal family represented, like order and respectability, were jokes." He felt that in the press, even the conservative press, there was "a feeling that, you know, the royal family—well, their time's gone. Nothing to do with us. What are they? Oh, they're just an irrelevance."

Jay says that Lord Brabourne, the film producer married to Mountbatten's daughter, had come up with the idea for the documentary. According to Jay, Brabourne believed that "if only people could see what the royal family is like, they'd feel much, much better disposed towards them." Jay says he was much impressed that the Royals, though well used to cameras, were especially worried about what the microphones might pick up—not on their own account but because a stray comment might hurt other people.[20] They need not have worried. Cawston, in Jay's reckoning, was a great diplomat as well as a great filmmaker. Though the BBC had a "very strong republican element" at the producer level and higher up, the film was considered a great coup. As a result, the BBC exercised a good deal of self-censorship in their effort not to offend, "a sort of deferential sense of respect and obligation towards the monarchy and there was no doubt who was the boss in the operation."

When it was shown in June 1969, *Royal Family* became easily the most-watched documentary in the history of British television. Twenty-three million people tuned in to BBC to see the first showing, in black and white; another fifteen million watched it when it was shown on ITV in color.[21] An estimated 68 percent of British adults watched the film.

The reaction was everything the Duke of Edinburgh could have hoped for. Even the *New Statesman*'s republican-leaning television critic John Holmstrom found that the Queen, "who doesn't always look very appealing or animated on newsreels, emerges as a warm, engaging and even girlish person, capable of little giggles of motherly pleasure." He concluded that Cawston and Jay should be given knighthoods: "They'll certainly have added a decade or two to the life of the British monarchy."[22] The *Spectator* welcomed the film and mocked the idea that by letting in the cameras the monarchy had devalued itself: "If the sight of the Queen making salad is thought to dissolve the magic of monarchy, what about this sort of comment: 'His late Majesty, though at times a jovial, and, for a King, an honest man, was a weak, ignorant, common-place sort of person . . . his feebleness of purpose and littleness of mind, his ignorance and his prejudice.' " The *Spectator* then revealed that the remarks came from its own obituary on William IV in 1867.

The Queen seemed pleased by the huge audience figures and the general reaction. Perhaps at the Duke's suggestion, the Queen gave her appearance fee and share of the profits, £60,000, to the British Academy of Film and Television Arts, a sum that helped it move to its current headquarters in Piccadilly. In retrospect, however, there were faint indications that letting in the cameras was a tricky business, especially since they provided images that would stay in people's minds long after the subjects of the film had changed. Stuart Hood, the *Spectator*'s television critic, felt that the documentary had been "the apotheosis of home movies" whose purpose must have been "to promote the idea that one family is very like another. It may even presage a move to a Scandinavian type monarchy."[23] If the first proposition was tenable, the second was certainly not the message intended. In any case, the Queen never gave permission for the documentary to be rebroadcast in full after its year of release.

Those who suggested that *Royal Family* was intended as a riposte to inquisitive politicians, or even to bizarre rumors about the supposed ill-health of the Queen and younger princes, were told this was all nonsense. But there is little question that the film had been meant as a prelude to the investiture of Prince Charles as Prince of Wales, which took place on July 1, a few days after the documentary's broadcast.

⟞⟐⟝

Prince Charles had by now undergone much of the training his father had wanted for him—head boy at Gordonstoun, further toughening up in an Australian outback school, RAF jet training and university. In 1969 he was at Cambridge studying history, and the next step would be the navy. But before that he was to be introduced to his public role. The investiture was, in its way, as ambitious an attempt to project a modernized monarchy as Cawston's film. This time, however, the choreographer was not the Duke of Edinburgh or a BBC producer, but one of the younger and newer royals-by-marriage, Princess Margaret's husband, Anthony Armstrong-Jones, who had become Lord Snowdon after their wedding in 1960.

The child of a barrister and a woman from a notably artistic family, Armstrong-Jones had become a successful society and royal photographer. Thanks to another upwardly mobile Welshman, David Lloyd George, the ancient practice of investing Princes of Wales had been moved to the spectacular setting of Caernarvon Castle and turned into a patriotic spectacle as long ago as 1911. The romantic Lord Snowdon, appointed by the Queen Constable of Caernarvon, decided it was the perfect opportunity to design a contemporary royal pageant that would be both theatrical and television-friendly.

The castle would be refurbished. Giant stages would be erected.

The largest clear plastic structure ever made would be created, all to show off the young prince. As his ambitious plan developed, Snowdon began a struggle with the more traditionalist Earl Marshal, the Duke of Norfolk. A wickedly perceptive article in the *New Statesman* saw this as a fight between old monarchism and the new ways, between "the greatest expert in ceremonial nonsense outside the Vatican" and Snowdon's "Mary Quant" worldview: "One could search the universe in vain for two men who have less in common . . . the Duke knows the exact degree of precedence between, say, an Irish countess and the eldest son of an English baronet; he can spot an incorrectly dressed Herald Extraordinary at a hundred yards flat; but he has neither the desire nor the talent for designing canopies and pennants, has no knowledge of textiles and the uses to which they can be put; he is not trendy and has no wish to be."[24]

By 1969 it was at last the sixties in the full meaning of the phrase, and so Lord Snowdon won the battle. The investiture was indeed a carnival of color and modern design, meant to show Wales as being both romantically ancient and also, with its Severn Bridge and nuclear power stations, determinedly modern. On the day of the ceremony an astonishing 250,000 people thronged the streets of the small town, and the television coverage—with a young, oddly vulnerable-looking Prince Charles repeating his vows of fealty to his mother in both English and newly studied Welsh—was spectacular. Philip Howard, writing in *The Times,* caught the mood of rapturous excitement: "There were proud peacock processions, frequent fanfares of silver, snarling trumpets, coveys of red dragons . . . hymns, harps and heraldry, choirs carolling, brass bands booming, dodders of druids and bards . . . lions rampant, regimental goats. . . . It was the greatest television spectacular in history, a carnival to entice tourists to Wales for years."

So it was. And yet it was not quite the unvarnished success for the monarchy that Lord Snowdon had hoped for. Welsh nationalism was on the march, and the mood was more militant than ever before. An "explosive device," later found to be a dummy, was discovered under a railway bridge on the royal route. Two naval mine-sweepers patrolled the entrance to Caernarvon harbor, and a team of frogmen on board the Royal Yacht was prepared to search for underwater bombs. There was a gelignite explosion at Abergele, where two men were killed, apparently by their own bomb. In Cardiff Post Office, six sorters had a narrow escape when a parcel bomb exploded, the fourth bombing in the city in three months. Among the crowds there was scattered booing and a few eggs were thrown.

None of this amounted to anything like the significant unrest emerging in Northern Ireland, nor would the "Free Wales Army" amount to a serious threat when some of its adherents later faced trial. But the mood had changed from the unrestrained enthusiasm the Queen had enjoyed when she announced during a visit to Cardiff in 1958 that Prince Charles would become Prince of Wales, or when she traveled to Caernarvon in 1963. Welsh national pride was no longer automatically loyal to the British idea. The Scots had shown flickers of nationalism when students stole back the Stone of Destiny, used during Coronations, from Westminster Abbey on Christmas Day 1950. Now Welsh nationalists were causing trouble too. Monarchism relies on common symbols, reliably beckoning common responses. By the end of the 1960s, different parts of the United Kingdom were beginning to lean away in different directions. Suddenly the center seemed less sure of itself, and less powerful.

THE SWINGING SEVENTIES

Though the 1970s was a difficult time for the British state politically and economically, these were in general good years for the Windsor dynasty. The Cawston film, the settlement of the financial argument, the advent of Prince Charles as a public figure, the emergence of Princess Anne as a horsewoman good enough to compete at the Olympics—all these added up to a family success story.

Prince Charles was in his action-man phase. A trained RAF jet pilot and then naval officer, he seemed to be relaxing more into his public role, and he had already taken on important royal visits to Japan, South America and the United States. He was learning to make speeches; intermittent speculation in the media about girl-friends was still genial, even friendly, in tone. But under the surface, the story was darker. While beginning to find his own place in the Windsor dynasty, Charles had become increasingly cut off from his parents. He had been unable to form a close relationship with his father, and although in awe of his mother, he found her mostly focused on her job. Charles, it must be said, does not have the sunniest of temperaments, and one of the issues raised time and again by people who know the royal family is the question of "what went wrong." Inevitably, the same people also wonder about the extent to which the Queen can be blamed for her oldest son's unhappiness.

Often we find it easier to empathize with ancient historical times than our own recent past—nothing, it seems, is as far away as the world of our grandparents. The Queen had been brought up in a largely male world, dominated by ritual and duty. She had close and loving parents, but from a very young age, her responsibilities had been drummed into her. The address she delivered in South Africa on her twenty-first birthday was the speech of a true believer—in monarchy, nationhood, God and destiny—but the vision of service it offered left little room for an ordinary relaxed family life. Time management rules her every moment; her diary is her most unrelenting master. Charles was her first child, and the Queen had had no brothers or close childhood male friends. So it should hardly be a surprise that she delegated much of the job of looking after Charles to Prince Philip. And given that Philip had found Gordonstoun and the navy a delight and an inspiration, it's understandable that he hoped that Charles would feel the same way about both institutions. But individual temperament matters enormously, and Charles was simply very different.

As he began to think of himself as a future monarch, Charles became increasingly independent-minded. Though two charitable trusts connected to the Silver Jubilee of 1977 were raising money for good causes, he was becoming interested in the idea of his own Prince's Trust, which would disburse grants to individuals, as well as organizations, in an effort to give deprived teenagers a fresh start in life. Though some of his interests and values contrasted with his parents' (his fascination with Eastern spirituality, for instance), he had also learned a great deal from them, and from the very same institutions he had quailed from. He believed in physical challenges, self-discipline, order and authority. Though he recoiled from the joshing, alpha-male atmosphere of the navy, he was a traditionalist when it came to the military, and to its commitment to ceremony and protocol. He loved the humor of the radio show called *The Goon Show*, which was routinely referred to as anarchic, but he was quick to rebuke secretaries for spelling errors or to blast equerries for minor failures. As he began to take a more active and prominent public role, then, the Prince was already a complex figure.

In some ways Charles is strikingly like his father. Prince Philip's interest in science is not shared by his son, but they both painted when younger. They are both passionate about the natural world—the Duke of Edinburgh through his lifelong association with the World Wildlife Fund and his efforts to raise awareness of over-population, and his son through his equally strong concern for the world's wild spaces and rain forests. They were both close to Lord Mountbatten; they both shoot, and stalk, and read poetry. They both take a serious interest in things military, and both want do to something practical for young people.

For years Prince Philip had been bored at ceremonials, and he had long endured the pain of being maliciously misquoted (or some-times accurately quoted, which could be bad in a different way), and of having to bite his tongue. Now his son was experiencing the same tribulations. But the difference was that Prince Charles was complaining, quite loudly, though at this early stage only to friends and to staff. Even so, during these years the royal family was at its most united. The Queen began to sound more relaxed. Her role as "head of our morality" fit well with a new image of her motherliness, and she had a very strong team around her.

The key non-family position around the Queen is that of private secretary. One of those who has followed the court all his working life describes it as "the only appointment in the Royal Household that really matters a damn." Adeane, Lord Stamfordham's son, and a personal link to the court of George VI, finally retired from the job in 1972. The obvious man to replace him was Martin Charteris, who had been the Queen's private secretary when she was Princess Elizabeth and was with her in Kenya when she learned that her father had died. But the Lord Chamberlain, Lord Cobbold, had introduced a rival, Philip Moore, a pilot who had been shot down during the war and risen through the civil service. In 1966 Moore became the Queen's assistant secretary. According to one who knew and partly admired him, he was somewhat stiff and overtalkative: "She got frightfully impatient with him at Balmoral. She wanted to rip through the papers, and select the most important ones; Moore would plod slowly through everything."

When Charteris realized that the job might go to Moore, he did a rather brave thing. He went to the Queen and confronted her. Who did she want as her next private secretary? "You, of course," replied the Queen. In effect, Charteris then told her to get on with it. Later on, in 1977, Moore did get the job, but the appointment of Charteris gave the Queen one of the wittiest and shrewdest senior advisers she has ever had, during one of the most difficult periods for her realm.

Charteris arrived at a time when the attitude in the British press toward the royal family was hardening. Ann Leslie, one of the great reporters of her time, covered her first royal tour for the *Daily Express* in 1968, when the expected method of reporting was simply to note the color and style of the Queen's clothes and make some anodyne remarks. From the first, she says, the press were not made welcome: "Mao Tse Tung in China used to classify his enemies in various gradations and journalists were the ninth stinking category of enemies, and in a way the Court feels that about us, and I don't blame them, really."[25]

Meanwhile, the press were becoming more confrontational. Leslie says the journalists and photographers found that 1968 tour, which was to the Caribbean, "stunningly boring and tiring," largely because of the transport problems caused by the need to get ahead of the Royal Yacht. In Dominica, while Prince Philip was opening a hospital, the matron told him about the terrible mosquitoes and he replied along the lines of, "Well, you have mosquitoes, we have the press." The reporters and photographers revolted. Leslie remembers: "We ordered him to apologize. . . . We pointed out to his horrified press secretary that actually he needed us more than we needed him . . . and if he didn't behave and stop insulting us we would snap our notebooks shut, put our cameras down on the ground—or we'll start photographing close-ups of tropical flowers." The Duke succumbed and came over to apologize, after which, says Leslie, "he was rather unnervingly charming to us. We're not used to that."

At the time, Leslie was working for a keenly royal newspaper, and she went on to write for another, the *Daily Mail*. She describes her readers as "definitely the 'knit your own Royal' and 'Royal biscuit-tin' types; to begin with, there was no danger that the irritation of reporters would spill into hostile news stories. But, she adds, "then along comes Murdoch, who is of course a republican."

Harry Arnold, one of the reporters who caused many teeth to be ground at the Palace, says he believes the Queen's reign saw a revolution in the attitude toward the royal family. Asked what caused it, his reply echoes Ann Leslie: "In two words—Rupert Murdoch." Arnold was there on the day in 1969 when the Australian tycoon bought the *Sun*, and he became the paper's first royal correspondent seven years later. He says that it was clear from early on that Murdoch, who had developed classic Australian republican views, wanted the Royals to be treated as just another story and given no special favors. But, says Arnold, Murdoch was always more interested in selling newspapers than in promoting republicanism.

Arguably the Royals have done more for Fleet Street than Fleet Street has done for them. For a long time the shift in the press's attitude toward the royal family would not directly affect the Queen, who was generally regarded as so popular as to be untouchable. More often, it was focused on her husband or her sister, and later her children. Arnold recalls, with some glee, a gaffe the Duke made during the first royal visit to China, when he told some British students they would be "slitty-eyed" if they stayed too long there; the fact that the Queen seemed angry with him the next day was regarded as a further coup.[26] This new aggressiveness by the British popular press was perhaps inevitable once it became clear that Murdoch's less reverential, cheekier attitude toward the Royals—along with his page-three girls, shorter stories and terrible punning headlines—was a winning formula. One by one his critics became his imitators.

Harsher treatment by the press only exacerbated the worst problem the Royals faced, which was that they seemed increasingly out of touch with the times. No one could possibly associate the Queen and her immediate family with the new mood and trendy culture of the sixties and seventies. They sought solace in Scottish glens and mountains, with guns and rods. They dressed formally and traditionally. They were more comfortable with dogs, horses and military types than with rock music, film stars and designers. The Queen Mother retained a lively, if unadventurous, interest in the arts, but the same could not be said for her daughter, who had giggled at Wagner, quite enjoyed farces, and drew the line at serious literature. Partly because their values and tastes were so traditional, the royal family was loved by, and in some sense represented, a broad swath of middle-class and working-class traditional Britain—the church-going, prudent, self-disciplined and patriotic people who still formed a majority.

But the monarchy did not represent the new social forces, both heroes and villains, reshaping the country. Despite the odd OBE lobbed at a pop star, and sometimes lobbed back again, the royal family during the Queen's middle years was considered by many to be painfully old-fashioned. Charles grew his hair a little longer. There were halfhearted attempts to suggest that Princess Anne was fashionable in her minidress and beehive. But the performance was never convincing. The Queen, with her corgis and headscarf, was the antithesis of the age's signature tone, a brittle metropolitan trendiness tinged with revolutionary ideas about utopias and a fascination with self-analysis. Most monarchists who observed the growing distance between the Royals and contemporary culture would say, "and a good thing too," but dangers lurked when the court seemed even older than its years. A culture war and a generational conflict were raging, and the House of Windsor was all on one side.

But there was one glaring exception: Princess Margaret. She had struggled to recover from the brutal destruction of her love affair with Peter Townsend; later, she emerged as the funniest, most open and theatrical of the Windsors, though she shrewdly understood the role she was being forced into. She told the writer Gore Vidal, one of her many intellectual friends, that if the first of two sisters was the Queen and the source of all honor and goodness, the other "must be the focus of the most creative malice, the evil sister."[27] In the early years, she was merely the wild one, the sister who went dancing into the small hours in London nightclubs, had a series of romances, and defied convention by smoking in public. If her sister and mother expected anything particular of her, it was that she might marry one of the wealthy heirs in whose company she was often seen while partying at Windsor or in London. And she did have royal duties of her own. She was colonel of a dozen regiments in Britain and other Commonwealth countries; further, playing something of the role that Diana would later on, she was a keen patron of charities, particularly those concerning children and the disadvantaged. But these responsibilities did not amount to a life.

She lived with her mother in Kensington Palace. Because of the long saga of her involvement with Peter Townsend, most of the obvious suitors were already married by the time she was free again, and she came to think she would always be single. Then she met Anthony Armstrong-Jones, who at the time was a rising young photographer with royal connections. They conducted their romance in semi-public without Fleet Street noticing, which would have been unthinkable later on. But only when Margaret was told by Townsend in December 1959 that he was about to marry a Belgian woman did she finally accept Armstrong-Jones. She told him "yes" the following day, and before they married, he moved from his bachelor pad in Pimlico Road to Buckingham Palace. The wedding took place in May 1960, the first big royal television event since the Coronation.

Princess Margaret and her new husband then began a life that provided a startling contrast to the home life of the Queen's. Armstrong-Jones—soon Lord Snowdon—worked hard to do his bit as a royal worker, learning the duties of consort from Prince Philip. He even learned to shoot, a skill that was, and still is, expected of people who mix with the Windsors. But he and Margaret moved in a very different set from the rest of the royal family. She stopped traveling in a stately Rolls-Royce and took to a Mini, or rode with Armstrong-Jones on his motorbike. Their circle included Peter Sellers and his wife Britt Ekland, Greek shipping tycoons, the Aga Khan, the ballet dancer Rudolf Nureyev, rock stars like Mick Jagger, actors such as David Niven, the hairdresser Vidal Sassoon and the designer Mary Quant, alongside the more predictable rich aristocrats. They holidayed in Sardinia, Venice and the Caribbean. Predictably, Princess Margaret became an easy target for Labour republicans who did not quite dare snipe at the Queen but found they could call her sister extravagant and lazy—and worse—and get away with it.

For better or worse, Margaret and her husband became the one part of the extended Windsor family that seemed in tune with the more relaxed spirit of the age. They brought a sense of style and a bubble of fun. Unfortunately they seemed unwilling to work very hard at their marriage. Both were soon having affairs, causing them to be gleefully pursued by the paparazzi. At the center of what appeared to be a glamorous and hedonistic world, there was coldness, sadness and mutual humiliation. Princess Margaret and Lord Snowdon began to spend more and more time apart, often leaving their two children in Britain. (Happily, both grew up to be thoroughly normal and well-balanced adults.)

One place the photographers could rarely reach was the small Caribbean island of Mustique, where the couple had honeymooned. It was owned by one of Margaret's longtime friends, Lord Glenconner, Colin Tennant, whose family had been influential during the industrial revolution in Scotland, and who was extremely rich after selling the family business. He had originally bought Mustique as a hideaway, but he then turned it into a luxurious holiday resort that was frequented by rock stars and the superrich. Tennant offered Princess Margaret some land to build a house on the island, and soon it became her favorite hideaway, as well as a place British newspaper readers associated with exotic but mysterious naughtiness. Tennant played his part in this drama with much enthusiasm: on his fiftieth birthday party, attended by Princess Margaret (dubbed the Princess of Misrule for the occasion), he was crowned king of the island, while local youths paraded around wearing gold-painted coconut shells as codpieces. This "anti-kingdom" provided a stunning contrast to the decorum and seriousness of her sister's court, and Margaret encouraged the comparison by surrounding herself with a little court of flatterers and hangers-on, who adored her wit but whom she would often flatten with a swipe of Hanoverian hauteur. Meanwhile, Snowdon pursued his own life, working ever harder and seen with a wide array of other women.

In 1973, when she was forty-three, Margaret was introduced by Tennant at a lunch in Edinburgh's Café Royal to a twenty-five-year-old Welsh charmer named Roddy Llewellyn, a man whose life had been a muddle and a struggle up to then. Margaret's affair with him would last eight years, and it scandalized many because of the gap in their ages and Llewellyn's modest means.

With this story, the press opened the floodgates and began following the royal family's every move. In 1976 the *News of the World* covered its front page with a story about Princess Margaret and the young Welshman. The spotlight did no favors for Margaret and Snowdon's dying marriage; killed by the affair, it ended in divorce two years later.

Princess Margaret's story did not end happily. Like her father and grandfather, she was a heavy smoker; she was also, like many of her generation, a heavy drinker. The combination, and an accident which left her with badly scalded feet, produced a dramatic deterioration of her health in later years—at one point she was treated for alcoholic hepatitis and in 1985 had part of her left lung removed. She suffered strokes and lived in seclusion at Kensington Palace before dying in 2002 at age seventy-one. The men in her life all remarried; even the apparently doomed Llewellyn became a successful television gardener and inherited the family baronetcy.

Often the butt of scathing jokes and dismissive abuse, Princess Margaret's life illustrated the difficulty of coping with the pressure of royalty without a strong work ethic and an abnormal amount of self-control. She was badly treated when it mattered most, and she struggled to find a way to live happily. When considering Margaret's many troubles, her sister's words about the importance of duty and marriage uttered so long ago seem poignant. The Queen has been a paragon of duty and determination, but in her marriage and the security of her role, she has been lucky too.

FRIENDS AND FOREIGNERS

If "the sixties" were not, for many people, the reality of life in the actual 1960s, then "the seventies" did not feel like the 1970s as actually experienced by those leading Britain. It is hard to imagine anyone less trendy, unbuttoned and in tune with the times than

Edward Heath, who won his election victory in June 1970. Because the Queen was at the Ascot races, he was not summoned to the Palace until seven p.m.

Previous Tory prime ministers had been grander figures. Here was a man from the lower middle class who had no interest in grouse moors, horse racing or indeed country life generally. Heath was a different kind of Conservative. One way he showed it was by his treatment of the Queen. Immediately, he had a favor to ask of her: the royal family was giving a party at Windsor for Lord Mountbatten and the Queen Mother, both seventy. Would she mind if he was late? As he told the story later: "She threw back her head and laughed, saying that all the family had been discussing whether or not I would still be able to come."[28]

But the relationship between the two developed, and like later premiers, Heath found that his weekly audiences, at six-thirty p.m. on Tuesdays, had the omertà of the therapist's office: "It was always a relief to be able to discuss everything with someone, knowing full well that there was not the slightest danger of anything leaking." He would talk about politics but also the personal affairs of fellow politicians and foreign leaders. Northern Ireland and his attempt to "join Europe" were early topics. Afterward, he would stay for a drink with her private secretary—initially Sir Michael Adeane, and then Martin Charteris.

Heath already knew the Queen and the Duke of Edinburgh from informal lunches, though he was as socially awkward with royalty as with any other branch of the human family. In his memoirs, he recounts an early lunch when he was sitting next to Princess Margaret, who spent the first two courses talking to another guest. "She then turned to me. I had always been taught not to initiate a conversation with a member of the royal family. So while awaiting her opening gambit I just looked back, and remained silent. So did she." On the third go, he asked her whether she had been busy and got the acid reply, "That is the sort of question Lord Mayors ask when I visit cities."[29]

This story suggests the sort of difficulties the Queen must have had with Heath: "She did not find him easy," says one former civil servant, "but who did? That was Ted." Yet she worked hard at the relationship, paying her first formal visit to Chequers in October 1970 to see Heath and President Nixon, who was there for talks. At Balmoral, Heath was politely asked about his latest yacht-racing exploits and answered at considerable length.

But Heath, to his credit, was prepared to offer unwelcome advice if necessary. In 1971 the Commonwealth heads of government conference, a biennial event the Queen cares passionately about, was due to be held in Singapore. The Canadian prime minister had established the expectation that the Queen would go to these meetings even when they were not held in the UK. But Heath felt she should not go, because the Commonwealth was at war with itself due to the confrontation between Rhodesia and the "frontline" black African states. The Queen put up a counterargument, saying that if the conference was being held in London, as it had been until then, she would have been present and the situation would have been just as explosive. Heath retorted that London simply had a different atmosphere. The grand buildings and the proximity of Buckingham Palace and Windsor would make it likelier that people would be on their best behavior. In Singapore she would meet each of the warring leaders at a time when it was almost impossible to arbitrate between them.

This incident offers a key example of the Queen's limited ability to knock heads together at the top of the organization. She simply cannot go against a British prime minister who has dug his heels in. On October 15, 1970, Heath wrote a letter advising her formally not to go; however reluctantly, she agreed. Five days later, Adeane wrote back, saying that since the Queen's only interest was to help the Commonwealth and "as it seems probable that her presence on this occasion might well lead to controversy and embarrassment, she agrees that it would be better to stay away." In the event, it proved to be a rough conference, and Heath believed that he had saved her from "political and personal unpleasantness."

The Queen has a long memory, however, and later she got in some gentle verbal revenge. In 1992 Heath, long retired, was at Buckingham Palace discussing the first Gulf War with the Queen and the U.S. secretary of state James Baker. A real row bubbled up between the two men, since Heath, in a much criticized visit, had traveled to Iraq to see Saddam Hussein himself and warn him to get out of Kuwait. Heath told Baker he should have done the same. The Queen intervened and said Baker could not have gone to Baghdad. Why not, Heath asked the Queen. *He* had been able to. " 'I know you could,' said the Queen, 'but you're expendable now.' "

Heath's greatest political work during his three years in office was to secure Britain's entry into the European Economic Community. Some believed this change would have significant implications for the Crown, since Britain was joining a supranational organization, many of whose members assumed they were well on the way toward political union. The sovereignty of the sovereign, never mind the nation, was at least in question. In Britain, constitutional opponents of the project saw the entire structure of the "Crown in Parliament" under attack, a historic surrender of a thousand years of proud independence. Yet there is not the slightest sign that the Queen or other Royals objected. Far from it, in fact: the Queen dutifully lauded her government's achievement in speeches, and she suggested in her 1972 Christmas broadcast that the Commonwealth family of nations was now joining hands with another extended family. This statement was well meaning and pious but, given the rivalries, implausible.

Heath celebrated Britain's formal membership in the EEC in January 1973 with a "Fanfare for Europe" gala concert at Covent Garden, followed by a dinner at Lancaster House. The Queen and Prince Philip were guests of honor, and Heath recorded that "my heart was full of joy . . . at the recognition which Her Majesty the

Queen had given to our country's great achievement."[30] The Queen did seem to be comfortable with British membership in the EEC, despite the unease it caused some members of the Commonwealth concerned about their agricultural trade, and lingering questions about her own role. Perhaps she reflected that the Swedish, Dutch and Danish monarchies had managed perfectly well in the new bloc, never mind the reviving Spanish monarchy.

When Heath's crisis-stricken government, exhausted by its battles with the trade unions, finally gave way and he called the first of the 1974 elections, the Queen was at the other end of the world, enjoying a February tour of the South Seas. As the election campaign raged at home, she traveled through Pacific island territories, New Zealand and finally Australia, before flying back to London for the close of polling. There she faced a new dilemma, not this time a question of party leadership but of parliamentary arithmetic. The voters had returned a hung Parliament, in which Wilson's Labour Party, not Heath's Conservatives, had the largest single bloc of seats. As when Gordon Brown faced a similar outcome in 2010, the Palace stuck by the constitutional doctrine that the prime minister remained prime minister until he or she had resigned. And just as Brown hung on until it was clear that Labour could not form a workable coalition with the Liberal Democrats, so Heath spent an agonizing weekend trying to stitch together a deal with Jeremy Thorpe, the Liberal leader, before finally resigning on the Monday.

In theory, the Queen had the power to invite anyone she liked to try to form a government, but it was so overwhelmingly obvious that the right choice was to invite Wilson back that there was no real decision to make. Several exchanges of messages between Buckingham Palace and Number Ten followed, but there was no sense of constitutional crisis, still less a concern about the sorts of dangers that swirled around the Macmillan or Eden successions.

For the Queen, the more serious mid-1970s political challenge came not in Britain but in Australia. The crisis that played out there in 1975 boosted republicanism, and it demonstrates the dangers of the Queen's theoretically political role when others try to exploit it. Australia's prime minister was the intellectual and fiery Labor politician Gough Whitlam. His government had introduced numerous reforms but was in deep trouble, hit by scandals and struggling with an economic crisis. He had a majority in the lower house, but not the upper house, the elected Australian senate. His Liberal Party opponent, Malcolm Fraser, decided to use the senate to block Whitlam's budget bills, thus effectively bringing the government to a standstill and forcing a general election. The Queen became involved because her representative in Australia, the governor-general Sir John Kerr, intervened. He abruptly sacked Whitlam and appointed Fraser prime minister.

Whitlam wanted to appeal to the Queen directly but his dismissal came so quickly that he was unable to use this constitutional right because he was no longer prime minister. Kerr, whom Whitlam believed was acting in concert with Fraser to ditch a properly elected Labor government, acted using the same "reserve" powers of the monarchy that would allow the Queen, in theory, to force out British prime ministers. But the words that matter are "in theory"— few people imagined that Kerr would go so far as to actually exercise his powers.

Kerr was not, it should be emphasized, a grandee governor-general sent out from St James's with a plumed hat, fine command of ancient Greek, and long family tree in the West Country. He was a tough Australian lawyer from a working-class Sydney family who had risen through the law, specializing in trade-union cases. Kerr had spent the war in Australian intelligence and then wanted to be a Labor politician himself, though he later drifted to the right. He had been appointed by the Queen but had actually been chosen by none other than Whitlam.

The Queen was so little involved in Kerr's decision to dismiss her Australian prime minister that Kerr did not even tell her about it until after the fact. He wanted to protect her from controversy, he said later; a governor-general was expendable but a Queen was not. Still, he had acted using her authority and in a way that infuriated many Australian socialists. Whitlam emerged from the parliament building to greet an angry crowd, and he began his speech by referring to the official proclamation calling for an election: "Well may we say 'God Save the Queen' because nothing will save the Governor-General." He then told his supporters to "maintain your rage and enthusiasm" for the election ahead. The Queen was asked to intervene, presumably by sacking her new governor-general and reinstating Whitlam, on the grounds that the sovereignty of her people had been infringed. But that would have been an even more provocative reassertion of personal authority, and she declined to get involved.

Though this incident and others encouraged Australian republicanism, nothing dramatic has happened in the years since Whitlam was removed from office. The 1986 Australia Act formally severed any rights of the UK to interfere in Australian politics, and five years later the Australian Republican Movement was formed. References to the Queen were removed from the Australian Oath of Allegiance. Australian barristers ceased to be Queen's Counsel. In 1991 a new Australian Labor prime minister, Paul Keating, who had served under Whitlam, called for the Australian flag to be redesigned, dropping the Union flag from its edge, and began moves to prepare for a republic.

The Queen watched these developments almost silently. When she arrived for her visit in 1992 she invited Keating aboard *Britannia*, and before he could deliver a prepared speech told him that she was the last person who would stand in the way of Australia becoming republican. Now, she said, I gather you have fifty-four nationalities in Australia today. There must be a time when I am completely redundant; you will let me know, won't you? Keating, according to those present, was both silenced and disarmed. During the same trip, he fell foul of the British media by committing the solecism of putting an arm around the Queen, but under the circumstance that was a more protective gesture than she might have expected.

The following year Keating set up a Republic Advisory Committee, which led to a Constitutional Convention to thrash out the fine detail of how a "resident for president" might actually be chosen. After a change of government, the referendum was finally held in 1999, and the Australians, to general surprise, stuck with the Queen by a 55 percent majority. Yet if one of the major realms of which she is sovereign is ever to reject her, or her heir, Australia is the likeliest candidate. Julia Gillard, the country's current prime minister, is a republican (though hard-liners are suspicious that she is "soft" on the subject), and so was her predecessor Kevin Rudd. Both suggested that she should be the last monarch of their country—a poignant thought, given that she is due to visit Australia in fall 2011, just months before her Diamond Jubilee year, for the Commonwealth heads of government meeting. Yet polls on the topic show that public opinion remains divided, and Prince William is one of the most popular royals in Australia since his mother.

Canada, which replaced a Union-dominated Red Ensign with a national maple-leaf flag in 1965, was going through a similar reevaluation during this period. Complicating matters, however, it had a large French-speaking and increasingly separatist minority in the province of Quebec. During the 1960s and 1970s, the rise of the Parti Québécois gave an angrier and more urgent edge to republicanism, though it also had the effect of cementing the monarchy's popularity in the more strongly English-dominated provinces of Canada. In 1964, the Queen had an early, firsthand experience of the problem during her visit to Quebec, when activists staged a number of protests, including ones where long lines of people silently turned their backs to her. During the same visit, there were also reports of assassination plots against her. But the Queen was back in Quebec for the opening of the 1967 Expo fair, and again in 1976 for the opening of the Montreal Olympics. She also had to deal with the impish, charismatic and unpredictable

Pierre Trudeau, Canada's independent-minded premier from 1968 to 1979 and 1980 to 1984.

Trudeau is a fascinating example of a public figure who begins as a rebel and then metamorphoses into a mildly conservative figure. He had been an anti-conscription protestor during World War II, a French-Catholic intellectual interested in Marxism, and a persistent enemy of Mackenzie King, Canada's pro-British wartime leader. As prime minister, he became known for stunts such as sliding down the banisters at Buckingham Palace, doing an impromptu dance behind the Queen, and meeting John Lennon on his world peace tour. Given his background, many in Britain asked whether he was also a republican.

Yet in office Trudeau had to confront not only Quebec separatism but also several extremist groups. Over time, he developed into a tough operator, determined to keep Canada united, if by now bilingual. He denied being republican, and continued to invite the Queen to Canada. When Whitehall expressed some uncertainty about the wisdom of her going, British ministers were reminded that it was none of their business. She was Queen of Canada and Trudeau was her prime minister, just as much as Douglas-Home, Wilson or Heath. Later, during his 1980s term as prime minister, Trudeau decided that Canada's constitution should be "patriated"—that is, properly written down and established for and in Canada, rather than as an appendage of British law—and as evidence of support for his position he said the Queen approved. In his memoirs, Trudeau said he had been impressed by her grace in public and the wisdom she displayed during private conversations.

The 1982 patriation, which included a Canadian Bill of Rights and Liberties, did not lead to serious new questioning of the monarchy and is now a cornerstone of Canadian identity. Canada's political evolution provides a classic example of the wisdom of the gentle, unprotesting retreat of British power, just as the Queen's handling of Trudeau helped ensure that a politician who represented a potential threat to her authority ended up as a supporter of it. But Canada's feeling about the monarchy continues to develop. During Trudeau's era, the notion of vesting Canadian sovereignty in the governor-general, and so remaking the country as a republic, began to be seriously discussed. An active republican organization, Citizens for a Canadian Republic, has long argued that when the Queen dies, the monarchical connection must end and a native-born Canadian become head of state. By 2010, when the Queen again visited Canada, opinion polls showed that a clear majority, 58 percent, believed that the country should sever its ties with the monarchy after her death.

In the 1970s, monarchical issues that arose in Australia and Canada were debated in Britain, too. The thought of "losing" such large pieces of the monarchy caused much unease. Yet the ambiguities of the Queen's role could not be ignored. Was she purely symbolic or were there situations in which she not only could intervene in politics to resolve a crisis, but ought to? How could one distinguish between her role as head of different states if their interests collided? Since Britain did not have an elected second chamber, there could be no precise parallel to the Australian crisis that had ousted Whitlam, but questions surfaced about how the Queen might act in Britain if the parties or Parliament were stuck. Suppose Harold Wilson, who returned as prime minister in 1974, had suddenly resigned. Should the Queen appoint an interim prime minister to allow "the Queen's business" to continue smoothly?

This question caused much debate between the Palace and Downing Street. The formula that finally emerged, devised by Martin Charteris, was that the outgoing prime minister must stay in office, resigning only as party leader. The party would then choose a new leader, at which point there would be a seamless switch-over, thus leaving the Queen entirely out of it. This was exactly what happened when John Major resigned as party leader to confront his Tory critics: he remained prime minister while the contest went on, even as he assumed that he would continue to be prime minister after he had flushed out his enemies. And when Wilson shocked the political world by announcing his resignation in 1976, he did indeed stay in office while Labour conducted its election for a new leader. (Jim Callaghan beat out the left's much-loved intellectual Michael Foot, and in short order, Callaghan became prime minister too.) In neither case was the Queen involved.

Wilson's announcement spawned a score of wild-eyed theories involving blackmail, Russian spies, and corruption. His loyal press secretary, Joe Haines, is convinced that Wilson's discovery that he had early-onset Alzheimer's disease was the true reason for his exit. If so, he must have indicated this to the Queen privately in September 1975 during his annual Balmoral visit. Apart from Wilson's wife, the Queen was the first to know that he was determined to resign the following March. On December 6, 1975, he told her at his audience that he would leave around March 11, and later the same day he said at a dinner given by his lawyer Arnold Goodman that "I mentioned that matter to the Queen" so that nobody could later say he had been pushed into it at the last minute. Even so, the conspiracy theorists had a field day when the resignation announcement came.

On March 23, 1976, the Queen and Prince Philip went to a farewell dinner at Number Ten, a convivial evening that went on until nearly midnight. She had done the same for Winston Churchill, but for no one since. They had been through a lot together, and her attendance at the dinner was a mark of considerable respect and affection. Wilson was not a great prime minister. He had spent so much time dodging and tacking to keep Labour united that he was rarely able to grasp the great issues and change the direction of the country. But he had governed during a time of ferocious social upheaval, of political unrest, middle-class paranoia and intergenerational strife—and he had kept the show on the road. As the quintessential "sixties" politician, he remained a resolutely old-fashioned and unhip figure—podgy, dressed for comfort not fashion, phlegmatic and traditionalist. And despite the convulsive change occurring all around him, he stayed true to his monarch.

"He adored the Queen, he really did," says one senior Whitehall figure who worked with him.

The Wilson years were marked by scandals and conspiracy theories, but the Queen managed to keep well clear. She clearly liked him, but she cannot have liked some of what he did. Asked to approve a seat in the House of Lords for Marcia Williams, Lady Falkender, Wilson's controversial secretary and gatekeeper, the Queen rolled an eye: "Must I?" But she complied.

ROYALISTS AND REPUBLICANS

Two major moments of royal stocktaking occurred in the seventies, the Queen's silver wedding anniversary and her Silver Jubilee of 1977. Jubilees, culminating in the Diamond, have been among the most characteristic celebrations of the Windsor dynasty. The first "modern" Jubilee took place in 1809 when writers and politicians agitated for something to mark the fiftieth anniversary of George III's accession. Much as it did in 1977, this Golden Jubilee came at a moment when the country was badly in need of cheering up. The Napoleonic wars were at their height, and in Britain they brought high taxes, reduced imports, wounded soldiers and physical isolation. In Spain and Portugal, the Peninsular War was grinding grimly on. George's reign had seen the great naval victory of Trafalgar four years before, but he was also associated with the loss of the American colonies, and by this time he was almost blind and suffering grievously from rheumatism.

The idea of celebrating his exceptionally long reign was seized upon as a national dance of defiance. George III's Jubilee was hailed with services of thanksgiving around the country, ox roastings, and formidable amounts of beer. Special food was issued to soldiers and sailors. The King freed all debtors to the Crown. Many other debtors were released from prison, after being fed copious amounts beef and plum pudding. Deserters were pardoned. Prisoners of war, except for the French, were released and sent home. George himself celebrated with prayers and fireworks at Windsor, while in London huge crowds turned out for a thanksgiving service at St. Paul's, afterward thronging the illuminated streets, dressed in patriotic garterblue sashes.

All this provided a great boost to the King's popularity. Within a year he had begun the sad descent into madness and dementia—which made necessary the Regency Act and the rule of his fat, rebellious son—but the notion of the jubilee had been established. The next long-reigning monarch was Victoria, whose Golden Jubilee of 1887 occurred in an entirely different atmosphere. At the very zenith of Empire, this anniversary was grander, more military and more imperial, and it was celebrated in India, Australia, New Zealand, Canada and Africa, as well as in Britain. With her Jubilee, the Queen left behind her years of seclusion as "the widow of Windsor," and it did much for her popularity, too. The ceremonies in London included a gathering of the vastly extended royal family network of Europe, a parade of Indian troops behind the famous gold coach in which the crownless Victoria sat and waved, and a service at Westminster Abbey. Disaster was averted when a serious Irish terrorist plot to blow up the Queen, the government and assembled notables failed, partly because of London's unreliable public transport system. Around Britain, there was enough collective memory to repeat the ox roastings, feasts, beer drinking, bonfires and dances of 1809.

Victoria was still reigning in 1897 when her Diamond Jubilee was celebrated in similar fashion, though this time Britain marked the anniversary with more looking back and the first tremors of suspicion that her age of dominance might not last forever. In the first half of the twentieth century, the most significant such celebration was the Silver Jubilee of George V in 1935. Again the anniversary occurred at a time of national gloom and uncertainty—among the most fulsome messages of congratulation was one from Adolf Hitler. The by now familiar ritual of beacons, fireworks, ox roastings, parties and church services was repeated, but not all was the same.

When the King and Queen visited the slums of east London, the royal coach and horses were followed by enthusiastic roller skaters and cyclists, and they were greeted by a sea of flags and cheering faces. (One sign in a particularly dilapidated area read simply, "Lousy but Loyal.") After this enthusiastic reception, George reflected, "I'd no idea they felt that way about me: I am beginning to think they must really like me for myself." This was probably not false modesty. Living in an era long before regular polling, the royal family was relatively isolated from public opinion, and only a major occasion allowed for a substantial encounter with the people.

By the 1977 Silver Jubilee, then, Britain could work from an established tradition. The country knew what jubilees were for: they were moments of stocktaking and reflection, about both the state of the monarchy and the state of the nation. Jubilees were bad news for oxen and good news for brewers; they had become dates in the national life not unlike milestone birthdays or diamond weddings in family life. The historian David Cannadine makes a simple but powerful point about them:

> If you live in a republic—let's take the United States of America—and you think about the period of history that the country's chopped up into, it is four years for a president, eight years if you're lucky, and then it's a hundred years, for centenaries or centennials, and that's about it; whereas if you have a monarchy, especially if you have the present Queen, who has reigned for twenty-five years, then fifty years, then sixty years, what you get is this sequence of jubilees which provides you with the opportunity for structured retrospection . . . that otherwise you don't have.[31]

In 1977 one of the questions prompted by the jubilee was: after the overblown romantic optimism of the "New Elizabethan Age," how had the Queen and the country done? The Windsors were unscathed by scandal. The behind-the-scenes efforts by Palace

officials to avoid controversy had been largely successful. The previous year, the Queen had celebrated her twenty-fifth wedding anniversary by reminding her listeners of the bishop who, when asked
what he thought of sin, replied that he was against it; in the same way,
she said, she was "for" marriage. And her "family monarchy" was
intact. Divorce had become a national addiction, and the young
behaved with much greater sexual openness. But, Princess Margaret
apart, the Windsors were straitlaced and together. Prince Charles
was seen most often in uniform at the bridge of naval vessels or in
helicopters, or on a polo pony. Princess Anne had married Captain
Mark Phillips three years before, at Westminster Abbey. Phillips
declined an earldom and their children, Peter and Zara, would grow
up outside the glare of publicity, though the couple would later separate and divorce.

Princess Anne was already one of the unflashy stars of the family. A superb horsewoman, she took part in the 1976 Olympics as
part of the British team, riding her mother's horse Goodwill. (She
says today that it is a rare, possibly unique, case of the same person
breeding both horse and rider.) She had her father's bluntness and
plenty of guts. In March 1974, on her way back from a charity film
screening, she had been the victim of an attempted ransom kidnap
on Pall Mall. The kidnapper shot and wounded three men, including her driver and her protection officer; he then told the Princess
to get out of the car, to which she replied "not bloody likely" before
bolting out of the other side and eventually being helped by members of the public.

If the royal family was in good shape at the time of the Silver
Jubilee, the country was not. With strikes and severe limitations on
basic services haunting Heath's domestic premiership, and with
union militancy returning with added edge during the Wilson-
Callaghan years, many wondered whether Britain was even gov-
ernable. Day after day the press reported alarming economic news,
dire threats about inflation, and the continuing menace of a Soviet
Union that seemed more powerful and threatening than ever. On

the right, hostility to the idea of joining the EEC, fear of communists infiltrating industry, and despair about the cycle of terrorist violence spinning out of control in Northern Ireland produced an almost paranoid mood.

As with her grandfather's twenty-fifth anniversary in 1935, the Queen's Silver Jubilee provoked some MPs to call for a limited celebration because of the tough economic times. The leftist and republican minority was more vocal than ever, though not, according to the polls, any larger. The journalist Philip Howard asked how seriously Britain should take the radicals, who felt that monarchy had become, as he put it, "a soporific for a geriatric society, and comic relief to the death-rattle of a nation"? He concluded that despite all the current problems, "There is a great advantage in having your official head of state above competition and so above party contention. Constitutional monarchy is, paradoxically, a democratic institution: by giving your official head of state no power, it makes her representative of all her subjects, particularly the weaker ones."[32] By the beginning of the Silver Jubilee year, it was unclear how widely that assessment was still shared. And as ever with monarchy, there would be no clear line between the popularity of the private family and the usefulness of the institution.

§

On the liberal and left side of the political divide, the mood was mutinous. For the first time in the Queen's reign, living standards had actually fallen during the previous two years. Inside the Labour Party, Trotskyites and Marxist local authority bosses seemed to be gaining influence. In the jubilee year, communists would organize their own celebration, socialists would distribute "Roll on the Red Republic" badges, and students would hoist red flags over Ruskin College, Oxford, to commemorate the sixtieth anniversary of the Bolshevik revolution. These agitations may have added to the gaiety of the national conversation, but they did not really amount to a hill of red beans. Photographs of the Queen were removed from some town halls. A few cities and communities, such as Manchester, decided to "waste" no money on celebrations or decorations, and effectively boycotted the event. Summing up the change in attitude, the *New Statesman*, which at the time of the Coronation had produced such a reflective and nuanced argument for the monarchy, now ran an anti-jubilee special edition mocking the Queen as "the doll in the golden coach."

In different ways the views of both right and left were the reflections of elites; gauging, and now remembering, the mood of the majority—many of whom are less inclined to give voice to strong views—is far harder. The best assessment, based on personal memories and conversations, might be summed up as simply a feeling of a loss of innocence. The optimistic uplift of the 1950s, essentially romantic and conservative, and the naive peace-and-love hopes of the 1960s, passionately espoused by the counterculture, seemed equally discredited. The culture had become ruder, cruder, and more violent. Union confrontations had become angrier. In Northern Ireland, the early idealism of the equal rights marchers had given way to a cycle of vicious killing, torture and banditry. Even in popular music, twang and sugar had been elbowed aside by the raucous insurgency of punk. Where in this picture did Queen Elizabeth II and her family fit? All in all, it did not seem an ideal time for a party to celebrate hereditary monarchy.

The jubilee year had begun with a long round of Commonwealth tours, but the government was dubious about, and initially hostile to, a big national tour. The celebration in Britain didn't really get under way until early summer, with loyal addresses from the Houses of Parliament. Speaking to MPs, the Queen made a sharp-edged reference to the fact that she had been crowned Queen of the United Kingdom of Great Britain and Northern Ireland. Scottish nationalism was on the rise, fueled by the discovery of North Sea oil, and her words caused some offense.

But as the domestic tours began, including most riskily to Northern Ireland, it became clear that people were very much in the

mood for a party. As in 1809 or 1935, all the current anxieties made
the jubilee more desired, not less. On June 7, about a million people
gathered in central London to watch the Queen and her family go
by coach to St. Paul's for a thanksgiving ceremony. (As at the Coronation, people had camped out overnight while waiting for the
Queen's carriage.) Harking back to George III, a chain of 101 beacons had been lit around the country—no mean feat, considering
the awful weather. Innovations developed for the jubilee included a
river tour of the Thames, larger-than-ever fireworks displays, and
the painting of London buses silver.

At her speech to a banquet in the capital's Guildhall, the Queen
drew attention to the disappearance of the Empire that had still
been visible at her grandfather's Silver Jubilee. During her reign,
she said, "I have seen, from a unique position of advantage, the last
great phase of the transformation of the Empire into Commonwealth and the transformation of the Crown from an emblem of
dominion into a symbol of free and voluntary association. In all
history this has no precedent." It was an unusually frank assertion
of her personal enthusiasm for the Commonwealth, but was there
also a message about the domestic meaning of monarchy? Here too
the Crown no longer symbolized power, but democracy. It was a
message that would have perplexed her ancestors. The Crown's
strength was its weakness? Its meaning was that it did not mean too
much?

These paradoxes were little discussed by most of the celebrants.
More than anything, 1977 would be remembered as the year of the
street party. Streets were closed to traffic so that long snakes of linen-
covered tables could be laid out; bunting and flags crisscrossed
between top-floor windows. Sandwiches, biscuits and cakes were
piled high, record players were brought out into the blustery open,
neighbors uneasily reintroduced themselves, and there was some
embarrassing dad-dancing. At London's biggest jubilee party, held at
Alexandra Palace, up to 160,000 people emptied 180 barrels of beer.
Some areas, such as well-heeled and liberal Hampstead, seemed

emptier of street celebrations; one journalist noticed that "the wealth-
ier the street, the less likely it is to have a party."[33] Maybe so, but for
millions, the collective effort involved in closing streets, introducing
neighbors, organizing food and drinks and putting up decorations
was a delightful, energizing and nostalgic surprise.

The jubilee, an exercise in what could be called virtuous nostalgia, reminded people of the national family feeling that had existed
in the immediate postwar years and now seemed to be falling away.
Amid the consumerism and political bickering, people turned toward
each other again, discovering an imagined community perhaps, but
one with real warmth. The most visible addition to that community
were the immigrants from Asia and the Caribbean, who in 1977
made up about 3.3 percent of the population, or 1.8 million people;
to the surprise of some, the jubilee celebrations were as keenly supported, perhaps even more so, by the new Britons. Looking back
now, it's clear that the jubilee refreshed and reasserted the meaning
of constitutional monarchy and helped produce a resurgent feeling of royalism that, four years later, would culminate in the wedding of Charles and Diana.

Wilson's successor, James Callaghan, reveled in his part in the
1977 celebrations. (He particularly enjoyed the Review of the Fleet,
since his father had been a rigger on an earlier Royal Yacht, the
Victoria and Albert, during the time of George V.) A traditionalist
with a naval background, Callaghan continued the tradition of
Labour Party super-patriotism. Like Wilson, he brushed aside the
attempts of Labour left-wingers to abolish the Civil List or make
the Queen pay income tax. His weekly audiences were said to be
"genial and relaxed," and the Queen offered him moral support
over issues such as the continuing sore of Rhodesia. Callaghan, for
his part, tried to interest the Prince of Wales in the world of politics, getting him to sit through a cabinet meeting and attend a session of Prime Minister's Questions. But Callaghan felt, probably
rightly, that Prince Charles was not much interested in the formal

side of constitutional politics, preferring his own causes. In White-hall the experiment was judged a failure.[34]

The end of the 1970s saw several further blows to the royal family. The worst was the murder of Lord Louis Mountbatten by an IRA man, Thomas McMahon, when Mountbatten was on his small wooden fishing boat off the coast of County Sligo in the Irish Republic. He had a summer home there and had been long warned of the danger by the Irish police, especially since the area was also popular with IRA men on holiday. On August 27, 1979, while on a lobster-potting and mackerel-fishing expedition with friends and family, his boat was blown to pieces by a remote-controlled bomb. He died shortly afterward of his injuries. Also killed were two teen-agers, one of them his grandson Nicky Knatchbull, the other a local boy, Paul Maxwell. His daughter's mother-in-law Lady Brabourne, who was eighty-three, died the following day.

Nicky Knatchbull's twin brother, Timothy, then fourteen, was also on the boat but survived. He and Nicky had been inseparable while growing up, and the two were so alike that at times even their parents struggled to tell them apart. Timothy Knatchbull remem-bers it as a glorious summer day in the middle of an idyllic holiday, part of a routine he had known since a toddler. Mountbatten was his hyperactive grandpa, still at seventy-nine always at the center of games and projects, and on that day looking forward to the catch of fish, crabs and perhaps lobsters. "We had been going for a few minutes—beautiful, flat, calm sea, not a cloud in the sky. . . . There was this almighty bang, just a recollection really of a thud . . . and the next thing I remember is lying on the bottom of another boat." He could hear worried Irish voices and felt intensely cold. In the hospital in Sligo, his mother lay opposite: "Her face was unrecog-nizable, held together by 117 stitches twenty in each eyeball. My father lay in a nearby ward, his legs horribly smashed up with wounds from top to toe. Between the three survivors we had three working eyes, no working eardrums." After three days in intensive care he awoke to find his sister Joanna, who told him: "When you arrived in the hospital you were unconscious. You woke up. Nicky never did." At that moment, he says, he knew the unimaginable had happened, "and I knew really in an instant that either I was going to survive or I would never get over it. . . . I looked at her, she looked at me, and as her eyes filled with tears I followed, and crumbled."[35]

It was the worst terrorist attack the royal family had ever suffered. Ironically, according to government papers held at Dublin's national archive, Mountbatten had told the Irish ambassador as early as 1972 that he was in favor of a united Ireland and would have been happy to assist efforts toward reunification. Of the murder, Gerry Adams, who was then vice president of Sinn Fein, told *Time* magazine that the IRA had "achieved its objective: people started paying attention to what was happening in Ireland." Adams told the magazine's Erik Amfitheatrof that "the IRA gave clear reasons for the execution. I think it is unfortunate that anyone has to be killed but the furore created by Mountbatten's death showed up the hypocritical attitude of the media establishment. . . . What the IRA did to him is what Mountbatten had been doing all his life to other people; and with his war record I don't think he could have objected to dying in what was clearly a war situation."

Lord Mountbatten, in the words of the writer Kenneth Rose, "was eulogized as a Renaissance man and buried like a medieval emperor." His murder outraged the country; among others, it deeply affected Prince Charles, who in his journal described reacting with "agony, disbelief, a kind of wretched numbness, closely followed by fierce and violent determination to see that something was done about the IRA."[36] He reflected that he had lost someone who could tell him unpleasant things, a man who "combined grand-father, great uncle, father, brother and friend." Mountbatten had indeed been closer to the Queen's heir than almost anyone else, advising him on girlfriends, warning him against his tendency to self-pity, and stiffening his sense of duty. Later, the memory of the

murder must have made it particularly hard for the Queen to swallow her feelings and accept that a future prime minister, Tony Blair,
would develop a cordial relationship with Adams as part of the Northern Ireland peace process.

As it happens, Timothy Knatchbull's account of the bombing and
its aftermath also provides unusual insight into the Queen, because
shortly after he began his recovery he experienced at first hand the
warm and mothering side of her that the rest of the country hardly
ever sees. With his mother still completely incapacitated in the hospital, he and his sister Amanda were invited by the Queen to Balmoral
to help them return to health. After being delayed by a fogbound
aircraft, they arrived at the castle between two and three a.m.; the
driver warned them everyone would have gone to bed long before,
so they should sneak in and find their bedrooms on their own. As
Knatchbull reports:

> None of it. We arrived through the door and we make a quick
> left turn and I looked down this long imposing corridor and the
> sight that greets me is of the Queen, Prince Charles at her side,
> and she's sort of steaming up the corridor at us . . . it's difficult to
> describe but it had this sort of feeling of a mother duck gathering
> up her lost young. And just a total look of care and concern on
> her face—from Prince Charles as well. And it was a wonderful
> moment, total surprise. And they led us to the back of the house
> where they had soup and sandwiches—no one else around . . .
> just the two of them . . . and they really wanted to go into their
> default setting of love and care, of asking about family, of plying
> us with soup and sandwiches and wrapping us up in a sort of
> motherliness coming from the Queen.

Knatchbull and his sister tried to prevent the Queen from taking them to their rooms and starting to unpack their cases. "She
was in unstoppable mothering mode, leading Amanda and me
down the corridor, pulling open the drawers, getting clothes out."

Only with some difficulty was she persuaded eventually to leave them and go to bed herself. In the days that followed, the same pattern persisted. The Queen sat the teenage boy next to her at meals, oversaw the dressing of his wounds, and sent him to bed when he looked tired. "She was brilliant. She was able to draw me out. If I felt a little lost she'd catch my eye and turn the conversation towards me. And within ten, twenty, thirty seconds she had me at the heart of the conversation again, throwing out ideas, chatting, laughing. This is the gift of truly remarkable motherhood and generosity." It left him with "a strange warm glow that's really never left me. And it's about the care, the loving tender care that the Queen [has] as a mum."

Others who have been family friends of the Queen also comment on her motherly instincts. One man had been stalking at Balmoral; late off the hill, he found the Queen pulling her Land Rover to a halt and embracing him with relief. The Queen's own children have learned to be circumspect about intimate family time, but they say this picture of their mother is accurate. Princess Anne, for instance, said she learned early that her mother's absences from home were part of "the service life." She had learned that it was "not a personal thing—she's not going away because she didn't like you or, you know, there's something wrong with the system; it's because there are priorities and you will get your time, and that's what happened." Speaking in an interview with real feeling, Princess Anne added that Knatchbull's experience was for her an expectation: "As all mothers, she's put up with a lot and we're still on speaking terms so I think that's no mean feat!" It was, she thought, "pretty good mothering" achieved inside a strict timetable but one in which quality made up for quantity: "The quality of the time that you get is something that you make yourself."

In the late 1970s, the demands on the Queen's time were in no way diminished. These were years of constant IRA threat and attack. As Queen of the United Kingdom of Great Britain and Northern Ireland, she was acutely aware of the blood-soaked and unhappy condition of the territory named in the final two words of her title. A vicious war was being fought between Irish republicans, hostile to everything the Queen symbolized, and Irish "loyalists" who loudly proclaimed their passionate devotion to the monarchical state while drawing its soldiers and police into death and danger every day. In Northern Ireland, as nowhere else, the symbols of the Queen's reign, from cap badges to letter boxes, had become controversial. The prefix "Royal" was either a rallying point or provocation. As the security risk increased, her visits to Northern Ireland had become steadily more difficult and briefer.

The physical threat to the Queen was now even more firmly in everyone's minds. On June 13, 1981, while the Queen was riding her beloved horse Burmese at the Trooping of the Colour parade, a youth fired shots at her, and everyone's first fear was IRA assassination. The youth was mentally disturbed; the shots were blanks; the Queen showed icy courage and expert handling of her horse. Royal life went on. Then, the following July, another disturbed man, Michael Fagan, managed to climb over the railings at Buckingham Palace and make his way to the Queen's bedroom. Again the immediate question was, "What if the IRA . . . ?" Again the Queen displayed impressive sangfroid; when Fagan appeared, one hand bloody after he slashed it with a broken ashtray, she eventually managed to leave her bedroom and get help when he asked her for a cigarette.

Just days after the Fagan incident, two IRA bombs brought death almost to the front door of Buckingham Palace. On July 20, members of the Household Cavalry, on their way from their Knightsbridge barracks to change the guard, were hit by a nail-bomb attack. Two soldiers died; seven horses were also killed. Another bomb went off under the bandstand at Regent's Park where the Royal Green Jackets were playing to tourists and relaxing office workers. The two attacks killed eleven people and injured fifty more.

Increasingly, the Queen lived in a world that challenged her private motto, "I have to be seen to be believed." Politicians were also at risk, of course, and before long Downing Street would be hemmed in by security railings and London would resound to the throb of police sirens as ministerial cars accelerated through traffic behind motorcycle escorts. And although the Queen has always been protected by some of the most experienced officers in the country and has consistently heeded their advice, security arrangements for the entire royal family became still more vigilant. But even during the worst of the danger, she never canceled and never stopped showing herself in public.

⚬══✦══⚬

Money

In the mid-1980s, a quiet and still mostly unknown Palace revolution got under way, as reformers upended the old "country house" atmosphere of the court, took back control of much of the day-to-day running of the monarchy from the government, and radically increased its efficiency. Questions about the royal family's finances had flared up regularly during the Queen's reign, and although Whitehall initiatives to "keep the Queen out of politics" would briefly calm things down, a residuum of public doubt always remained.

The real cost of the monarchy is a maddeningly complex subject. The Queen's money comes from three sources. First there is the Civil List, funds that are paid by the Treasury to the monarchy for its upkeep. The Treasury's money, in turn, comes from the revenues of the Crown Estate—property owned by the monarchy—most of which has been paid straight to government. Second, the Queen has a private estate that funds much of her other spending. And third, there are her private investments. (These two types of income are together known as the Privy Purse, which for some conjures up the image of a huge velvet handbag.) All three of these revenue sources come gnarled and knobbly with complicated history.

The Crown Estate comprises the lands owned by Kings and Queens since the Norman Conquest of 1066, and in some cases earlier than that. Throughout the Middle Ages, as the cost of running a more populous and complicated country slowly rose, the money from these lands was used by rulers to fund their personal government, and many estates were given to noblemen in return for their support, particularly when rebellion threatened or weak monarchs had to buy popularity. Through the centuries, the scale of these once-vast Crown lands shriveled. But even today they remain a large holding, worth around £6.6 billion and including everything from forests and farmland to some of the grandest streets in London. The Crown Estate has 450 farms, many acres of Scottish grassland, more than half of Britain's shoreline, all the seabed out to the twelve-mile limit, the quarries that produce the soft white Portland stone so much of grand Britain is built from, great forests in the West Country, and swaths of Regent Street and St. James's in London's West End.

Originally the revenues were simply collected by the Crown, but in 1760 George III agreed to turn them over to his government, in return for a "Civil List" payment from Parliament for his expenses. (From 2000 to 2010, for instance, the Crown Estate paid £1.9 billion into the Treasury.) But this way of operating has enabled MPs to regularly monitor and debate royal spending, which has also provided an opportunity to discuss the monarchy itself. Prince Charles, for one, has long chafed at this oversight and, as one of the higher-spending and more ambitious members of the family, he would prefer that the Crown Estate revenues revert to the royal family, giving them independence from politicians. It's highly unlikely that he will get his wish.

For decades the Civil List was a nagging problem for the Queen and her ministers. Inflation, combined with a more aggressive press, turned the annual increases into, in the words of one insider, "an increasingly painful running sore." Every year there were front-page stories about the Queen's "pay rise" and the extravagance of the Windsors. During the Thatcherite 1980s, for instance, when the rest of Britain was being vigorously evaluated in the name of effi-ciency, many asked why this ancient system was not also being looked at. Meanwhile, the whole issue was becoming confused with the second main source of royal income, the Queen's private wealth, and whether she should pay tax on that.

The royal family's private fortune is a hard-to-disentangle mix of wealth which is theirs, wealth that isn't but belongs to the Crown, and wealth that is somewhere in the middle. The wonderful paint-ings and jewels are the Queen's in the sense that she looks at them and wears them whenever she wants to. But she cannot sell them. They pass down, some for private use, some to be looked at in pub-lic spaces. Castles and palaces range from those never lived in by members of the royal family, to country houses, which are their private property.

The Queen's main source of independent income comes from the Duchy of Lancaster. Dating back to a grant of land made by Henry III in 1265, the Duchy now holds farmland across the north of England, very valuable buildings in London between the Strand and the Thames, offices and shops in a number of other British cit-ies, the tiny Victorian railway station that is featured in Harry Pot-ter films, and much else. Smaller than the Crown Estate, the Duchy's asset value was £323 million in 2009, and it currently pays the Privy Purse (the Queen's account) a little over £13 million a year. Out of this, she now funds all the Royals except for herself, Prince Philip, and the Prince of Wales. (The Duchy of Cornwall, founded by Edward III in 1337, supports the Prince of Wales and his family: its income is slightly higher than that Lancaster's, around £15 million a year. Like the Queen, the Prince cannot make profits by selling Duchy assets.)

The Queen also has private investments, though no one knows

their value. (In 1993 Lord Airlie, then Lord Chamberlain, said on her authority that the lowest figure publicly discussed, £100 million, "is grossly overstated.") But whatever the Queen is worth, polls in the 1990s consistently showed rising public hostility to the Queen's exemption from income tax, leading some to conclude that the Royals were an expensive luxury the country cannot afford.[1] It is not hard to see how dangerous the combination of these feelings, and the unfolding royal family scandals, might have been to the future of the monarchy, at least as a grand and relatively expensive national project. Those years were a genuinely difficult time for the Queen and the mission she had dedicated herself to since girlhood. In the end, however, these financial issues did not cause serious damage to the monarchy, an achievement that can be credited above all to two royal reformers, Lord Airlie and Sir Michael Peat.

David Ogilvy, the 13th Earl of Airlie, is a crucial figure in the story of the royal family toward the end of the twentieth century. A tall, handsome man, immaculately dressed and softly spoken, he is almost entirely unknown to the wider public, which is how he likes it. Airlie, a contemporary of the Queen's, is a Scottish landowner and Old Etonian who served in the Scots Guards during the war, and he has estates in Angus not far from Balmoral. He became a family friend early on and had a long career in banking that ended in November 1984 when he left the chairmanship of Schroders and went to work at the Palace. These were the high days of Thatcher radicalism, and it is hardly surprising that a banker found the monarchy behind the times. The Royal Household's spending was outstripping the Queen's income and she was digging deeper and deeper into a dwindling reserve; looking back, one person who worked for the royal family at the time says, "We were simply running out of money."

Airlie suggested that the Queen call in outside consultants. Peat Marwick Mitchell (now KPMG) were chosen to do "a complete review, top to bottom, with total latitude." For an institution so

used to running on private, traditional lines, this was a big step. But
the man chosen to lead the review, Sir Michael Peat, was much
more than an ordinary bean counter. A product of Eton and Oxford
whose great-grandfather had founded the firm, Peat was bald, lean,
fiercely intelligent and iconoclastic. He too had royal connections;
as a younger man, he had worked with his father on the audit of the
Privy Purse, and like Airlie, he would switch from the world of
finance to work full-time at the Palace. In the summer of 1986, Peat
and Airlie unleashed something like a private Thatcher-era revolution inside Buckingham Palace. If in 2012 the monarchy seems in
good financial shape, that is not all the Queen's achievement: the
Queen's fixers are part of the tale.

By the end of 1986, Peat and his team produced a 1,380-page
report that contained 188 detailed suggestions, from cutting footmen and administrators to cheaper ways of entertaining. "Like a
knife through butter" was how one Palace source described Peat's
effect on the royal finances. In the wake of his report, the Palace canceled bloated catering and transport contracts, ended a slew of petty
corruptions, brought in modern management and better people,
slashed overhead costs, and took back many of the functions then
being run by the government. The members of what was described
as "the country house set" that had been running the Royal Household by and large disappeared.

As one observer put it, the old guard had been nice and charming in their way, with their shoes always polished to a blinding degree
by valets. They were good company at excellent dinners and always
ready to join the royal family for shooting and fishing at Balmoral
or Sandringham. But they had allowed the state to take over more
and more of the job of running the monarchy, resulting in a lack of
independence, energy and enterprise at the Palace, a form of "genteel ossification." In the late 1970s, the Labour prime minister Jim
Callaghan had wanted to fully nationalize the operation of the
monarchy under a special Department for Royal Affairs. Airlie and

Peat were determined to go in the opposite direction and liberate the Royal Household from direct Treasury control. To a degree that has never been fully understood, they privatized the Queen.

They started by negotiating a new deal with the Treasury, which they struck in 1990 during Margaret Thatcher's final months in office. One senior official, who had been involved in earlier rounds of negotiation involving the Queen's finances, insists: "The attitude of the Treasury was not that we wanted to make great savings in the Civil List because frankly it was chicken-feed. This was an establishment manoeuvre to protect the Queen. We wanted to have a Civil List review as rarely as possible." As part of the deal, the Queen agreed to strip the minor Royals from the Civil List and to pay for them herself. From this point on, only she, Prince Philip and the Queen Mother would receive money directly from the Treasury. The rest would be funded from her private income, mainly the Duchy of Lancaster money. Overall, however, the effect was to give Airlie and Peat their chance to take over most royal management themselves. As Airlie put it, "We wanted to be more masters of our own destiny."

Annual deals regarding the Civil List had made it impossible to plan ahead. Both sides, Whitehall and the Palace, decided that a ten-year agreement would be the obvious solution. The major challenge was finding a way to accommodate inflation. Inflation had been rising sharply for several years, and since everyone expected that to continue, the deal was based on the average inflation rate of the previous decade, 7.5 percent. In fact, because inflation fell, the deal was more generous than intended, and the Queen was able to build up a cash surplus of £35 million by 2000. But after the ten fat years came the ten lean, and the surplus—which had been rolled over—proved invaluable.

By the time David Cameron's coalition government looked again at the royal books in 2010, the Queen had received an unchanged annual payment for twenty years. Behind the scenes courtiers were quick to ask what other parts of the state had been able to live within a cash-frozen budget for two decades. But much more important was that for twenty years—years covering the worst crisis for the monarchy since the abdication—the Queen was spared the annual fulmination about her expenditures from the press and republican politicians. Had the reformers not done their work before in the 1980s, the series of disasters experienced by the royal family could have led to a severe downward spiral, which though it wouldn't have meant the end of the British monarchy, it almost certainly would have caused a radical diminishment.

In 1989–90, Airlie and Peat also managed to take back day-to-day control of the major palaces from Whitehall. The Lord Chamberlain now took responsibility for Buckingham Palace, St. James's Palace, Clarence House and Windsor Castle. The cost of running the Royal Household was slashed, while the staff numbers were radically increased. In effect, Peat multiplied the size of the royal machine but spread out the cost, squeezing what he used to call "the inefficiency reserve"—the dripping, bloated costs of mismanagement by government officialdom. For the Royal Household, this change was a big gamble. As one of those involved put it, "We had to collect a team almost overnight. We didn't have anybody—we may have had the odd plumber, but we had to start afresh."

The Queen, acting as chairman, was heavily involved throughout this process. One who worked closely with her during this period says: "The Queen's very businesslike. You send a memorandum and it's back the next day, or certainly within twenty-four hours. She's intuitive and has good judgement; and whenever I go to see her, I have to remember that she has more experience than anybody else and that she knows more than I do. At the end of the discussion, I always felt better. She is very calm, cool and collected about these things."

Airlie made other significant changes to the structure of the Queen's little state-within-the-state. Most important, perhaps, he redefined the role of the Lord Chamberlain, who became a chief executive, or mini prime minister, overseeing a monthly committee of the five heads of the different departments. His role is hard to describe, but it is meant to be a mix of strategic manager, adviser to the Queen, liaison between her and the Prince of Wales, and operations executive. The official job description lists two qualities that are particularly important: the Lord Chamberlain should "have the confidence of the Queen" and take "a wise and balanced approach" to his work.

The job tends to go to a male aristocrat near retirement age. Lord Chamberlains are vague about who exactly recommended them for the position, but they will always have met the Queen before and will be interviewed by her. She told one, "If I am going to do my job, I have to have very good people working for me; and it's got to be a nice atmosphere because if you work in that atmosphere, people want do their best for you." If this makes the work sound genteel, then it is. But if it makes the job sound gentle, then it often is not. Until 1968 the Lord Chamberlain, assisted by former naval officers with conservative views, was responsible for censoring plays. More recently Lord Chamberlains have had to bring the Queen some of the worst news and most difficult decisions about her family, which often involves plain speaking about her sometimes errant children.

Airlie, at the Queen's request, also looked at the other great conundrum, whether she should pay income tax. To start with, Airlie insisted in his conversations with the government that she should not pay inheritance tax for "sovereign to sovereign bequests"; exemption from this tax would ensure that the Crown Estate could pass essentially unaltered from reign to reign. The Treasury agreed, but even today the decision rankles. Further, he proposed that the Queen pay income tax and capital gains tax on her Duchy of Lancaster money, and on her private investments. The government agreed to this proposal as well.

In the end, the cost of the monarchy is not a serious economic issue for the country. Instead, it is a clear indicator of the monarchy's popularity. The old ways of somewhat complacent senior courtiers, excessive numbers of footmen, unchallenged grace-and-favor apartments, and a general vagueness about priceless possessions such as the Royal Collection were not in themselves the problem. But as MPs discovered in the expenses scandal of 2009, what seem comparatively small issues can come close to destroying the reputation of entire institutions.

So what, in the final count, does the monarchy cost the British? In her 1959 book *How the Queen Reigns*, the journalist Dorothy Laird calculated that the government grant to the Queen "amounts to between twopence and twopence halfpenny per person in the United Kingdom each year. That is the cost of one cigarette."[2] On a roughly similar basis—taking into account grants, the Civil List and annuities—what the government describes as its total support for the Queen as head of state (£32.8 million in 2011) now works out to be the cost of two cigarettes. Furthermore, the Queen now pays a large amount of taxes on her private wealth, which she did not do in 1959.

Looking at head count, the amount spent on entertaining, and Royal Household salaries relative to other London-based wages, the Queen today does not operate more extravagantly than before; indeed, less so. The more important point about the cigarette comparison—today it might be more apt to say that the per-person cost is less than half the cost of a cappuccino at a high street chain—is that it is very small, especially when compared to a rough figure of £23,000 as each Briton's current share of the national debt.

During 2010–11, the question of how the British monarchy is financed was revisitied and, once again, the Queen was closely involved. Soon after the election in 2010, Prime Minister David Cameron's office came up with the idea of paying for the monarchy through a percentage of the Crown Estate revenues—15 percent—rather than a specific sum voted every ten years or so by MPs. This would help take the funding decision out of politics. But this approach raised two obvious questions. First, would it have the effect of removing the financing of the monarchy from Parliament's view, thus hiding it from public scrutiny? Second, if the Crown Estates were well run (and they included potentially major new revenues from, for instance, offshore wind farms), might not the Crown become ever richer? To resolve these issues, the Queen agreed that her spending would in future be scrutinized each year by a committee of MPs. And to prevent the Queen or her successor doing too well out of future profits, the monarchy agreed to set up a system of reviews and caps on money held in reserve.

Throughout this review, Palace figures say the Queen was clear that any recipe for future profligacy would be unwise; as one person puts it, "she is very aware that she rules by consent." And the Queen seems unsentimental about money, as evidenced by the fact that she has willingly made big changes—ending the Civil List, agreeing to being taxed and taking more direct responsibility for the Royal Household's spending. Meanwhile, her income from private investments remains important to her—but mainly to finance her continuing involvement in breeding horses and horse racing.

Since the new arrangements agreed to by the Queen will carry over into the next reign, there is a decent chance that the long and vexed question of paying for the British monarchy has finally been settled. But this presumes responsible management of the royal family's finances: if any future monarchy is perceived to be a spendthrift, particularly in hard times, politicians will undoubtedly return to the issue. It's a sign of the times that the monarchy, the finances of which were once nearly a taboo subject, is now scrutinized as if it was just another corporation needing government oversight.

※

PART FIVE

Into the Maelstrom

A wide variety of experienced politicians, civil servants and courtiers who observed at first hand the Queen's relationship with Margaret Thatcher agree: it was (long pause, pained expression) "difficult." Here were two women of similar age but very dissimilar backgrounds; previously strangers, they were conjoined during the most tumultuous and confrontational years of postwar politics.

Among the most radical of the Thatcherite thinkers were some whose contempt for the old, flabby institutions of a weary, over-socialized country reached even to the monarchy. They (naively) tended to see the United States as a model in politics and econom-ics, a briskly invigorating meritocracy where wealth was made, not inherited. They disliked the Queen's tolerance of left-wing dicta-tors in the Commonwealth and had no more patience for the easy life and unchallenged rituals of the court than they did for BBC executives or tenured academics. Ardent young men from think tanks saw "Margaret" as their real queen, and even older gurus of the right, such as Enoch Powell, warned that the Queen's overseas ambition was mere swollen pride. In the 1970s, the Marxist left had derided the monarchy and the Queen had been assaulted on punk T-shirts. In the 1980s, the hostility of right-wing radicals was as serious. In a strange twist, by then many on the left had begun to delude themselves and believe that, deep down, the Queen was secretly on their side.

Margaret Thatcher herself gave no suggestion of anti-Queenism, at least in public. In her memoirs, she said that "stories of clashes between 'two powerful women' were just too good not to make up" and she praised the Queen for her conduct of the weekly audiences. These, said Lady Thatcher, were no mere formality: "they are quietly businesslike and Her Majesty brings to bear a formidable grasp of current issues and breadth of experience."[1] The Tory revolutionary was so punctilious and respectful of her monarch it was almost embarrassing. She curtsied lower than the Queen thought necessary. "It was the starchiest relationship. She was deferential, much too deferential. The Queen was not requiring so much," said one longtime observer. "The Queen had some most amusing and well-observed lines about Thatcher," says a family friend.

Throughout her reign the Queen's relationship with prime ministers had been with men, either older than herself and to be respected, or younger and to be helped by almost maternal listening. Here was someone different. Some senior Whitehall sources believed that there was an early "stiffness" between the Queen and Mrs. Thatcher. Several say that each of them found the choreography of having two women at the apex of British life slightly awkward, which was why they rarely appeared together. There were early and earnest discussions about which of the two should go to which national events. Some officials recall meetings to make sure the prime minister was not wearing a similar outfit to the Queen's; others say no. And Thatcher's refusal to leave with the rest of "the ladies" at the end of dinners caused some discussion before she came to Balmoral; the informality of the outdoor barbecue was an obvious answer.

Fortunately the relationship was helped along by several ice-breakers, none more effective than Denis Thatcher, whose role as prime ministerial consort was not so different from Prince Philip's. He was equally adept at intervening to protect his wife at tricky social moments and making himself scarce when she had state business to attend to. Denis Thatcher got on well with the Queen Mother, enjoyed a drink as much as she did, and was punctilious about royal protocol. This went some way toward making the annual Balmoral visits easier, though unlike other prime ministers, the always-impatient Margaret Thatcher used the trip north to Scotland to get through party business as well. Before arriving at Balmoral, she would visit Tory officials in Edinburgh, stay with Sir Hector Laing, the genial leading elder of Scottish Toryism, at his estate, and perhaps manage a meeting of North East Scottish Conservatives.

This dedication to efficient time management was noted, with some wry amusement, by the Palace. Once Mrs. Thatcher arrived, there was also the problem of entertaining such an uncountrified and work-focused visitor. Asked whether the prime minister would be joining the rest for a walk on the hill, the Queen drily replied, "I think you will find Mrs. Thatcher only walks on the road." And later, when Denis Thatcher suggested to his wife it was time to retire for bed—the Queen has a strict 11:15 p.m. curfew—she apparently replied with a puzzled: "Bed? What we would do up there?"

After a first evening dinner at the main house, a black tie occasion with local guests, the ritual second evening of each Balmoral visit features a barbecue organized mainly by Prince Philip. It takes place at a cottage or sometimes a summerhouse on the estate and begins with the Duke setting off in a Land Rover with a special trailer, ingeniously kitted out with cutlery, plates, glasses, drink and food. "When you arrived there, Prince Philip would be cursing away getting the barbecue going, and the Queen laid out the knives and forks and the equerries got the whisky going, and the seating plan was not at all hierarchical," says one participant.

Prince Philip would arrive with a beautifully cooked but very rare piece of beef, "which didn't suit Margaret at all, she hated rare meat," and the Queen would ensure that she was sitting next to a new, or relatively junior, guest, to put them at ease. Another visitor recalls "feeling as if I was in some kind of virtual reality" where the Queen and Prince Philip were "playing at being normal people."

Once, as the Queen handed around and then gathered in plates, Mrs. Thatcher, upset to see her monarch doing a menial job unaided, kept trying to leap up to help. Eventually the Queen hissed: "Will somebody tell that woman to sit down?" The story seems emblematic of their relationship: a prime minister with a strong sense of authority and deference only trying to help, and a Queen who cannot help feeling irritated by her. A similar story is told about the annual diplomatic reception at Buckingham Palace, a mammoth two-hour affair, crowded and intensely hot. At one of them, Mrs. Thatcher felt faint and had to sit down. The following year, it happened again. The Queen, physically tough and, as one person who was present put it, moving through the crowd "like a liner," glanced over at her prime minister and said, "Oh look! She's keeled over again."

But as Mrs. Thatcher's time in office went on, the Queen became more used to her and a mutual affection steadily grew. A senior Buckingham Palace official at the time recalls being struck by how vigorously they would talk together. Another says: "The Queen always saw the point of Margaret Thatcher. She understood that she was necessary." One longtime courtier remembers hosting a private lunch for the Queen and Lady Thatcher, after the latter's retirement, and finding that "the Queen was much more fond of Margaret than I realized, though amused by her." During the same lunch, when the former prime minister began lecturing the table on how she would be dealing with the unions if she were still in charge, the Queen quietly said, "Well, I think it's time to go." Another former adviser says that the Queen greatly admired her as someone who had fought her way to the top: "As someone who inherited her position, she is interested in meritocrats."

The most interesting question is whether the royal family in any way opposed the principles of Thatcher's conservative revolution. True believers in the government and some on the left always suspected that it did. As evidence, some would point out that Prince Charles was inclined to be interested in urban poverty. Lord Charteris, the private secretary who perhaps knew the Queen best of all his tribe, told the historian Peter Hennessy in retirement: "You might say that the Queen prefers a sort of consensus politics, rather than a polarized one, and I suspect this is true, although I can't really speak from knowledge here. [Regarding that last point, Hennessy thought Charteris was dissembling.] But if you are in the Queen's position, you are the titular, the symbolic head of the country, and the less squabbling that goes on in that country, obviously the more convenient and the more comfortable you feel."[2]

A much harder-edged version of this point of view surfaced in July 1986 in a front-page story in the *Sunday Times*, owned by the Australian-American republican Rupert Murdoch. The Queen's then press secretary, Michael Shea, had given an extensive interview to the journalist Simon Freeman and been so blithe about it that he had boasted to other Buckingham Palace officials there would be something "pretty good" in the paper on Sunday morning. The paper's editor, Andrew Neil, had brought in its veteran political editor Michael Jones to work with Freeman, and the result seemed sensational.

The Queen, the article reported, thought Mrs. Thatcher uncaring, confrontational and socially divisive. More, the Queen had worried about the social fabric of the country during the miners' strike, was unhappy about Britain's agreement to serve as a base for U.S. aircraft during the bombing of Libya the previous year, and did not agree with Mrs. Thatcher over the vexed question of sanctions against apartheid South Africa. (The Queen apparently sided with the pro-sanctions majority of Commonwealth members, not with Britain's prime minister.) The Queen, said the newspaper, was on the warpath: she was "an astute political infighter who is quite prepared to take on Downing Street when provoked." To back up these assertions, the newspaper insisted that its wide-ranging analysis of the Queen's pro-consensus and anti-Thatcherite views had been fully vetted by the Palace, and that the Palace had been well aware that these views would be publicized.

Especially since it touched directly on the Queen's constitutional position, the story caused considerable damage. When it broke, Mrs. Thatcher was in Edinburgh, staying with the Queen at the Palace of Holyroodhouse for the Commonwealth Games, which had been badly disrupted by the decision of many countries to stay away in protest at Mrs. Thatcher's South African policy. The Queen placed Michael Shea between the two of them at dinner. After he had apologized to Mrs. Thatcher, Shea later said, she patted his arm and told him: "Don't worry a thing about it, dear. I know it's a lot of nonsense."

Inevitably, a nasty argument broke out. Shea denied the story completely, saying that reports "purporting to be the Queen's opinions of government policies were entirely without foundation." Neil, for the *Sunday Times*, hit back, and came close to accusing the Queen's private secretary, Sir William Heseltine, of lying about the source of the story—a claim that still rankles in Palace circles to this day. Yet Shea had certainly briefed Freeman. He had not, he later told the historian Ben Pimlott, had a prior briefing with the Queen herself, nor had he heard her criticize the prime minister. Whatever the truth of the matter, it's reasonable to assume that if the Queen had talked bluntly about her feelings toward prime ministers, someone would have overheard her and eventually reported it. One veteran finds it highly unlikely that she would speak so harshly of Thatcher or any prime minister: "She would consider that completely unconstitutional, just out of court." Officials who were in the Palace at the time feel that Shea had a slight tendency to grandstand and had been led to go too far by the wily journalist. But as is the way at the Palace, nothing was said and Shea was never publicly criticized. He did, however, leave the job shortly afterward.

One person who was a close observer at the time agrees that while the Queen was "pro-consensus" and heard firsthand about the difficulties of miners' families and other hard-pressed communities during the days of strikes and riot, she was by no means unsympathetic to Mrs. Thatcher's aims. "The idea of saying that there 'is no such thing as society' is anathema to the royal family. They could never agree to that. But the time had come for a tempestuous force like Mrs. Thatcher and I think the royal family and the Queen particularly, would give her every credit for that."

For the most part, relations between the Palace and Downing Street were good. Mrs. Thatcher's redoubtable and controversial press secretary, Bernard Ingham, was regarded as a real friend by the Queen's advisers. Unlike later Labour prime ministers, Mrs. Thatcher made a point of staying for a whisky or two after her weekly audiences—"though with a certain impatience," says one observer— in order to ensure that Buckingham Palace felt in the loop. By the end of Mrs. Thatcher's time in office, according to courtiers who observed them, the Queen was genuinely sorry to see her go. Indeed, the Queen invited Mrs. Thatcher to join the Order of Merit—a great honor, and one in her personal gift.

৵

During the Thatcher years the biggest single event for the royal family was undoubtedly the wedding of the thirty-two-year-old Prince Charles and Lady Diana Spencer on July 29, 1981. The focus of extravagant press coverage, the wedding came, rather as the Queen's had, during a difficult year. In 1981 it was not postwar austerity but the high unemployment, continuing inflation and social divisions of the early Thatcher period that people needed to be distracted from. And distraction they got.

Diana's arrival on the global stage also marked a new phase in the relationship between the royal family and the media, one that was dominated by the love affair between Diana and the public, with the press as panting middlemen—and it ended, of course, in disaster. Robert Lacey, the journalist and pioneering biographer of the Queen, puts it this way: "I think the reign of Elizabeth II will be looked back on above all in terms not of the particular political crises but of the way in which the monarchy adapted to the media, was nearly brought down crashing down by the media—I'm thinking of what happened at the time of Diana's death—and has since emerged into calmer waters."[3] He argues, rightly, that one can see the entire history of the twentieth-century monarchy in terms of its struggle with the media, from George V's rebranding exercise in 1917, through the abdication crisis, George VI's struggle to master radio broadcasting, and the emergence of a more critical and even impertinent press in the postwar period.

Only twenty when she first came to the attention of the public, Diana was the daughter of parents who had divorced but whose family had multiple royal connections. Her older sister had been married three years earlier to the Queen's assistant private secretary, Robert Fellowes. Prince Charles had briefly dated another sister, Sarah. The Spencers had royal bloodlines of their own that, legitimately and illegitimately, ran back to the Stuarts. They were familiar with the world of hunting, polo and country life. And Diana's father, Lord Spencer, had been an equerry to George VI and to the Queen in her earliest years on the throne.

Diana had no string of previous lovers who might bring embarrassment and cause problems with the Act of Succession. She seemed artless and, to most people's eyes, a perfect choice. He had met her shortly after the murder of Lord Mountbatten when she had told him how sad and lonely he had looked at the funeral, and now the two seemed to be genuinely in love. Charles was serious about marriage as a commitment that would last a lifetime; he also seemed to have no illusions about what a difficult choice he would be for her. The press, of course, would be ravenous, especially since the question of who Charles would finally marry had been a near obsession for years. Sure enough, once Diana visited Balmoral and Sandringham and the story about a possible match was out, she was hounded by photographers and survived by dint of shy smiles and downcast eyes. The Prince was urged by family and friends to make up his mind as quickly as possible, and after only a little hesitation, he had proposed. Yet they met less than two dozen times before they were married.

Later events made hindsight about this marriage one of the few British growth industries left. Prince Charles was not only a dozen years older, but his tastes were much more traditional than most men of his age. He harbored a deep streak of pessimism and had long been close to an early girlfriend, Camilla Parker Bowles, though she had married several years before. He was cultured, sensitive, spiritual and driven by duty, though he hated some of what that involved. Between proposing to Diana and his marriage, he was absent for many weeks on an extended royal tour to Australia and America—just the kind of duty his mother had been criticized for when she had left him behind as a child.

Diana, by contrast, enthusiastically embraced the emotional pop culture of the early 1980s. Her only experience of the outside world was the comfortable one of posh girls in west London, satirized at the time as "Sloane Rangers." She could not possibly know what life as a Windsor would really be like. As a consequence of the substantial differences in their age, interests and background, the success of their marriage would inevitably require an optimistic throw of the dice.

The belief that Charles and Diana's marriage would significantly strengthen the royal family was shared by the Queen and the Duke of Edinburgh, uncountable numbers of fervently monarchist subjects, almost all of the media, and the royal couple themselves. The only political heckles came from the left, who resented the possibility that Mrs. Thatcher's government, then at its pre–Falklands War low, might gain a patriotic boost from the celebrations. In the event, Charles and Diana enjoyed their day as global celebrities—it is estimated that nearly three-quarters of a billion people around the world watched their wedding ceremony—and then continued for some years as an apparently successful couple, producing the next heir, Prince William, with commendable promptness.

The Prince of Wales's story over the next few years became the story of his marriage. Behind that, though, was another story, one that carried at least as much constitutional weight: the Prince of Wales's politics. In the conventional partisan political sense, he has no politics and understandably gets irritated when it is claimed otherwise. He has tried hard all his life to avoid political tags or direct interventions in the main themes of political argument, such as the economy, Britain's membership of the EU, the Iraq War, or the size of the armed forces. He is certainly no socialist. Yet he has strong views on a number of issues—such as the environment—that are close to "real" politics and getting closer by the year. And on those subjects his views have been growing more strongly conservative (in the more literal sense of the word) as he has grown older.

In the Thatcher years, Charles's views brought him into conflict with Tory radicals, rather than socialists, and it was during this period that he developed his habit of writing critical letters to ministers. He also spent increasing amounts of time on his charitable work, above all the Prince's Trust, which led to an association with an outspoken architect named Rod Hackney, who drove the more radical end of the Prince's work. After a conversation on a train between the two of them was leaked and then confirmed to the newspaper by Hackney, Charles found himself in the middle of a serious row. He had, reported the *Manchester Evening News*, become worried that he would inherit the throne of a divided Britain, split between haves and have-nots. This sounded very much like an attack on Britain's radical prime minister, and Mrs. Thatcher's office was furious. Charles apologized to the prime minister but afterward denied the accuracy of the story: writing to Hackney, he said these were "overtly political phrases of a kind I would never, ever use because I know exactly what the political reactions are likely to be . . . it is essential that I operate in this field of community architecture, inner city housing, deprivation etc. by steering my way very carefully through a political minefield."[4]

The Prince may have been chastened but he was not deflected. He continued to push the cause of small business and regeneration, particularly in some of the more deprived black areas, and he badgered Mrs. Thatcher to meet minority community leaders, which she eventually did, though no major initiative followed. During these years, his office was growing in size, he had established his own country base at Highgrove in Gloucestershire, and he was beginning to take a closer interest in the running of the huge farming estates owned by the Duchy of Cornwall. The private meetings between Buckingham Palace staff and Downing Street devoted more and more time discussing and divining the thinking of the Prince of Wales.

The Queen, however, kept herself well away from the controversies of the high noon of Thatcherism. To this day we have no knowledge about whether she sympathized with "the Iron Lady" or her critics in the European Union, nor do we know whether she had qualms about the loss of British—and her—sovereignty to a Brussels-led superstate. Leftish and liberal observers may have convinced themselves that, deep down, the monarch was no Thatcherite. The latex-puppet satirists of *Spitting Image* encouraged that notion by showing her with a Socialist Workers Party badge and a bust of Lenin, which was a good joke. But if the poor state of the Opposition led many to believe that, in some obscure way, the Crown was a buffer to the Crown's ministers, no one could point to hard evidence to support this theory. And the Queen's respect for Mrs. Thatcher was undeniable: when the prime minister lost her job in a dramatic and very public humiliation, the Queen made her feelings of strong sympathy very clear.

THE STORM BREAKS

In the spring of 1987, the Palace press office could have reasonably expected a relatively easy time ahead. The Commonwealth was experiencing problems overseas, but in Britain, these seemed to be golden years for the royal family, a time of renewal and optimism. The press remained entranced by the spectacle of Charles and Diana. Princes William and Harry were toddlers now, and their mother no longer looked so gaunt or unhappy as she once had. The royal couple had performed brilliantly during a tour of the Arabian Gulf the previous autumn, and they would dazzle the media again during their visit to Australia the following January to celebrate the country's two hundredth anniversary.

Prince Andrew, meanwhile, had married an old acquaintance of Diana's, Sarah Ferguson, who with a polo connection to the Royals through her father seemed eminently suitable. Nicknamed "Fergie," she was almost instantly written into the newspapers' Windsor soap opera as the cheerful, unstuffy royal recruit who would become a pal for Diana. When he married in July 1986, Andrew became Duke of York, a title with special meaning for the Queen and Queen Mother since it had been George VI's, and his father's too. Some of those close to the family believe that Prince Andrew, despite his occasional scrapes, has always been the Queen's favorite. Watching the two of them together joking and gossiping, one can easily believe it.

The House of Windsor's self-confident mood was particularly apparent in the decision to make a television show for 1987 under the direction of Prince Edward, the youngest of the Queen's children and an enthusiast about the world of broadcasting. The show, called *It's a Royal Knockout*, was intended to reveal the younger generation of Royals romping and cavorting with celebrities such as Rowan Atkinson, Meat Loaf, and Barbara Windsor, and the proceeds would go to charity. Some senior courtiers, including the Queen's private secretary, William Heseltine, objected to the enterprise but they were overruled.

When the show was broadcast on televison, it was greeted with universally negative press. Princess Anne was particularly embarrassed and Prince Edward, confronted by derisive newspapermen, walked angrily out of the subsequent press conference. This experience ought to have been a warning sign of the dangers of playing a media game without very careful preparation. But the alarms about the generational change in attitude toward the royal family were largely ignored. "There was a general feeling that if it's for charity, it's OK. Frankly, we had got cocky," says one of those involved.

This debacle was soon the least of the monarchy's worries. Behind the scenes, a very dark drama had been unfolding, one that would embroil the House of Windsor in its worst crisis since the abdication and turn these years at Buckingham Palace into a desperate period when firefighting almost overwhelmed reform. The Queen had long been puzzled by Diana's moodiness and odd behavior, yet she and Prince Philip had done their best to welcome her into the family. But Charles and Diana were deeply unhappy, consumed by the long misery of a marriage that was failing. Both were having affairs. Charles was deeply involved with his original love, Camilla Parker Bowles, using aristocratic retreats and silent friends to arrange their trysts. Diana had found solace for her loneliness in James Hewitt, a soldier, and later James Gilbey, a car salesman. The Prince and Princess engaged in terrible arguments, sometimes in the comparative privacy of Highgrove, the Prince of Wales's Gloucestershire retreat, sometimes in front of gossipy outsiders. Rumors and echoes of the trouble began surfacing, but they remained sufficiently vague for the Queen and Duke to ignore what was happening.

According to Jonathan Dimbleby, author of Charles's biography, neither of his parents raised the marital problems, or Diana's behavior, with him. A book by the journalist Anthony Holden, which in 1988 told some of the story, was brushed aside. Not unreasonably, many at the Palace felt that the difficulties would blow over—after all, many marriages go through hard times. "I don't think one could over-estimate the drama of the relationship between the Prince and Princess of Wales; everybody knew there were problems but no one believed that it was going to end as it did," says one senior figure. The royal family's personal troubles finally spilled into the open during 1992. The year began in January with the publication of old but embarrassing pictures showing the Duchess of York on holiday with a Texan friend, Steve Wyatt. Although not explicit, they laid bare how rocky her marriage to Prince Andrew, who was endlessly away on his naval duties, had become. Soon thereafter, Prince Andrew told his mother that his marriage was over.

The truly disastrous story to come was prefigured with more press photos, this time of Diana alone and lonely during a visit to India. Most famously, she was photographed looking forlorn while sitting in front of the Taj Mahal, that monument to married love. Diana had a keen eye for an image and she had effectively collaborated with the press photographers to send a public message.

In March came the formal announcement that the Yorks were to separate. The following month brought the announcement that Princess Anne, the most private and hardworking of the Queen's children, and her husband, Mark Phillips, were to divorce. All this was bad enough, but the real firestorm erupted with the publication in June 1992 of Andrew Morton's book, *Diana: Her True Story*. The book changed everything. And because Diana had collaborated with the writer, not simply with photographers, she had smashed all the old codes of privacy.

Had the Prince and Princess of Wales experienced their marital troubles twenty years earlier, they probably would have been ignored by the media and been given time to try to sort out their problems in the deep quiet of their own home. By the 1980s that reticence was no longer possible, particularly given the readiness of the Princess to talk so openly. She had grown up in the new celebrity-driven media climate, in which public voyeurism and the celebrity exhibitionism were lolling on the same sofa, two kissing cousins. The dangerous urge to be "understood" was one she found irresistible. Later, even Prince Charles—needled and jabbed all his life by a half-amused, half-censorious press—would decide he wanted his side of the story told.

Among Palace officials, 1992 is remembered as the worst time in the history of the modern monarchy—worse even than the very difficult days after the death of Princess Diana in 1997. It didn't help that the story of the failing marriage broke at a time when the press and public wanted a diversion from depressing politics and daily life. Britain was in the teeth of a recession, governed by a prime minister in trouble. Though John Major had confounded the pundits and won a clear mandate on a big national vote, by spring 1992 he was working with a slim majority in Commons and a divided party.

Twenty years on, it is possible to see with greater clarity what the Queen drily described at the time as her "annus horribilis" with greater clarity. The sequence of family breakups; an increasingly intrusive and unforgiving press; the Windsor Castle fire which fueled public debate about the royal finances; a government that was too weak and unpopular to offer much help to a Queen in difficulty—all this was very bad luck. One or two of these events could have been managed easily enough but, like the famous "perfect storm," each amplified the rest. Worse, this consuming crisis seemed to have fallen upon the Queen, if not quite out of a clear blue sky, at least out of a typically English one of light clouds and sunny spells. But that was an illusion: in fact, it was the culmination of fundamental problems reaching back through the previous two decades.

The first of these lay at the heart of the Windsor dynasty. Marriage had been central to the Queen's Christian mission since she addressed the Mothers' Union rally of young wives at Westminster in 1949. As she said at the time: "We can have no doubt that divorce and separation are responsible for some of the darkest evils in our society today." She followed this remark with a trenchant attack on materialism and selfishness. It may be difficult to imagine that some believed that postwar, austerity-shadowed Britain was threatened

by self-indulgence or conspicuous greed, but in those years empha-
sizing the sanctity of marriage probably seemed a safe enough message. After all, in the early years of her marriage the Queen had been
a "fairy-tale princess" in her own right and, as she bore children, she
continued to be portrayed as the ideal of young British motherhood.

Presenting the monarchy as an emblem of personal moral recti-
tude had also followed closely on the "we four" unity of George VI's
time. Inevitably, perhaps, the royal family became a social example
as well as a constitutional mechanism, not least because its political
role had never been substantial enough for true monarchism to thrive.
In the early years of the Queen's reign, all this seemed straightforward enough. Marriage was a sacred bond; anyone who broke it
was considered so heinous that divorcées were kept well away from
the royal enclosure at Ascot or royal garden parties. Even Princess
Margaret had been barred from marrying her first love on strictly
traditionalist grounds. Yet within a few years of that stern decision,
standards were clearly slipping, and by the early 1990s the Windsors
were as afflicted by changed attitudes to fidelity as many other British
families.

By now the Queen's wide-eyed, serious-looking children had
grown into adults struggling with old human dilemmas about how
to be happy. Sexual frankness, the pill, society scandals and relax-
ations of the divorce law were pushing Britain away from the
Christian certainties of the Mothers' Union and toward a world in
which a fulfilling romantic and sexual life was being treated as virtually a human right. Once, the moneyed and aristocratic world
had tended to view lovers and adultery as a price worth paying
when appearances needed to be kept up. Something of those blasé
male attitudes persisted among older Royals such as Lord Mountbatten, who is said to have helped Prince Charles with early trysts.
Now, what had seemed like wise discretion to their parents looked
to a new generation like mere hypocrisy. The post-1960s morality
of authenticity, openness and "being true to yourself" had pushed
aside tact and restraint.

Alongside this had come the utterly changed mood in the press. Buckingham Palace people have tended to blame Rupert Murdoch, often labeled as a "Republican and vulgarian," for this shift. That is not quite accurate: although it is true that his *Sun* and *Sunday Times* newspapers—closely followed by his *News of the World*— were the most aggressive tormentors of monarchy during this period, mockery and intrusive reporting sold newspapers only because public taste had grown coarser or at least less deferential. The *Sun*'s Kelvin Mackenzie might make menacing jokes about "whacking the Germans" (by which he meant the Windsors), but other editors were also publishing both fawningly obsequious columns and savagely destructive news attacks. The Queen herself was almost always seen as beyond reach, though she was occasionally lampooned for not paying taxes or gently mocked by cartoonists. Her children, however, had been demoted to the level of celebrities, meaning they took their place in the endless "set 'em up, knock 'em down" game that chewed up and spat out rock musicians, actresses and television stars.

However persecuted members of the royal family felt, the British press had reverted to its oldest traditions, which are robustly scurrilous. The comparatively self-censoring and high-minded newspapers of the 1930s through to the late 1950s, which the Queen and Duke had grown up reading, were the product of an abnormally serious geopolitical time. Now politicians were once more being splattered with dirt, cackled at and abused—as was anyone else who caught an editor's eye. By breaking the print unions and returning an invigorated press to its pungent origins Murdoch had only changed the industry's economics.

By running a serialization of *Diana: Her True Story* in the *Sunday Times*, Murdoch ensured that Morton's book would receive maximum publicity and inflict maximum damage. An urbane former tabloid reporter, Morton provided an account of serial attempted suicides by the Princess—including one when she was pregnant with the heir to the throne—and of self-mutilation, wrist slashing, and bulimic vomiting. He portrayed a marriage dying because of Charles's infidelity, a collapse hastened by the coldness and mental cruelty of the Windsors. In all, the book delivered a direct, passionate, brutal (and unfair) attack on the Queen, the Duke of Edinburgh and the Prince of Wales, portraying them as dysfunctional to the point of inhumanity.

Vividly written and extremely detailed, the book's most sensational claims were filleted and repeated by the *Sunday Times* in the days following their initial publication of the excerpts. Millions of people, and many other journalists, simply did not believe them. The claims were seen as "too much" and simply could not be true. But before the newspaper published the excerpts, its editor, Andrew Neil, had been convinced by Morton that not only was his book based on a series of reliable sworn statements by friends of the Princess, but that she had directly authorized them to help the writer.

The decision to publish had been approved by Andrew Knight, the head of News International in Britain, and by Rupert Murdoch himself. Some saw it as a republican plot, but this is too narrow a view. Although Murdoch may be no friend of the royal family— nor indeed of other British institutions—this was finally a decision for his editor. Andrew Neil published the serial because this was a huge story that would sell a lot of newspapers. And Neil, who had been the paper's editor for nearly a decade, was fully aware of the storm he was sailing into.

At first the Prince decided not to hit back. He wanted to believe that his wife was not complicit in the book's preparation, or at least that she had been betrayed by overly talkative friends. As the storm howled, the Palace had no idea how to respond; there seemed to be nothing to say. Its first move was to downplay and in part deny Morton's assertions. Next the Palace encouraged Lord McGregor, the then chairman of the toothless Press Complaints Commission, to protest at the "odious exhibition of journalists dabbling their fingers in the stuff of other people's souls in a manner that adds nothing to legitimate public interest in the heir to the throne."

McGregor uttered these words after checking with the Queen's private secretary, Sir Robert Fellowes, who was also the Princess's brother-in-law. McGregor asked Fellowes to confirm that Diana had not been the source for the book; in turn, Fellowes checked with Diana, who assured him that she had not been involved. In fact, she deceived this upstanding and old-fashioned royal servant: she had indeed passed the key material to Morton. Later, she barely tried to deny it. First she staged a public meeting with a former flat-mate who was one of Morton's key witnesses; then, when asked by the Queen's press secretary to sign a statement repudiating the book, she refused to do so. Fellowes, whom the Queen had known since he was a small boy, was put in an impossible position. He apologized to McGregor and honorably offered to resign. Wisely, the Queen turned him down.

As rival editors and others attacked Andrew Neil for irrespon-sibility, intrusion and almost everything else short of high treason, the Princess of Wales had to face the Queen, the Duke of Edinburgh and her husband in private. Fixated by what had gone wrong in her marriage—"the star in her own private movie," as one observer put it—she had not perhaps realized how deep her treachery seemed to the older Royals. Prince Philip, by the accounts of those close to the family at the time, worked hard to help the errant Princess and find ways to mend the marriage. He wrote her kind and perceptive letters, which she then showed to friends and complained about. (Later, the Duke's letters were stolen and published.) Diana also engaged in a detailed correspondence with the Queen Mother, who had many reasons to understand her plight, having been brought into the royal family as a titled commoner herself, and who had suffered setbacks in her early years.

(Sadly, the whole correspondence between Diana and the Queen Mother was destroyed. In 1993 Princess Margaret spent an entire week burning letters and other papers in an effort, she told friends, to clear out the chaotic and "hopeless" state of her mother's writing room, which was full of attaché cases overflowing with letters.

Before taking this task upon herself, Princess Margaret asked the Queen Mother: "Do really want to keep these old things?" After getting a noncommittal response, she had set to with the help of rubber gloves, plastic trash bags, and a pinafore, collecting a treasure trove of royal history and burning it in Kensington Palace's private gardens. Among the items thought to have been destroyed was the manuscript of an ode to the Queen Mother by Benjamin Britten. One writer asked Princess Margaret if by any chance she had found any letters from him? Oh yes, she replied. And had she burned them? Oh *yes*, was the answer.)

Confronted by her heir's broken marriage, the Queen counseled a six-month hiatus. Yet her son believed that separation was inevitable. The final break came over a comparatively minor argument about which parent should have the two young princes during rival weekend breaks at Sandringham and Highgrove. In the months that followed, the Palace tried to respond appropriately to what one senior official called "an unfolding human tragedy," but almost nobody was able to cope. Press officers and officials remember feeling exhausted, beaten down and almost disoriented by the volume of criticism. "It was a complete feeling of being in the bunker, the original bunker mentality," says one. A senior official adds: "It was a wretched business. . . . It went on and on. It was worse than 1997. People got a bit punch-drunk and it stopped one thinking positively."

How could things get worse?

꜀ꙷ꜄

On November 20, 1992, fire broke out in a chapel at Windsor Castle and tore through much of the most historic part of the structure, badly damaging the state dining room and three other key rooms. Paintings and other valuables were saved, but beautiful and ancient furnishings and fabrics went up in smoke. "A horrible November afternoon, dull and drizzly and the fire roaring across, heading for the Queen's apartments," remembers one senior official. "The next week was ghastly," says another. "The Queen was very bruised by the fire. It was her home. It was very close to her, very intimate. I remember going across the Rose Garden carrying Prince Philip's sock drawer." The fire took 250 firemen fifteen hours to control and eventually damaged a hundred rooms.

The Queen had spent her teenage years in the castle, and throughout her life she had spent family weekends, entertained friends and received world leaders there. It meant much more to her than Buckingham Palace, which has always been "the office." After the fire, she was caught by the television cameras, looking stricken. Prince Philip, who was on a visit to Argentina, did what he could to comfort her by telephone. Prince Andrew helped ferry as much of the priceless collection of paintings and furniture out as he could.

An immediate wave of sympathy for the royal family followed the fire, but soon many people began asking who would pay for the repairs. The affable Heritage Secretary, Peter Brooke, prematurely announced that the taxpayer would pick up the bill for the restoration, since the castle had not been insured. But when the cost was estimated at £40 million, the public reaction turned hostile, raising once again the long-running issue of the Queen's wealth. The mood was so angry that the cabinet minister Douglas Hurd delivered a speech warning that the British were in danger of treating their constitutional monarchy as "some trifling toy" that could be tossed about in public debate without causing it harm. "Sex and money; money and sex," says one senior figure, "as in life it always is." The combination was toxic. Had the Morton revelations never happened, it is likely that public sympathy for the Queen's financial position in the wake of the fire would have been greater.

What had really stunned the Palace was the Princess's decision to tell all, which broke a tradition of royal discretion that had lasted, with the solitary exceptions of the Duke and Duchess of Windsor, for centuries. Throughout the Queen's reign she had struggled to negotiate the boundary between public and private. Marion Crawford's betrayal, which upended her childhood in public, still rankled.

In the years since the Palace had been extraordinarily sensitive to the dangers of eavesdropping staff or bribe-taking footmen. Yet at a time when crowns and scepters had lost their luster and human stories were replacing them, the Queen understood that the monarchy was in the popularity business. On one hand, she had been pushed by relatives, including everyone from Lord Mountbatten to Prince Edward, for more openness about "the real Queen," with television companies, authors and journalists demanding to know ever more. On the other, she no doubt fully comprehended the wise words of the great Victorian constitutionalist Walter Bagehot, whom she had studied as a girl and who had warned against letting too much sunlight shine on the magic.

Less than four weeks after the fire, on December 9, 1992, the Palace announced the separation of Charles and Diana. John Major blandly told the House of Commons that the split would have "no constitutional implications." Major went on to say: "The succession to the Throne is unaffected by it . . . and there is no reason why the Princess of Wales should not be crowned Queen in due course. The Prince of Wales's succession as head of the Church of England is also unaffected." Even Major's own staff were unimpressed. One says: "They were making statements such as, 'She can be Queen,' which looking back was complete nonsense. In everyone's mind there was this image of a future Coronation, with Charles and Diana arriving separately."

The Prince, meanwhile, was being blamed particularly for the breakdown, and especially with Camilla Parker Bowles in the background, some MPs were deeply skeptical about his future role as head of the church. Major worked hard to bridge the rift sufficiently to ensure that the Prince and Princess still carried out some official duties together. But his government did not demonstrate the automatic and full-throated support for the battered House of Windsor that would have been expected from previous administrations.

This was hardly surprising. On September 16, 1992, which came to be known in the financial press as "Black Wednesday," the pound had fallen out of the European exchange rate mechanism. In one fell swoop, Major had lost his economic policy and foreign policy, not to mention much of his personal authority. Afterward, he seriously considered resigning as prime minister, and as the fall went on, his position didn't improve much. A Downing Street observer at the time says:

> You were torn two ways. There was to some extent a normal sympathy in a Conservative government for the monarchy . . . but it was a government so battered and knocked about politically that there wasn't spare energy, and a will to go over the top; and there was considerable fear, too much fear, of the media. So because it was a media-driven "annus horribilis," Downing Street in my view pulled its punches and was more responsive to media criticism, for instance on tax, than another government would have been.

The relationship between a constitutional monarch and her prime ministers is symbiotic: the monarchy sometimes needs cover and support from the government, just as the government of the day needs the authority of the Crown. In Britain, their authorities are often indivisible; the monarchy is weakened by weak governments and is given confidence by successful ones. When the Queen greets her prime minister each week, she has a vested interest in that individual doing well. The politics and policies of an elected leader, whether Labour or Tory, matter less than the authority of that leader and thus the authority of the state which the Queen heads. It was the Queen's considerable misfortune that the breakdown of her heir's marriage occurred at the same time as her government, riven by disagreements over Europe and recession, was also unpopular.

That awful year even ended badly: the Queen's 1992 Christmas message was leaked and printed early in the *Sun*. But the following year proved that the Queen and her advisers had not lost their capacity to learn and change in response to bad times. In April 1993 the Crown announced that to help cover the restoration costs of the Windsor fire—a massive program supervised by Prince Philip involving rebuilding and improving parts of the ancient building, as well as straightforward restoration—Buckingham Palace would be opened regularly to the public. Tickets were priced at £8, and originally the scheme was meant to last for just four years. It proved a huge success, drawing around 400,000 people a year and necessitating the development of new facilities and a better Queen's Gallery to show some of her art collection.

What started as a stop-gap measure to raise cash turned into a major new source of income. By 2002, revenue from Windsor Castle and Holyroodhouse, both run by the Royal Collection Trust, totaled nearly £17 million a year. More important, though, was the symbolism of opening the great palaces to visitors. What were once rather stern walls and spiked railings now welcome the curious; chilly old Buckingham Palace now sometimes seems almost cozy. The hideous notion of allowing the public in, which once so affronted Winston Churchill, has proved uncontroversial and popular.

As the shock waves from the Morton revelations continued, however, the feud between Charles and Diana proved anything but cozy, and caused even more controversy. The Prince of Wales decided to hit back by authorizing a biography by his friend the broadcaster Jonathan Dimbleby. Dimbleby was given deep access to the Prince, who provided his private diaries, state papers, and long recorded interviews. *The Prince of Wales* threw new light on Charles's strong political views and his unhappiness about his childhood, but most of the initial attention focused on Charles's account of his failed marriage to Diana and his admission in the book and an accompanying television interview of his ongoing affair with Camilla Parker Bowles.

Charles's decision to cooperate with Dimbleby in the book's preparation was unheard of from a modern Royal. The effect was devastating: when the Queen read through the galley proofs of the book, she was observed to be pink with shock and bemusement. The code of silence, even of dissimulation, when journalists were around had been central to the monarchy's self-protection. But the book completely overturned that long tradition. Not only was the Princess of Wales shown as unbalanced and paranoid, but Prince Charles did further damage by revealing in hurtful detail his thoughts about the failure of his parents in his own upbringing, explained in paragraphs that verged on the cruel. One royal servant, who has long supported and still admires the Prince, described his agreement to collaborate with Dimbleby as the single worst decision of his adult life. Yet again, the monarchy's curtain had been ripped aside, but this time by a future King.

As the scandal unfolded, powerful forces arrayed themselves against one another. The key advisers at Buckingham Palace were men who had had long careers as royal servants, or in Whitehall, or in the City, but who had little experience of the raw end of modern British life. Their watchwords were tact and loyalty. They saw their job as protecting a discreet and cautious Queen who had firmly old-fashioned views; they also took direction from her husband, who for good reasons had a deep suspicion and dislike of journalists. During the good years for the monarchy, they had become complacent. Nothing in their experience could have prepared them for younger members joining the royal family and then conspiring with the press to put the most sensitive private matters into the public arena. Yet had they been paying attention to the fast-changing world of the media, and to the new pressures on more junior members of the family, they might have seen the dangers ahead.

Against them were the journalists, editors and proprietors in the media industry, all of whom competed with one another for survival and felt little obligation to the British establishment. Journalists had been trained to pursue and disembowel celebrities and were using new technologies to steal information. The big newspaper companies were often owned by overseas proprietors who did not live in Britain, and few of their editors had much interest in honors or an association with the monarchy. Now largely a money-driven hierarchy, Britain's press increasingly resembled America's.

THE LIGHTNING STRIKES

The story of Charles and Diana's separation and divorce, and then Diana's other affairs, screamed from newspapers and magazines for more than four years. As the drama continued, the Windsor dynasty was in danger of becoming a sideshow to a soap opera it had spawned and could not control. The Queen and the Duke of Edinburgh suffered through various phases. First they tried to reconcile Charles and Diana. Later, with the rest of the world, they watched and waited to see whether a "separate but allied" life could be sustained by their son and daughter-in-law.

The Queen had few illusions about her son: on this subject she has often been, if not salty, then at least peppery. Lord Hurd, the former foreign secretary, said of her during the "annus horribilis," "I was surprised by the very great frankness with which she would talk about it—the problems—and how different people were coping with them in her family. She would only talk in a group she trusted."[5]

Another who was with the Queen at the time says, "I think she really did go through hell. She found Diana frightfully difficult and was terribly sad when the children were 'protected' from her; and then all the tantrums at Sandringham and so forth, which she couldn't really cope with." The Queen was unused to extreme displays of emotion: aside from her father's famous rages or "gnashes," she had not encountered them before. Diana, showing a remarkable lack of understanding, told politicians that the Queen needed to be persuaded to be more "huggy." The generational gap between what the actress Helen Mirren, who played the Queen in that Oscar-winning film, calls "the noble generation" of buttoned-up public-service Britishness and the country of the late twentieth century had never seemed wider.

Too much of a fairy tale to last: Prince Charles and Princess Diana curtsey to the Queen after their marriage in 1981. (*Getty*)

The future: "Granny" with Princes William and Harry, 1987. (*Getty*)

The lowest point: the Queen waits to make her "annus horribilis" speech at London's Guildhall, after the marriage breakdowns of two of her children and the devastating Windsor fire, 1992. (*Getty*)

Responding to the eruption of grief: the Queen back in London after Diana's death in 1997, when critics accused her of failing to read the national mood. (*Getty*)

A royal website: the Queen goes digital at a school in Brent, 1997. (*Getty*)

The Queen Mother waves to the crowds on her hundredth birthday, watched by the Queen and Princess Margaret. Their deaths, close together, robbed the Queen of two of her closest confidantes. (*Getty*)

The Queen's enthusiasm for the Commonwealth has helped her become a successful head of a nation being reshaped by immigration. London East End crowds during the 2002 Golden Jubilee. (*Getty*)

A genuine triumph, which surprised media cynics: the Queen's portrait in a Golden Jubilee–bedecked Brentford window. (*Getty*)

A golden mist: Terence Cuneo's Coronation portrait. (*Royal Collection*)

Monarchy taken seriously: a sketch by Pietro Annigoni for his famous portrait has an almost Renaissance feel.

(*Royal Collection*)

More informal times: Michael Leonard's popular 1986 portrait of the Queen with her corgi, Spark. (*Credit TK*)

Lucian Freud, the greatest portrait painter of the Queen's reign, insisted on many hours of sitting and was never known to flatter his subjects. (*Royal Collection*)

"I think she loves being Queen," commented one senior politician. The Queen and the Duke of Edinburgh at the Braemar Gathering in Scotland, 2008. (*Getty*)

A military family, as well as a royal one: Prince Harry, Prince Andrew, the Queen, the Duke of Edinburgh and Prince Edward watch an RAF flypast to commemorate the sixtieth anniversary of the end of World War II, 2005. (*Getty*)

Touchy-feely with new friends: Michelle Obama gets personal with the Queen, 2009. (*Press Association Images*)

One of the most significant and moving visits of her long reign: the Queen with the Irish President Mary McAleese in Dublin, 2011. (*Getty*)

All families have troubles, but families mend and grow: the Queen watched by Kate Middleton, the Duchess of Cambridge, at the Garter Ceremony in 2011. (*Press Association Images*)

But what does she think of us? (*Getty*)

Through it all, the Queen carried on with a heavy routine of the usual engagements and the formal turning of the royal year. Her advisers, meanwhile, found it very difficult to exert any control over Diana's behavior. After she moved out of the family home, Prince Charles's Highgrove House, the Palace could cut her out of most royal engagements, and limit her to an apartment in Kensington Palace and a modest office at St. James's Palace. They could not make her go away. Her husband's friends and the "royal set" maintained a frosty, hostile wall of turned backs and unanswered letters. But Diana had her friends too. What remained of wealthy, "society" London divided into two camps, his and hers. And with the boys now at boarding school, Diana became isolated, lonely and dangerous.

Diana's triumphs overseas, including photogenic trips to publicize aid work in Nepal and Zimbabwe, and a notably successful visit to Paris, were depicted by her supporters as rivaling, and upstaging, visits and speeches by her husband. Her office consciously tried to build her up as an autonomous, alternative kind of princess, one who would speak openly about her eating disorders, weep with the bereaved, and clasp the sick. Her emotional openness—or exhibitionism—was completely alien to the Queen.

That would have been difficult enough. But Diana, like Charles, was searching for real love. She was furiously jealous of the boys' nanny, Tiggy Legge-Bourke; later, she was obsessively interested in whether Charles would marry Camilla Parker Bowles. She began a series of affairs, some serious, others not, which were conducted with cloak-and-dagger secrecy but became increasingly dangerous. Partly as a result of her complicity in Andrew Morton's book about her, she was considered fair game by tabloids and foreign magazines in ferocious competition with one another. And Diana encouraged this blood sport: she would leak to one journalist or editor, then find the rest of them infuriated and after her.

Diana was a past mistress of the art of being photographed for a purpose. But now there was a new private army of freelance photographers—known as "paps"—who sold their wares to the highest bidder in a global market. They had no masters who could be summoned for a dressing-down or pleaded with by phone. Editors could use their pictures without explicitly endorsing the behavior needed to get the images. The paps were as aggressive as piranhas; car-chasing motorbike boys, they were skilled at pushing and provoking their subjects to elicit a vivid expression of rage or fear. Pictures of Diana were soon fetching so much that almost anyone who could provide access to her seemed to be willing to accept a bribe.

Hollywood stars have coped with this sort of thing for years, but they are usually surrounded by regiments of bodyguards, minders and the privacy that huge wealth buys. The royal family, similarly, have long had their palaces and protection squads. But although Diana had protection officers too, she was relatively exposed. Worse, she continued to believe that she could play the media. She invited newspaper editors, columnists and executives to Kensington Palace, asked their advice, flattered them and flirted with them. When she met the up-and-coming Labour leader Tony Blair, she boasted to him about her ability to manipulate the newspapers. At a dinner with Blair, Alastair Campbell (Blair's media adviser) and mutual friends in January 1997, Diana said she had now met almost all the important editors. She also spoke about the power of images. "You have got to touch people in pictures. They can take a lot from you, but they can never take away the pictures," she told them.[6]

Obviously taken with Diana, Blair explained that "compassion" would be a key theme of the Labour campaign and said "we had a lot to learn from her." He said later that she offered to advise New Labour—an extraordinary act for someone in her position. He also said he was wary of her, but he acknowledged her shrewd sense for how to handle the media: "Occasionally she would phone and say why such-and-such a picture was rubbish or what could be done better . . . she had a complete sense of what we were trying to achieve and why."[7] Alastair Campbell believed that Diana was pursuing Blair, or at least bedazzled by him. More important, they imagined themselves to be Mistress and Master of the Media Universe, and deluded themselves into believing that journalists could be endlessly manipulated into giving flattering coverage. Both would learn the bleak truth about that, Diana before Blair.

Even in 1995, two years before he became prime minister, Blair felt the Queen had good cause to be worried about Diana, calling her an "unpredictable meteor" in the Windsors' "predictable and highly regulated ecosystem." Diana was trying to radicalize the image of the monarchy, he thought, much as he was trying to change the image of Britain: "For someone as acutely perceptive and long-termist about the monarchy and its future as the Queen, it must have been deeply troubling." As Blair understood, the Queen knew the monarchy had to both stand for tradition and also evolve, but in a steady and controlled way.

Diana's risky game with the press continued. In any given week, she could out-picture and outsmart Prince Charles during private competitions for coverage. But when stories of her possessive and aggressive behavior toward one married man or another hit the papers, she promptly went to war to defend herself—and lost. Then came a book based on letters to her earlier lover James Hewitt, soon known in press shorthand as Love Rat, and stories about other liaisons.

Hoping to turn the tables on Prince Charles and those in the media who had decided she was unhinged, Diana decided to allow Martin Bashir of the BBC's *Panorama* program to interview her in November 1995. It was a decisive moment. She had been advised against it by almost every one of the friends she consulted. Her agreement to be interviewed was kept secret from royal circles; the BBC director general John Birt did not even inform his chairman, Lord Hussey, whose wife was a close friend of the Queen. Birt, who went on to work for Tony Blair, later said that the interview "marked the end of the BBC's institutional reverence, though not its respect, for the monarchy."[8] After recording the interview, Diana informed the Queen that it had taken place, though she gave no further details.

Diana's interview with Bashir was broadcast on Charles's birth-day and watched by 23 million people. In it, Diana cast doubt on the Queen's competence in handling her relationship with her people and suggested that Prince Charles might not be able to adapt to being King. Switching between third and first person, Diana said: "She won't go quietly, that's the problem. I'll fight to the end because I believe that I have a role to fulfil, and I've got two children to bring up." (Diana had played her good mum card often with photogra-phers, taking the boys to theme parks or films; how she thought this was consonant with displaying her marital woes to the world is mys-terious.) After careful practice, she delivered a series of devastat-ing one-liners to the British public—most famously, she spoke about there "being three of us in this marriage" and her desire to be "a queen of people's hearts." During the interview, she admitted to her adulterous affair with James Hewitt, but was not asked about others. Her private secretary, Patrick Jephson, who had been trying to rebuild bridges with the royal family, resigned from his job shortly after-ward.

The Bashir interview was an explosive upping of the ante and a direct challenge to the Queen, as well as to her son. In its immedi-ate aftermath, polling companies recorded large majorities in favor of Diana's decision to participate in the broadcast. She seemed to have "won." Pressing her attack, she libelously mocked Legge-Bourke and then refused to attend the family Christmas at San-dringham.

Finally the Queen decided that things had gone too far and that Charles and Diana should divorce. She talked to John Major and to the Archbishop of Canterbury. At first, Diana refused a divorce, but this was soon followed by a struggle over the terms. She had emotional support from the Duchess of York, then divorcing Prince Andrew, and the tactical support of a bright young lawyer, Anthony Julius. Diana demanded a huge lump-sum settlement—£17 million—plus high annual support. She also wanted to keep the honorific title Her Royal Highness. (Though "HRH" does not mean anything legally, it is a mark of closeness to the Queen, reserved for inner members of the family only. Losing it would mean that she would be formally cast out, and would not, for instance, have to be invited to state occasions.) Eventually Diana won on the money and lost on the HRH. The settlement, formalized in July 1996, forced the Prince of Wales to borrow a substantial amount of money from his mother and gave Diana complete financial independence. It also gave them both something they had not had for many years, the chance for personal happiness.

Diana made it clear that she intended to be a rival, unofficial "royal," and she still had plenty of media and public support behind her. She would now be able to marry whomever she chose, and that person would have a family link to the future King. Her first lover after the divorce was an eminent Pakistani heart surgeon, Hasnat Khan, who ended the relationship after a few months. The second was Dodi al-Fayed, son of the maverick, foulmouthed Egyptian owner of Harrods. Meanwhile, Diana continued to glow as a global star wherever she appeared. She returned quickly to her high-profile charity work with AIDS and leprosy victims, and to her campaign against land mines in Africa. (She told Blair, with icy calculation, that she had "gone for the caring angle.") And she was in no way hesistant to make political mischief, telling anyone who would listen that Charles would never be King and that the Royals were in trouble.

At a time when Labour was making much of the decision not to replace the Royal Yacht and Blair was touting a "modernization" theme that could clearly hurt the monarchy, Diana's assertions caused real anxiety at the Palace. Yet her position was not as strong as it appeared to nervous courtiers. Charles too felt liberated, and he was now openly being seen with Camilla Parker Bowles, who had divorced. Many felt that Parker Bowles could never be Queen; many felt they could not marry. The Queen herself bided her time; somehow the monarchy carried on.

Despite a series of devastating shocks, the House of Windsor had managed to survive. Then came the worst shock of all.

꙳

Diana's death in a Paris tunnel was an accident. True, blame for the accident must be assigned to humans, including the driver of her car and the paparazzi harassing her and Dodi al-Fayed from motorbikes. But she was not murdered. She was not the target of shadowy forces. The events of that dreadful evening were not manipulated by Buckingham Palace, MI6 or the man on the moon.

How can we be so sure? Though it is hard to prove a negative, it is even harder to prove the existence of a conspiracy when, despite extraordinary effort, no one has produced a shred of supporting evidence. Anyone who has seen Buckingham Palace at work cannot possibly believe that the Duke of Edinburgh, say, could order any government body to do anything at all. The conspiracy theories about Diana's death do reflect two realities, however. The first is that she was much loved by millions of people, many of whom took her side in the media war with the Windsors. The second is that her death removed a nagging problem for the British monarchy. Had Diana lived, it is likely that her star would have slowly faded and that she would have lived the life of many wealthy and glamorous women who are not members of the royal family. Her former husband's remarriage would have been more problematic, however, and it's possible that her continued presence could have prevented it. Further, she would likely have been unable to resist taking sly potshots at Buckingham Palace, or offering unhelpful "advice."

All of which is speculation, because Diana died. Her death on August 31, 1997, shook the British so hard that many became slightly deranged. It was the end of such a bright, vivid life; it happened in such a grisly way; and it came so much out of the blue that it produced rage as well as shock. Not surprisingly, one target for the anger was the media, which had exploited Diana's troubles endlessly. In the immediate aftermath of her death, some photographers were spat on and their editors abused. But it was only a short step from blaming the newspapers to blaming the people who bought them for just these kind of stories—and that meant millions of the very people who were angriest.

It was perhaps natural, then, that the public's anger was quickly turned toward a different target. Who had been Diana's enemies in life? Who had stripped her of her royal title? Who had she repeatedly complained of as cold and heartless? The Queen and the Duke of Edinburgh had tried to save their son's marriage; so had the Queen Mother. And Diana was hardly guiltless. No matter: in a remarkably short space of time the Queen herself became the focus of anger, an unprecedented event during her reign. In many quarters, the public mood felt mutinous. The queen of people's hearts had become the anti-queen of the streets.

The real Queen was at Balmoral with her husband and their grandsons during those first days. As usual, they had taken the children to the Sunday church service at Crathie, and the whole inner core of the royal family gathered to help. Charles and Diana's sons were talked to, and walked with, and kept well away from television, newspaper or radio reports that would have upset them. Princess Anne was particularly helpful; so was the Duke. A cocoon was put around the grief-stricken children. Throughout her adult life, the Queen had had to tolerate those who criticized her for not being an active enough parent. (Her critics were often the same people who would have criticized her had she failed to carry out the full round of British and Commonwealth duties.) Now she chose to ignore media-stoked demands for her to travel to London and participate in a kind of state wake; instead, she concentrated on her grandchildren. What was the point of leaving Scotland to go to a closed Palace behind shuttered windows, she asked rather sharply, when she could be looking after the boys?

According to her family, the Queen enthusiastically embraced her role of grandmother, which became more important than ever after the breakdown of her oldest son's marriage. She missed the children who had fled the turreted nest. Princess Anne says of her mother that, having been at the stage "when you think you can't get the children out of the house quickly enough . . . you suddenly realize how quiet it is, and I think she quite missed that part of having children, so the grandchildren were very much enjoyed, all of them." They, and the various nieces and nephews, had delighted in the same places the Queen had loved as a child, and they had taken longer than her own children to distinguish between the Queen as monarch and the woman who was their grandmother.

In London, meanwhile, Prime Minister Tony Blair and his media team observed the public's increasing anger with alarm. Blair later wrote: "The outpouring of grief was turning into a mass movement for change. It was a moment of supreme national articulation and it was menacing for the royal family. I don't know what would have happened if they had just kept going as before. Possibly nothing, but in the eye of that storm, unpredictable and unnerving as it was, I couldn't be sure."[9] Blair identified with people who, when things were done by the book, "couldn't give a damn about 'the book' . . . in fact, thought 'the book' had in part produced the chain of events that led to Diana's death. . . . Public anger was turning towards the royal family."

The Queen's private secretaries remained in close touch with Blair's Downing Street office as they arranged for Diana's body to be brought back to London. They also began to discuss funeral arrangements. During long phone calls about how to arrange a suitable service at Westminster Abbey and what the role of Princes William and Harry should be, the Duke was angrily protective of the boys' interests.

Soon tensions arose between the Queen's advisers and those working with Prince Charles. (Buckingham Palace officials still express private anger at the behavior of Charles's spokesman at the time, Mark Bolland, who in their view seemed to suggest that had it not been for the Prince of Wales, no appropriate or special arrangements would have been made.) By then there had been quite a history of bickering and icy silences between the rival courts. In the end, the Queen's team arranged a special flight to retrieve Diana's body; they also quickly realized that any notion held by the Spencers that this might be a limited, private funeral was impractical. For a day or two, the Palace seemed to have things under control. Lord Charteris, that wise old hand, called up his successor Robin Janvrin to congratulate him: "You're getting this about right."

It was not so. The Queen's advisers were slow to grasp the astonishing scale of public anger. Alastair Campbell, always alert to a new mood in the media, telephoned the Palace and delivered a warning: "I don't know what those journalists are up to but it's something to do with the flagpole." Soon enough, the Palace flag became a small but telling issue. Protocol and long tradition spoke with one voice: only the Queen's flag, the Royal Standard, flew over Buckingham Palace, and then only when the Queen was there. (When she arrives at the Palace, the flag shoots up the pole as she passes through the gates, a ritual of careful observation and timing conducted by the Queen's Flag Sergeant, a soldier from the Household Cavalry.) The Royal Standard never flew at half-mast—or only in theory, if a dead monarch was in the Palace, and the new one was not yet present.

This tradition made no allowance for the demands of public grief following Diana's death, which was given focus by television reports and provocative newspaper headlines. The naked flagpole came to symbolize a chilly monarch. Tear up the stuffy protocol, ordered the *Sun*, and many seemed to agree. Eventually the Queen asked that the Union flag—which had never flown above the Palace— should go up, and fly at half-mast. Thus was a new tradition begun, for it generally flies there now when the Queen is away and is lowered as a mark of mourning, as for instance after the attacks on the World Trade Center in New York.

As huge crowds gathered from Westminster to Buckingham Palace, and at Kensington Palace too, leaving bundles of cellophane-wrapped flowers, impromptu shrines, candles, teddy bears and hand-written cards, courtiers watched and waited. These were very strange days. Sober-looking men who had queued for hours to sign the condolence book at St. James's Palace reported that Diana was "appearing" in a painting of King Charles I. Busloads of people arrived from all over the country and camped out. An undercurrent of hysteria showed itself in the raw and weeping faces and expressions of anger.

One of the Queen's advisers noted the sound of the plastic wrapping on the flowers outside rattling in the wind at night: "it was the most sinister noise." Another returned from holiday to help and found "the nearest to a revolutionary atmosphere that I have ever witnessed. The silence of this extraordinary crowd milling around Buckingham Palace was dreadful. It was a difficult time internally at Buckingham Palace; and a terrible time outside it." Tony Blair made a pitch-perfect and emotional television speech on his way to church: "She was the People's Princess and that is how she will stay, how she will remain in our hearts and our memories forever." But New Labour did their best to help the monarchy get through this critical moment, and there seems to have been no whiff of republicanism from Number Ten. Even today courtiers remain grateful.

In his autobiography, Blair recounts a strange scene that occurred the last time he saw Diana, when she came to Chequers in July 1997. Blair had invited her to discuss what formal role she could play for his "new Britain"—wary he might have been, but he was still enthralled and wanted some of the Diana stardust to rub off. She brought Prince William with her, and the heir to the throne was obliged to play football with the police, staff and Blair family on the back lawn. "Poor bloke," reflected Blair, "I think he wondered what on earth she had brought him for and he didn't much want to play football but, like a good sport, he did." Meanwhile, Blair and Diana walked alone in the grounds while, he says, he challenged her about

Dodi al-Fayed, whom he had not met but felt "uneasy" about. Their conversation was in parts uncomfortable, but the visit ended warmly. Offering a rare glimpse of the role that Diana might have played had she lived, the scene also provides a reminder that Blair clearly felt a strong sense of identification with a celebrity being hunted by media critics. As he put it, either you attempt to feed the beast, or the beast eats you.

༺ঌঌ

Several courtiers were watching from inside Buckingham Palace as the Queen, the Duke and the young princes arrived from Scotland for Diana's funeral. From upper windows they could see the scene: "As the Queen came down in a car you could hear the crowd beginning to clap, and it was a bit ragged at first, and then it became warmer." As the Queen and Duke entered the Palace, they were talking about the crowd and the flowers, remarking on the strangeness of it all and what seemed like so many "*Daily Express* readers"—the heart of traditional Middle England royalism—on the march. And almost as soon as the Queen was back, the mood shifted again. A girl had come forward with flowers as the Queen walked through Kensington Palace. "Are these for Diana?" the Queen asked. "No, Ma'am, for you."

The Queen's speech on the eve of Diana's funeral was untheatrical, calm, even cool. She does not "emote"; no gallery has yet been found that she will play to. But she tried to explain her feelings in a way she never had before. Everyone had been trying "in our different ways" to cope. Along with shock, disbelief and anger, there was also "concern for those who remain." She looked her subjects in the camera's eye: "So what I say to you now, as your Queen and as a grandmother, I say from my heart." She then offered a graceful and carefully worded tribute to Diana as "an exceptional and gifted human being" who in good times and bad was able to smile and laugh, and inspire others by her kindness. Those who listened carefully heard slight barbs about the millions "who never met her, but felt they knew her," which was surely both an acknowledgment of her star quality and a hint that public Diana and private Diana were not quite the same.

Continuing, the Queen said that the royal family had been at Balmoral, where "we have all being trying to help William and Harry come to terms with the devastating loss that they and the rest of us have suffered." Yet the overwhelming message of the short speech was that the Queen had listened, understood and was doing her best to change: "I for one believe that there are lessons to be drawn from her life and from the extraordinary and moving reaction to her death." And she ended with a plea for unity under the Crown. Diana's funeral was a chance "to show the whole world the British nation united in grief and respect."

The speech and other small acts of acknowledgment before and after it—the flag, and then the Queen's own, unexpected, decision to bow her head in respect as Diana's coffin passed—were among the most important acts of her later reign. Diana's funeral was watched by 32 million people in Britain, second only in history—and only just—to the audience for England's 1966 World Cup victory over West Germany. No modern television event can match the effect of the Queen's Coronation (which was watched by 19 million people in Britain), simply because television can never seem so fresh or surprising as it did in 1953, and because the optimism of a country struggling to emerge from postwar austerity cannot be recaptured. But the impact of the funeral was similar in scale—and far bigger, of course, around the now television-saturated globe—than any previous event involving the royal family. Some 3 million people are thought to have gathered in London or waited on the route of the funeral cortege to the Spencer home at Althorp.

After a remarkable, moving and at times bizarre funeral service—which featured a mutinous speech by Diana's brother, Earl Spencer, that enraged Prince Charles and probably angered the Queen—the cause of the Windsors was no longer at question. Princes William and Harry, marching behind their mother's coffin with their father and grandfather, had touched the hearts of the British deeply enough to make the future of the dynasty, in their time, seem secure. The Queen had acknowledged the power and charisma of the most extraordinary woman the Windsors had ever brought into their family circle. The Queen's court style had unbent enough, and in time, to prevent the subrevolutionary atmosphere in the country from going any further.

Had things been done differently—had the flag never flown, the funeral been handled badly, and the Queen declined to explain or discuss—then in all probability, despite Blair's worries, nothing dramatic would have followed. No unruly mob would have stormed of the Buckingham Palace gates, no antimonarchy bill put before the Commons, no outward expressions of disrespect delivered to the sovereign herself. But the institution would have taken a terrible blow. The careful opinion polling done on behalf of the Palace would have brought bad news. Prince Charles might have found himself so unpopular that he would ask himself whether he wanted to try to be King. And the next time an argument about the cost of the Royals arose, it might well have gone badly for them at Westminster. It would have been rust and rubbing, abrading and verdigris—a dulling of the luster, a souring of the taste. In our times that is how monarchies decline.

The days following Diana's death in 1997 were a crucible. In part, they were a collective madness, a form of national hysteria that could never have been sustained for long. But if the Queen had responded poorly, they could have weakened her and her cause. Instead she emerged wiser, perhaps; sadder, certainly; but stronger, too.

THE PEOPLE'S QUEEN

Throughout this period, the Queen's relationship with Tony Blair—who was, after Margaret Thatcher, her longest-serving and perhaps most controversial prime minister—was evolving. One insider, who knows Buckingham Palace and Downing Street well, says the

Queen's relationship with Blair was not especially close. On the simple "Did he stay for drinks?" test, Blair, unlike Major, did not. But
the Queen did telephone Blair personally to congratulate him on the
results of the Northern Ireland peace process; as the insider said,
"I thought, I bet she doesn't do this often, and indeed she doesn't."
A senior civil servant at the time characterizes New Labour's attitude
to the monarchy as "complete ignorance, combined with a cheerful
arrogance that they could cope with it . . . they saw themselves as
modernizing people brought in to sweep away the old institutions."
Many in Blair's inner circle were fascinated with the U.S. presidency
and held the belief that the prime minister should become a more
presidential figure, which must have discomfited a constitutional
monarch.

In the early Blair years, the Palace's hunger for information
about this new government was particularly intense. "Buckingham
Palace didn't understand the Blair regime," says a former mandarin. "The Palace is very cut off and it was very hard for outsiders to
understand, for instance, the Blair–Brown feud, that cycle of rage
and fear." The lack of understanding was a two-way problem. In
advance of the 2001 general election, then a date still very much
under the prime minister's control, Alastair Campbell had been
instructed to leak the election's timing. Civil servants reminded
Blair's chief of staff, Jonathan Powell, that constitutionally the prime
minister had to go to the Queen and ask for a dissolution of Parliament; after a startled reaction, Blair hurried off to the Palace. On
another occasion, early on, Blair was reluctant to agree to the timing of a Commonwealth heads of government meeting and the
Queen confronted him. Says a former Whitehall mandarin: "The
Queen can be hugely formidable if she decides to be formidable."

Over time, the Queen impressed her personality upon her New
Labour ministers. On one occasion, the overseas development secretary, Clare Short, apparently left her mobile phone on during an
audience and it started to ring. "Do answer it, dear," said the Queen.
"It might be somebody important." On another, she is thought to

have gently put John Prescott, the distinctly non-monarchist deputy prime minister, in his place—quite literally. As he came over to talk to her, she dropped her voice. Straining to hear her, Prescott leaned down, and seemed to everyone present to have bowed low to his monarch. As for Blair himself, he appeared to enjoy his weekly audiences more and more, to the point where his staff began to tease him about his infatuation. One observer says: "She has phenomenal charm and I think the charm worked."

Blair's memoirs, however, went much further than those of any other prime minister by providing revealing stories about the Queen and what he thought of her. There is a playful quality to them, which did not go down well at Buckingham Palace, funny though some of the tales are. Mr. Blair discussed the routine of his visits to Balmoral, which he called "a vivid combination of the intriguing, the surreal, and the utterly freaky. The whole culture of it was totally alien, of course, not that the royals weren't very welcoming." He gently mocks the valets, the food and the artwork. As for the famous barbecue cooked by Prince Philip, "This, too, is governed by convention and tradition. The royals cook, and serve the guests. They do the washing up. You think I'm joking but I'm not. They put the gloves on and stick their hands in the sink. You sit there having eaten, the Queen asks if you've finished, she stacks the plates up and goes off to the sink."

Later, Blair ruminated over the night of the millennium celebrations at the "Dome" in east London, which did not go well. "I don't know what Prince Philip thought of it all, but I shouldn't imagine it's printable. I suspect Her Majesty would have used different language but with the same sentiment," the former prime minister wrote. During the show, Prince Philip pointed out that the acrobats overhead were working without safety harnesses, and Blair conjured a vision of one of them falling and killing the Queen: "I could see it all. 'QUEEN KILLED BY TRAPEZE ARTIST AT DOME' . . . 'BLAIR ADMITS NOT ALL HAS GONE TO PLAN.' "[10]

A harmless joke, a few pages played for laughs—but it has been a long journey from the adulation of Sir Winston Churchill. As with her other prime ministers, the Queen has kept her opinions about Blair very private. But it was New Labour, badly briefed by the outgoing Major government, that decided not to replace the Royal Yacht and, despite the cooperative behavior when Diana died, it is hard to find evidence of much warmth on either side. The Prince of Wales, meanwhile, has inveighed against political correctness and the blame culture so many times that it is safe to say he was not an unadorned admirer of New Labour. And the Duke of Edinburgh once denied to the writer Gyles Brandreth that he himself was a modernizer: "no, not for the sake of modernizing, like some bloody Blairite, not for the sake of buggering about with things," which is crisply self-explanatory.[11] Later he openly complained about the decision to scrap *Britannia*.

Blair's fantasy of a radically modernized monarchy, rebranded with Diana magic, came to nothing. Yet when one considers how many changes his government introduced that posed questions about the constitution or (like the foxhunting ban) infuriated individual members of the royal family, it is remarkable that the Palace responded with such restraint. New Labour expelled all but ninety-two of the hereditary peers from the Lords in 1999, established a Scottish Parliament and a Welsh Assembly, incorporated much more European law, and argued for abolishing the pound in favor of the euro. The Palace undoubtedly had its opinions, but there were no circumstances in which, under the Queen, it would get into a fight with democratically elected politicians.

This discretion was partly a response to New Labour's behavior toward the monarchy itself: when it came to the milestones that mattered most to the royal family, Tony Blair and his ministers were helpful and supportive. There had been gloomy head shakings about George V's Silver Jubilee, and more of the same about his grand-daughter's twenty-fifth anniversary celebration more than four decades later. In the winter of 2001–2, plenty of naysayers once again predicted a jubilee flop. The *Guardian* spoke of "panic at the palace" about the lack of organized street parties, and said the new Buckingham Palace website "bears a forlorn look. So far it lists a golden jubilee snooker and pool tournament in Plymouth, the planting of an oak in the village of Oxhill, Warwickshire, the planting of a jubilee garden at Cranmore infants' school in Shirley, Birmingham, the placing of small fountains all over London—and precious little else."[12] Palace officials downplayed the apparent lack of enthusiasm and were quoted saying that the number of people who turned out later in the year for the jubilee celebrations would have little bearing on the monarchy's popularity.

The anxiety about the Queen's Golden Jubilee was caused by the continuing reverberations of the disasters in the 1990s. Some feared that the "Cool Britannia" of the New Labour, though already out of fashion, was still a better description of how the country saw itself than was the aging monarchy. Nor did 2002 begin happily for the Queen. In February she lost her sister Princess Margaret, which was more of a blow than it may have seemed to outsiders. Though Margaret's life had been very different, the two sisters kept in close touch, talking almost daily. To this day, the Queen carries in her handbag a worn gold box for her sweeteners given to her by Margaret. One of the mourners at the funeral was the redoubtable Queen Mother; six weeks later, at age 101, she too died.

Neither death can be described as unexpected, but it was a difficult time for the royal family. The Queen's family say both Margaret and the Queen Mother had been essential sounding boards for the Queen. To lose both so quickly, says one member of the family, "was very hard and should not be underestimated." They would have expected her to cope, and she did. Some Palace officials, however, thought that in due course the Queen came to feel liberated, finally seeing herself as the sole Queen and so entering into a new phase of her life.

Prince Charles seemed particularly devastated by the Queen Mother's death, and he spoke more openly and emotionally about his grandmother than he had about anyone else. Her funeral obliged republicans and royal skeptics to think again about the monarchy's role in British culture, just as the Golden Jubilee would later on. The *Guardian*, now the dominant voice of Windsor skepticism, ran a headline that read, "Uncertain farewell reveals a nation divided," and its columnist, Jonathan Freedland, argued that the crowds outside Buckingham Palace were thin, with the queues to sign books of condolence almost nonexistent. Clearly this was no Diana moment. Freedland questioned the official period of mourning, which had been cut from thirteen days to nine: "Perhaps they anticipated the current mood and worried that the nation's grief would not last a fortnight. But is there any guarantee that nine days won't also come to seem excessive?"

In the event, the turnout for the funeral was huge and long lines of mourners queued up to pay their respects. The country's slow initial reaction was perhaps a combination of lack of surprise at the news and the gradual recollection of just how long Queen Elizabeth had served. A media spat fizzed and crackled around the event, as it often did around royal occasions, with the *Daily Mail* leading the attack on the BBC for showing lack of respect when a broadcaster announced the death wearing a burgundy tie rather than a black one. The display of fervent monarchism was becoming a media-created dividing line; while some considered it a sign of deep patriotism, others took it as shallow and meretricious. It was not a division the Palace itself particularly welcomed.

Later that year, the Golden Jubilee celebrations broke records. The only comparison could be with Victoria's Golden Jubilee, but that had occurred so long ago that lamentations about British imperial decline seemed meaningless. The echo of the Victorian Age was dimly audible, however, because the year involved an early royal visit to Jamaica, New Zealand and Australia, and then later on to

Canada. The Queen was greeted by enormous crowds; despite a few protestors, including Rastafarians in Jamaica and French Canadians in Quebec, the tours showed a vast reservoir of affection for the monarch in what had once been Victoria's Empire. But gusts of dissent offered a warning for the future. In New Zealand the prime minister, Helen Clark, declared that the country should become a republic. In Canada, the Queen was welcomed by the deputy prime minister, John Manley, who had said that, after her reign, Canada should end its connection with the monarchy.

Britain itself celebrated the jubilee with the now-customary rituals. The Queen addressed both Houses of Parliament, reflecting on the altered world since 1952. "We must speak of change," she said, "its breadth and accelerating pace over these years. . . . Change has become a constant; managing it has become an expanding discipline." Much of her address was devoted to the themes of stability, the importance of institutions, and the nature of the British themselves—"a moderate, pragmatic people"—which have been constants in her speeches for decades. The jubilee was an attempt to express both the monarchical and populist sides of the national character. There were the beacons, lit around the world this time, 2,002 of them; thousands of street parties; a procession with the State Coach down the Mall, where a million people gathered on the jubilee weekend; a service of thanksgiving at St. Paul's; a parade of Commonwealth costumes; and an RAF flypast, watched by the now-diminished royal family from the Buckingham Palace balcony. One of those present said he thought the Queen's expression of relief and pleasure at the success of the jubilee was the genuine reaction of a fundamentally shy woman.

So far, so predictable. This time, though, there was also a classical concert, the "Prom at the Palace" in the gardens of Buckingham Palace. It was the biggest event ever held in the gardens: 12,500 people listened to the BBC symphony orchestra and chorus and a galaxy of operatic stars. More striking, there was a "Party at the

Palace" celebrating British pop music, which was opened by the Queen guitarist Brian May playing his version of "God Save the Queen" from the Palace rooftops, before other gnarled veterans such as Paul McCartney, Eric Clapton and Tony Bennett played in front of the royal family and their guests.

Attempts by the Royals to embrace popular culture have not had a happy record. Something about the conjoining of state formality and youth-centered musical exuberance makes the well-adjusted adult cringe. Even the younger Windsors tend to be grouse shooters, polo players and military officers, which does not mesh well with the music of black and adolescent revolt. But of all the gambles in taste undertaken by the Queen's advisers during the 2000s, this one went off the most happily. Britain was a much more varied, knowing—even cynical—country compared to the Britain of her Silver Jubilee. But the celebrations of 2002, which also included a series of visits that crisscrossed the country, seemed to have firmly reestablished the popularity of the monarchy in general, and the Queen in particular.

⌘

These were the start of the Queen's quieter years, when there was more looking back in affection and less embarrassing turbulence; after the white water, the limpid pool. The year 2006 brought the Queen's eightieth birthday celebrations—a children's party at the Palace, fireworks, a family dinner at Kew, a thanksgiving service at St. Paul's. By now, inevitably, there was more focus on the eventual succession. In February of that year, Prince Charles took the *Mail on Sunday* newspaper to court over the publication of extracts from his personal journals, which he had circulated himself to friends and which were politically highly embarrassing. But the previous year saw a happy milestone in Charles's life: after years of speculation, he married Camilla Parker Bowles in a civil ceremony at Windsor.

Camilla had been divorced from her husband ten years before, but since Diana's death she had endured a difficult twilight status. There was much debate at the Palace and elsewhere about whether remarriage would be acceptable for the heir to the throne and the future head of the Anglican Communion, though the prospect of Camilla continuing as his "companion" seemed an even less appealing alternative. For some time, Charles's staff at Clarence House had been engaged in a careful operation to introduce the idea of Camilla as, first, his companion, and then likely bride. Most noticed the happier demeanor of the Prince of Wales and the down-to-earth cheerfulness of Camilla. Many merely felt sorry for them, regretting that they had not married half a lifetime before. A minority were Diana worshippers who could never forgive Camilla for any role she might have played in the breakdown of the Prince's first marriage, and who were dourly determined to ensure that she would never become Queen.

One observer says that in Buckingham Palace, the Camilla question "was there in the background all the time. There was a lot of private discussion with the Queen about her, and her role, and how much things could or couldn't be acknowledged." Camilla herself became very nervous when the Queen was likely to be present, as did Prince Charles. Even so, he was quietly determined. One senior official, contemplating a move to work for the Prince, was warned that if he wanted to work for the Prince of Wales he had to realize that three things were nonnegotiable. One was Camilla. Another was Charles's press spokesman, Mark Bolland. The third was the prince's factotum and private fund-raiser, Michael Fawcett. Fawcett, who formally left Charles's service but would remain influential, was regarded with particular suspicion by Buckingham Palace.

In general this was not a happy time between the rival establishments. The Queen viewed Prince Charles's extravagant behavior—for instance, when he was entertaining at Sandringham—with puzzlement and worry. The Palace read stories suggesting that, over private dinners at Highgrove, Prince Charles was telling people that his mother really ought to consider abdication before too long. These rumors were vehemently denied by Prince Charles's office, but they caused a lingering hurt.

The position of Camilla, a strong-minded and well-grounded woman, continued to be the central question. Even in the late 1990s, as one Palace observer put it, "there was a very clear view that nobody should be talking about her being the future Queen or even consort." As to remarriage, "the Queen's view was that it was probably going to come; she thought it was probably going to be after her lifetime." At least formally, this had been Prince Charles's view too. Before his divorce from Diana in 1996, his office said he had no intention of remarrying, a position confirmed in 2000.

Since then, however, the situation had become ludicrous. They were a proper couple. Camilla was living at Highgrove with Charles and was supported by him, a fact that had been publicly acknowledged in his financial records and by MPs. The arrangement was understood and accepted by both sets of children. Yet Camilla was not allowed to sit beside Prince Charles at public events and was not, for instance, allowed to join him for the family Christmas at Sandringham.[13] These occasions became extremely awkward for all concerned: if Camilla was present with Charles, the Queen was said to be acknowledging her as his mistress; if not, she was the victim of a "royal snub." By 2000, even as Charles was still claiming that he did not intend to remarry, it's likely that both he and Camilla wanted their marriage to happen.

The Queen's position was extremely delicate. Like her mother, she had enjoyed a strong and happy marriage, and she firmly believed in the sanctity of marriage. As Supreme Governor of the Church of England, she would risk offending many of its members, particularly on the traditional and evangelical wings, if she condoned the remarriage of two divorcees. Yet as Queen she knew that it would be more damaging to the monarchy if Charles succeeded her unmarried, while living with Camilla. Finally, as a mother, she wanted happiness for her son. How was all this to be resolved?

A slow dance began to bring Camilla more into the open. The Church of England itself helped the process along. The Archbishop of Canterbury, George Carey, pointed out that Christianity was about forgiveness and that failure was part of the human condition: "The natural thing is that they should get married." His successor, Rowan Williams, not only agreed but said that Prince Charles's remarriage as a committed Anglican would allow him to become the Church's Supreme Governor. Other clerics made similarly supportive statements. That removed one huge barrier.

The Church's position did not mean that the couple could marry in a conventional church service, however. Eventually Charles and Camilla took what was by then a familiar route, which was to have a civil ceremony, followed by an Anglican blessing. This produced a second problem: would the marriage be legal under English law? The original 1836 Marriage Act allowing civil marriages had specifically excluded members of the royal family, and it was not at all clear that later repeals and rewritings had changed this exclusion. Charles could have got around this obscure-seeming problem by remarrying in Scotland, as his sister Princess Anne had, but he wanted to be married at Windsor. A long and passionate, if ridiculous, debate ensued. Eventually the New Labour Lord Chancellor had to intervene to declare that the government believed that the marriage would be entirely legal. (Ironically, he relied in part upon the same human rights legislation that had often attracted Prince Charles's ire in the past.) As plans for the marriage slowly moved forward, laws and doctrines that had blighted the hopes of Princess Margaret and, before her, of Edward VIII were cast away like bridal confetti.

In recent years the Queen had rarely met Camilla. In 2000 she did so at a lunch Prince Charles gave for the birthday of the former king Constantine of Greece, but this was followed by reports denying that the encounter was evidence that the Queen approved of the relationship. By the time of the Golden Jubilee, relations had eased a lot and Camilla was occasionally being seen publicly with the

Queen. For the next few years, Prince Charles's advisers at Clarence House ran a deliberate campaign to soften up the public and the media to the idea of a wedding, complete with choreographed joint appearances of the couple and much sotto voce briefing.

Even so, preparations for the marriage did not go entirely smoothly. The official announcement was rushed out after a newspaper leak. A plan to hold the wedding in Windsor Castle had to be abandoned when it became clear that this would entitle other couples to apply to be married there too. The original timing of the ceremony had to be postponed because of the death of Pope John Paul II, whose funeral Prince Charles attended. And the rather silly argument about the legal status of the civil ceremony continued almost until the last moment.

The Queen warmly welcomed the marriage announcement. But on the wedding day itself, April 9, 2005, she did not attend the civil ceremony, which had been moved from Windsor to the town's Guildhall. This was not a snub; it was a mark of her strong, traditional faith and her constitutional position. And after the ceremony, the Queen made her feelings plain during a particularly witty and emotionally frank speech. She began with a joke, solemnly explaining that she had an important announcement to make: "Hedgehunter has won the Grand National!" Continuing, she then referred to her son and new daughter-in-law and the formidable fences faced by horses in that legendary horse race: "They have overcome Becher's Brook and The Chair and all kinds of other terrible obstacles. They have come through and I am very proud and wish them well. My son is home and dry with the woman he loves. Welcome to the winner's enclosure."

The Queen could hardly have put it better. These were not the words of a chilly matriarch but of a loving mother who had battled all her life with the chilly demands of constitutional propriety. In turn, and particularly of late, Prince Charles has spoken with genuine warmth and emotion about her—and not simply as Queen, but as his mother.

The marriage concluded what had been a very grim time for the Windsor dynasty, the only part of the Queen's reign when it seemed that the British might actually turn their backs on the monarchy. But because this is a family story, it of course never ends. The gap between the Prince of Wales's office at Clarence House and the offices of his parents at Buckingham Palace has not disappeared. There have been indications that the Prince of Wales's marriage has not been quite as happy as the couple had hoped. When the announcement of Prince William's engagement to Kate Middleton was made in November 2010, Prince Charles's somewhat curt response—"they've been practising long enough"—suggested to some friends that he worried that he was about to be overshadowed again, this time not by his parents or first wife but by the next generation.

Yet important lessons flow from the successful negotiation of the "Camilla problem" during the decade 1995–2005. First, if the weakness of monarchy as an institution is that it depends on the foibles of real families—families that periodically fail—then its strength is that families can also learn, grow, and repair themselves. Second, if the weakness of the British constitution is that it is a jumbled attic of historical artifacts, some of which remain useful while others are antiquated or downright embarrassing, then its strength is that one can rummage through it and pluck out whatever one wants—a new view of an old law here, a shortcut around an awkward doctrine there. And third, though the Queen remains wholly serious about her role, her status and the importance of precedence, she is far more flexible, adaptable and understanding than the official poker face of the British monarchy suggests.

❧

The Queen's next political hurdle came with the British general election of 2010, which followed the most sulfurous and unhappy period in British politics in many years. Parliament had been shaken by a scandal over a large number of MPs who had fiddled their expenses. Some would eventually face jail; many more decided not to stand again. Ordinary people, meanwhile, were struggling in an economic whirlwind caused by the incompetence of highly paid bankers and an addiction to borrowing by both individuals and the state. Britain's elites, in both politics and business, had rarely looked so discredited.

The great banking crisis of 2008–9 plunged the world's financial system into chaos and provoked a long period of slow or zero growth, national bailouts and heart searching—though not the global recession many had feared. The Queen responded with uncharacteristic public bluntness, using a visit to the London School of Economics to ask one of its economists, Luis Garicano, "Why did no one see it coming?" She followed this pointed query by summoning the governor of the Bank of England for a private meeting. Her much-reported question prompted a meeting of economists and others at the British Academy in June 2009, who debated the issue and wrote back to the Queen, "In summary, Your Majesty, the failure to foresee the timing, extent and severity of the crisis and to head it off . . . was principally a failure of the collective imagination of many bright people, both in this country and internationally, to understand the risks to the system as a whole."

The bright man who was blamed by many of Britain's voters, however, proved to be the Labour prime minister, Gordon Brown. The Queen had given him all the attention and personal respect of earlier prime ministers and warmly welcomed his two small boys to stay at Balmoral. But in the wake of the election on May 6, 2010, his party lost 97 seats and its majority. The Conservatives under David Cameron, meanwhile, fell short of the 326 seats they would need to govern alone. The possibility of a "hung" or indecisive result had already been much debated in Whitehall and at Buckingham Palace, because the polls showed it was likely. Memorandums had been drawn up, precedents investigated, but everything hinged on the numbers and the way political leaders behaved. As in 1974, the uncertain outcome raised the alarming possibility that the Queen would be drawn into political controversy, particularly if Brown tried to stay on for long while struggling to put together a coalition to keep out the Tories.

Though the Conservatives had won the most seats, 302, they did not have the automatic right to try to form a government at once. This meant that Brown had not only the right but the duty to stay in office until it was clear that some stable-looking arrangement could be negotiated. But how long would that take? The election result proved that the prime minister had lost the confidence of voters, and the condition of the economy remained horribly fragile. Cameron, meanwhile, had made a generous-seeming offer to the Liberal Democrat leader Nick Clegg and opened talks to form a Tory–Lib Dem coalition, founded on a compromise deal between the parties. Over a long weekend, the haggling on both sides continued, as the markets watched and waited. It was not until the following Tuesday that Brown finally resigned, in a speech of some dignity, having accepted that he could not form a stable administration. The coalition agreement—including a determination to govern for five years, which some thought undermined the Queen's traditional rights over dissolving Parliament—was accepted. The markets recovered.

Behind the scenes, officials at both the Palace and Whitehall exhaled. They had been engaged in intensive discussions about what to do to ensure that the Queen was not under pressure to try to fire one prime minister, or to appear to favor the interests of his successor. At Downing Street, Sir Gus O'Donnell, the cabinet secretary and a man who had served under successive Tory and Labour leaders, led a group of constitutional experts on one side of the debate. At Buckingham Palace, the Queen's team was led by Sir Christopher Geidt, her private secretary since 2007. A former diplomat, Geidt had taken over from Robin Janvrin, now Lord Janvrin. (Janvrin had had to negotiate the most challenging period of the Queen's life, and he was said to see his job as smoothing the latter part of her reign.) Geidt had won the Queen's strong personal confidence and is currently being credited for recent successes.

Geidt and the Number Ten team worked through different scenarios, the constitutional implications of different outcomes, and the circumstances in which it would be necessary to call yet another—no doubt highly unpopular and economically damaging—general election. The press was inclined to be highly critical of any attempt by Gordon Brown to stay in office, and the Queen could have found herself in a very tricky position. But due to close communication and diligent effort by Palace and Number Ten officials, the crisis passed. After it was over, the Queen paid a strictly private visit to O'Donnell's team in Whitehall to thank the civil servants in person.

After the Tory–Lib Dem coalition was accepted, the Queen called for Cameron to serve as her new prime minister. Though a younger man, he was not entirely without royal connections. He attended Heatherdown prep school at Ascot, Berkshire, where he once played a rabbit in a production of *Toad of Toad Hall*. Prince Edward, then eleven, played the part of Mole, and the Queen came to watch the performance. Cameron would be the Queen's first Old Etonian prime minister since Alec Douglas-Home in 1963, and the nineteenth to serve in the job from that school.

Those who think political life will be smooth and untroubled for the Queen are probably mistaken. The new government's defense cuts, which were a crucial part of the new chancellor George Osborne's plan to reduce the national debt faster and further than Labour would have done, produced great unhappiness and argument within the military. Given how connected the Windsors are to the military, the family could not have failed to follow the arguments about aircraft carriers without aircraft and fighter pilots facing redundancy. Senior military figures say privately that they "hope and expect" discreet royal lobbying. And other, equally difficult economic issues are likely to cause continued political disruption, which will inevitably come to the Queen's attention.

OUT OF THE RAPIDS

Friday, April 29, 2011, demonstrated that the British monarchy could still put on a world-class show. The wedding of Prince William to Kate Middleton was pitch-perfect in every way, outclassing even that of his mother and father. Whereas the Charles-and-Diana nuptials in July 1981 had been a fairy-tale event with an uneasy man and a very young, inexperienced girl at its center, a slight swagger of informality marked the occasion nearly thirty years on. Instead of a wedding in grand St. Paul's and a long procession through London, Charles and Diana's elder son was married at Westminster Abbey, which had been decorated with lines of trees. The newly minted Duke of Cambridge drove his Duchess away from Buckingham Palace himself, just the two of them in Prince Charles's green Aston Martin, which had been adorned with a learner's plate and various slogans by his younger brother, Prince Harry. It is hard to imagine his father doing something so relaxed.

As with that earlier wedding, which had been one of the most popular events of the early 1980s, enormous numbers of people poured into central London in advance of the ceremony. Many camped out overnight in order to secure the best spots, just as people had done for the Coronation in 1953 and other royal spectaculars. Despite dire warnings of rain and a cold start to the day, the weather turned out fine and—apart from an errant Guardsman's horse bolting and a verger caught by the cameras turning handstands down the aisle of Westminster Abbey after the guests had left—everything went according to plan. Some criticized the police for arresting a handful of anarchists and protestors ahead of time, but given the very real security risks from Irish republican extremists and others, they could be forgiven and even congratulated on the flawless marshaling of a million people.

Playing to a bigger and better-connected global audience, the wedding was seen by an estimated 2.4 billion people, almost three times as many people as had watched Charles and Diana's. These royal events provide rare national showcases; they determine how the British, like it or not, are viewed in China, California and Chile. The message being sent by this twenty-first-century monarchy was that London could direct a complex, highly sophisticated and visually stunning public event with no mistakes and a certain amount of wit, a year before the Olympics. The richly colored uniforms of the male Windsors and the glamorous, British-made dresses of the bride and her new family added to the Harry Potter effect created by swooping television shots in the gothic, leafy and stained glass—illuminated Abbey. The wedding hardly presented an image of the egalitarian, technocratic nation New Labour had hoped for but then failed to deliver. Nor, however, did it project an image of decline or self-doubt.

The British audience on mainstream television peaked at 24.5 million, while around the country fifty-five hundred roads had been closed for street parties, by now a firm tradition. The great British composer Arnold Bax once told his countrymen they should try everything once, "except incest and folk-dancing." Ignoring half of his warning, many streets were filled with Morris dancers and inebriated English people introducing themselves to their neighbors and trying Scottish reels. The day could be summed up as one of grand pageantry, but pageantry with a slightly informal twist, or a knowing smile. Many people in the crowds wore a T-shirt reading "Thanks for the Day Off" in the same typeface as wartime propaganda posters. Even the most republican of the newspapers, the *Guardian*, cleared most of its news pages for lavish coverage.

William and Kate's wedding was without question a very good day for the Windsors, and it proved that the British reacted as enthusiastically as ever to a happy ending and the prospect of a successfully self-regenerating dynasty. Perhaps the only sour note was that neither of the previous two Labour prime ministers, Tony Blair or Gordon Brown, were invited, though all the living Conservative ones had been. The excuse, which was that they were not members of the Order of the Garter, seemed thin, and some muttered that Clarence House used the occasion to take revenge for Labour's banning of foxhunting and the failure to order a new Royal Yacht. Others found this notion churlish, especially given Blair's help and support for the monarchy after Diana's death.

More generally, Charles and Diana's story had been such a roller-coaster ride for the monarchy, starting so spectacularly and ending so badly, that one of the questions about this wedding was whether it would avoid too many obvious echoes of theirs. The real difference, it turned out, was not in the choice of one location over another, but in the demeanor of the principals. Prince William smiled sheepishly but clearly enjoyed himself; Kate Middleton was poised and self-confident. At key moments, they chatted quietly about how lucky they were, and as they left the Abbey the newly created Duke of Cambridge told his Duchess, "It was amazing, amazing. I am so proud you're my wife." Around them Prince Harry grinned and muttered encouragement. At ease in their skins, these two attractive people had met at what they called "Uni" and were the same age. They had split up and made up. They had lived together—in what used to be called Sin but is now known as North Wales. At twenty-nine, Kate Middleton was old for a royal bride— nearly a decade older than Diana had been—and she would face the inevitable demands to produce an heir quickly. But that extra experience of life had undoubtedly been invaluable, and she seemed already to have the toughness, *savoir-vivre* and staying power that Diana Spencer had struggled to find.

In retrospect, the earlier wedding seemed like a naive explosion of frenetic patriotism at what had been, admittedly, a very difficult moment for Britain. In 2011, the country still faced plenty of problems. In some respects, they had got worse: with spending cuts meant to pay off an oversized national debt constricting the ecomony, and the long war in Afghanistan dragging on, no one could say these were easy times. But the new Conservative prime minister, David Cameron, was at a peak of his authority. Republican hostility to the spectacle of the wedding was so muted as to be almost invisible. The crowds in London were made up of much more than merely royalist sightseers. Overall, they seemed relatively young, and from every background. Had they carried different banners, many could have been at a summer rock festival or even on a march of trade unionists against the coalition government's cuts. Numbers of people in the crowd noted the Queen's expressions of delight as she returned to Buckingham Palace. Some even found it imaginable that there might someday be an Asian or black member of the royal family.

The wedding caused many to express particular pleasure that a middle-class woman had been welcomed into the Windsor embrace. Kate Middleton was not the first commoner in modern times to join the royal family; Lady Elizabeth Bowes Lyon and Lady Diana Spencer had been, strictly speaking, commoners, since they did not have royal blood. But as the daughters of wealthy landowners, the Queen Mother and Diana were not what most Britons would call commoners.

After Kate became romantically involved with William, she and her parents had gone through a long period of testing and apprenticeship in the odd world of royalty, and they had managed to say or do nothing embarrassing, despite teasing from twits and snobs. The Middletons were millionaires, but self-made ones who had built up a mail-order business for children's parties. Kate's father had been a flight dispatcher and her mother, the daughter of a shop assistant, had been an air hostess. Her mother's family was traced back to coal miners who had worked in pits owned by the Bowes Lyons, the Queen Mother's family. Though Kate had been educated at a private boarding school, Marlborough, and was doughtily learning to shoot, stalk and watch polo matches, her world was that of the aspirational, successful middle classes, not of landowners. She was the kind of woman millions of British women could identify with. Young women in the crowd waving signs reading "Harry's mine" were (mostly) joking but could go home afterward and feel the joke was not absurd.

Likewise, Prince William seemed much less removed from everyday life than earlier royals. His education at Eton and St. Andrews University was in some respects more "normal" than his father's or grandfather's. With his younger brother, he has been a regular at high-end London nightclubs, and a circle of affluent friends gives him security and support beyond "the Firm." Nevertheless, he travels in elite circles. At his wedding many of the guests, including the prime minister and the mayor of London, had attended his old school; so had some of the commentators describing the event. None of this need mean very much, so long as care is taken to avoid the impression of a closed ruling class, with morning coats, identical accents and similar views. That would undo the Queen's hard work to ensure she is seen as everyone's monarch—certainly not classless, but not politically tilted either.

For Prince William, the wedding contained messages and dilemmas that he will need to think about during what will presumably be a long apprenticeship before he becomes King. The British are now less class-conscious than ever before and far less formal. Negotiating the right balance between the reserve that royal mystique depends on and the openness that people expect has been difficult for his grandmother and it will be difficult for him. What jokes are acceptable? How does he dress? Which television programs, if any, does he agree to appear on? Should he give interviews to newspapers? Can he go on holiday anywhere other than secure royal estates or remote islands? After he finishes his career as an RAF helicopter search-and-rescue pilot, where will he make his home and how much royal work will he take on in the early years, when with luck he will have a young family to take care of? These are old questions, but for the monarchy they never go away, and the answers slowly, subtly change, generation by generation.

Handling these complex issues will be challenging, but thus far Prince William has demonstrated a sure touch. He is also married to a woman who, having faced a long period of testing by the press, is more streetwise than her predecessors. Some who know him have said that below that surface of smiling normality, Prince William remains coldly angry about the role played in his mother's death by the media. If so, who can fail to sympathize? There are no other obvious scapegoats for what happened. Afterward, his father looked after him and his brother warmly and well, and Charles and his sons now seem to have a good, easygoing relationship. And Prince William seems to be genuinely pleased that his father has found warmth and support from Camilla.

With respect to the press, William has more often calmed his father down, rather than the reverse. At a Swiss ski resort in 2005, unaware of the proximity of microphones, Prince Charles conducted the traditional photocall with a murmured commentary: "I hate doing this. . . . I hate these people." Observing the BBC's royal correspondent, he said: "These bloody people. I can't bear that man. I mean, he's so awful, he really is." All the while, his son urged him to keep smiling and attempted to lighten the mood.

The Duke of Edinburgh was a more open, optimistic man before feeling himself mauled and misunderstood by journalists, and then closing off. The Prince of Wales is said by friends to have been a funny, loving, open character before hitting a wall of hostility in the press, at which point he too shut the door to the media. Can the pattern be avoided a third time? Given the appalling blow of his mother's death, at such a vulnerable stage in his life and in the eye-scorching glare of global publicity, Prince William seems to have emerged as an astonishingly balanced man. But especially since both his grandfather and father have been demonized by sections of the press and public, it is too early to say how he will come to regard the media over time.

The recent phone-hacking scandal may influence his feelings. In 2005 both Prince William and Prince Harry had their mobile phone inboxes hacked into by a private investigator working for Rupert Murdoch's *News of the World*. They had plenty of company: journalists illegally hacked into the phones of hundreds, perhaps thousands, of targets, including those of a thirteen-year-old murdered girl, the bereaved relatives of victims of the July 2005 London bombings, and numerous politicians and celebrities. As public revulsion exploded, it pushed Murdoch into closing his 168-year-old Sunday newspaper, which for much of its life had been the biggest-selling paper in Britain. The scandal rocked the entire Murdoch empire and ultimately involved a number of the journalists and newspapers that had over the years most infuriated the Royals.

The fear of being eavesdropped on, entrapped or betrayed runs deep in the Windsor family, and most of its senior members have been conned or caught out at some time. Greedy or credulous junior Royals have been humiliated publicly, their secrets spilled at the highest levels. Even police protection officers upon whom the Windsors depend so heavily have been drawn into the web of suspicion. And since any senior member of the British monarchy has to live part of his or her life in the public eye, this is not a problem that can be shrugged off.

But it is not a problem for Prince William alone. What happened to the Duke of Edinburgh and Prince Charles—the spite and the jeering in the wake of unflattering media coverage—not only did them damage but also damaged the monarchy. It made them, and thus the monarchy as an institution, less open and more inflexible. If the British value the monarch—and they do—then the media figures who set the tone of at least some of the coverage (Twitter and the blogosphere have democratized much of the rest) must ask themselves whether they are making the country a better or worse place by hounding a future king.

William and Kate are tremendously popular now, but if the history of the modern British monarchy is any guide at all, the mood will at some point change and harder times will follow. Public fury about the behavior of some journalists and newspaper executives in 2011 may bring to an end the free-for-all behavior of the past few decades, especially now that the media itself has become the target of pitiless and unforgiving scrutiny. But scrutiny of the monarchy is unlikely to disappear; deference, and a belief in the virtues of privacy and reticence, will not return to make life easier for future kings and queens.

THE GOOD LIFE

It has been a good life. The Queen has moved among beautiful places and interesting people, and she has always known that she was here for a purpose. Almost every year, season by season, almost exactly the same things must be done, said and performed—Garter days, Maundy services, ambassadors retiring, prime ministers and civil servants to be seen, hospital wings to be opened and Commonwealth visits to be retraced. It is a public life of great predictability and minimal spontaneity. At the same time, it has been a private life with a lot of fun and warmth as well as the odd disaster. She has been an outdoor woman who has bred racehorses, gossiped with close friends, walked, shot and ridden, and been amused, as well as alarmed, by her family.

In her eighties she still rides and still stoutly refuses to wear a helmet. (Her daughter, Princess Anne, points out that for this habit to change, someone would have to be brave enough to suggest to the Queen that she rides unsafely enough to need protection.) Horses have been a refuge for her because they don't know she is the Queen. They are no respecter of rank, only of ability. The Queen and her sister were brought up to tack their horses and untack them, and brush them and pick stones from their feet. As a girl, her rooms were full of toy horses. The Queen's oldest friends remember horse games from the start of her life. One, Margaret Rhodes, has written:

"We cavorted endlessly as horses, which was her idea. We galloped round and round. We were horses of every kind: carthorses, race-horses and circus horses. We spent a lot of time as circus horses and it was obligatory to neigh."[14]

The Queen keeps in her head a great deal of information about the bloodlines of racehorses; she has a good memory for the kind of obscure details that even professional trainers need to check in books. Sadly, Carlton House, her much-fancied runner in the 2011 Epsom Derby (the only Classic she has never won), finished third because of a lost horseshoe. But there is always next year, and life has to offer further challenges. Meanwhile, her husband, now ninety, still rides four-in-hand carriages with verve, a sport that even a much younger man would find dangerous.

The Queen no longer stalks or shoots, but she takes a great interest in those activities as well, padding into the pantries at Bal-moral or Sandringham in the evening to check what has been killed. And as always, she stays on top of her papers. Former civil servants talk when they retire about the pain of "information withdrawal." With "dine and sleeps" at the palaces and the constant comings and goings of well-informed people—not to mention those secret papers—she has never experienced that.

For six decades, the Queen has been looking down from the top of the mast at the whole ship of state. In obvious ways she has been out of touch with daily realities, swaddled by the routine of court life, the constitutional job and the scale of the buildings she lives in. But if she does not carry the money with her head on it, she keeps a close personal eye on royal budgets, the salaries and daily running costs of the monarchy. By touring and talking endlessly to a wider cross section of people than most politicians or journalists ever meet, she is remarkably well informed. She has also done her share of sneaking out—sometimes, it is said, in an old, anonymous-looking brown car, chauffeured by that slightly wild driver, her husband. And she has seen the effects of family breakup at close quarters—rage, abuse, sorrow, regret. So she isn't swaddled, really. In private she can be spontaneously warm, but she never forgets her destiny and, when she needs it, she has a terrifyingly expressionless stare that could halt a tank at twenty paces.

The Queen is blessed with a strong constitution and the calm confidence of someone who knows she is useful. If she lives as long as her mother, she could reign for another fifteen years. That would make her the longest-reigning British monarch, easily outstripping that earlier great Queen, Victoria. The British monarchy remains physically Victorian. The palaces and their decoration still reflect the taste of Queen Victoria; the ceremonial uniform of the Guards remains essentially Victorian; most of the grand events of today are modeled on Victorian predecessors. But Queen Victoria was an empress, whose reign saw her small archipelago of damp, sooty towns and newfangled farms stretch its power across the world. She was Great Britain's figurehead during her confident heyday. Elizabeth II was dealt not this royal flush; her cards have been of a lower order. She has reigned during the final demolition of empire when the republican United States, formed in reaction to British monarchy, became the dominant world power. She may yet live to see China challenge for that role.

Queen Victoria had to do hardly anything to ensure Britain's continued expansion. She was more of an executive monarch, in the sense that she had to transact more of the state's business herself than her great-great-granddaughter. But Elizabeth II has traveled relentlessly to keep alive the spirit of the Commonwealth, the legacy of her imperial ancestress. She works at least as hard at her papers as did Victoria, determined to demonstrate her relevance to the politicians and civil servants who rule in her name. Unlike Victoria, who closeted herself on the Isle of Wight and at Windsor and Balmoral for so long she fomented republican feeling, the present Queen constantly shows herself. Queen Victoria, though a doughty woman, would have demanded smelling salts and headed for home in a carriage had she faced her descendant's schedule.

Being Queen these days is simply a harder job. The Duke of Edinburgh, who has seen the Queen's work at closer hand than anyone else, has reflected that it is a life no one would choose or volunteer for. His own job is not easy either: working behind the scenes to help keep "the Firm" together, he must support the Queen and act as head of the family. He is undoubtedly aware that any danger to the Windsors in the future will come not from political turmoil of the kind that created the dynasty in 1917, but from inside the family as it struggles to live in a fast-moving world of ravenous reporters and eavesdroppers. And Philip is a constant reminder that unlike the bereaved Victoria, Elizabeth has had the great good luck to have a long and happy marriage, which is part of the secret of her success. Like Victoria, she has produced a large family, who have had their share of scrapes. Like Victoria, her heir has had to wait until his own old age for the chance to reign, while struggling to establish an independent role.

The Queen understands that hers is a long-term role. She thinks back to wartime Britain when her father was King, and forward to a Britain of the 2040s when her grandson will reign. The ceremonies the public notice most are the irregular ones, the marriages and jubilees, but the one that matters most is the complicated constitutional pantomime of the State Opening of Parliament, in which the Queen represents the continuing state and therefore also the people who did not vote for the party in power, who loathe the prime minister of the day, or who perhaps did not vote at all. She represents the years and generations before the current government; she also represents the prospective governments to come. The state within her purview lasts far longer than any electoral cycle and its interests, like its people's interests, last longer than a mere government.

The Queen also responds to the mood of the times. When the recent banking crisis hit and the country faced a period of public austerity, the Queen cut the cost of monarchy by £3.3 million, froze salaries and slashed her travel bill. Average salaries at Buckingham

Palace are now lower than in other royal establishments. The Royal Flight, despite its name, is mostly used for military purposes and sometimes for conveying ministers around. The future of the Royal Train, which allows the Queen to stay overnight during visits around Britain and offers rare security, is now in serious doubt. (The Queen has already been seen taking an ordinary train seat to get to Sandringham for her Christmas break.) When Prince William and Kate Middleton made their first visits abroad, to Canada and the United States, they took a fraction of the staff that used to be thought necessary.

The Queen has been able to cast her net of goodwill very widely. She has supported the unsung heroines of the health service and the voluntary groups, the successful companies, the well-run towns. Since the Palace believes that the media, in general, exist to point fingers and criticize, the monarchy tries to correct that balance when it can and celebrate all the less newsworthy things that go right. Why does she endlessly visit small towns, industrial estates, colleges and relatively minor firms? Because nobody else does, and cheering people up is a substantial part of her job.

❦

Long ago, at the time of the Queen's Coronation, a journalist observed that the advantage of monarchy was that it allows people to both kill and keep its rulers, adoring the monarch while kicking out the prime minister. John Selden, one of the leaders of the other side during the great Crown-versus-Parliament confrontation of the seventeenth century, observed that a monarch was a thing people made "for quietness sake." Politically, the Queen has proved the truth of that notion. Despite economic turmoil, overseas war and terrorist violence, her reign has seen no dramatic breakdown of the political order. Swings from left to right, from radical to consensual, have happened with almost boring simplicity.

Critics of monarchy might say that this is precisely the problem. During the Queen's reign, Britain's power in the world—the country's ability to make things, to fully employ its productive energy—has declined. A less stable system might have allowed sharper turns; perhaps the British needed a bigger shock than they got in the second half of the twentieth century. Perhaps as a buffer, a reassuringly durable institution, the monarchy contributed to British complacency.

The Queen has certainly thought about all this. She has hinted in speeches over the years that she takes seriously the criticism, as well as the applause, that monarchy attracts. She has personally challenged policy makers about Britain's economic troubles and its decline as a world power. Closer to home, in family discussions several times a year, she has overseen the corporate strategy of "the Firm."

And the Queen has seen a staggering amount of change. In her lifetime, an Empire has become a Commonwealth; a military monarchy has watched the radical slimming and shrinking of Britain's military forces; an aristocratic system has been taxed and legislated out of existence; a firmly Anglican Christian monarchy has had to adapt to a multifaith and partly atheist country; a "family monarchy" insisting on its role as upholders of morality has been hijacked by adultery and breakup; and Royals brought up to show no emotion in public have struggled to adapt themselves to an exhibitionist, emoting, celebrity-crowded culture. Yet bizarrely, the British monarchy has emerged from all this not shredded and diminished, but strengthened. "The Royals" have been laughed at, dismissed, harangued, lectured and sometimes even ignored. But under the Queen, they have always bounced back.

It is no surprise, then, that accepting the need for constant change is deeply rooted in the family. The Queen has eliminated quite a lot of Royal tradition, from "the Season" to the once inflexible insistence on curtsies and bows. She stopped her children curtsying to her back in the 1960s, and she and her husband are well used to being greeted by a fixed eye and an outstretched hand. Even her voice has changed markedly over the years, becoming less brittle and aristocratic.

Her children have changed, too. Prince Charles, now in his sixties and clearly the most conservative senior Royal since his grandfather died, is a restless man, scratching away at the meaning of his life. His son Prince William appears to be what royal insiders fondly call The Natural—more in touch than his grandmother, less haunted than his father and with a reasonably level temperament. By taking into the family its first middle-class recruit, he is continuing the pattern of restitching the monarchy into the changing social fabric of Britain, the Windsor knit.

Is Elizabeth II the last of her kind? It is hard to imagine another monarch lasting so long on the throne of an important country that has changed as drastically as Britain has. Her life spans the lost and in many ways unhappy interwar years of jazz, depression and empire; the titanic struggle that nearly saw democracy capsized and fascism triumph; and the decades of growing material plenty, punctuated by national nervous breakdown. Her reign has lasted through international crises, from Suez and Vietnam, to Iraq and the "war on terror." When he crowned her, the Archbishop of Canterbury said: "The Lord give you faithful Parliaments and quiet Realms; sure defence against all enemies; fruitful lands and a prosperous industry; wise counsellors and upright magistrates; leaders of integrity in learning and labour; a devout, learned and useful clergy; honest, peaceable, and dutiful citizens." Over sixty years, she may at times have wondered how hard the Lord was listening. For better and worse, she has had to make the most of the politicians, clergy and citizens on offer.

Monarchy continues by acts of individual willpower and choice. Nostalgia makes us susceptible to the notion that the British monarchy has changed little or not at all. But this is hardly the case. From the OBE to the Duke of Edinburgh's Award Scheme, from Trooping the Colour to Facebook and Twitter, the Windsors are always on the move. The Queen's Official Birthday, when Trooping the Colour takes place and an Honors List is published, dates back only to her father's reign. The Maundy Service, so ancient, so cobwebbed by medieval history, was revived by her grandfather in 1932. Garter Day at Windsor, a splendid ceremony featuring the Knights in their ostrich and heron plumes and swaying blue mantels, is as gorgeous a piece of royal ritual as one is likely to see. Although it does indeed date to the reign of Edward III of England—in 1348 he initiated days of feasting and praying for this new order of chivalry—in its current form, after a very long break, it goes back only to the immediate aftermath of the Second World War, when it was revived by the Queen's father.

As the historian David Starkey has written, the mass investitures, which completely fill the Buckingham Palace ballroom, "are the most important and characteristic ceremonies of Elizabeth's monarchy. And they are without any historical roots whatever further back than the Windsor monarchy."[15] Reinventing tradition is a key tactic of the British monarchy.

Sometimes this reinvention is more about the present than the past. After the failure of the first version of the "family monarchy," which was based on traditional morality, the Queen had to produce a new version of it. When the Queen addressed the meeting of the Mothers' Union 1949 and said that "divorce and separation are responsible for some of the darkest evils in our society today," she was speaking to the widespread concern about growing self-indulgence and falling moral standards. She could not make the same speech today. Like millions of other British families, the Windsors found the gap between principle and life too wide. Now, after fracturing and then coming together again in a different form, the new family monarchy appears to be considerably more modern—and thus once again a reflection of the culture around it. Despite all the change, however, the Queen remains true to many of the beliefs she has espoused her entire life. Her annual Christmas broadcasts are shot through with a moral idea of the world, which emphasizes forgiveness, reconciliation and loyalty. In recent years, her bishops notice, they have become more religious, not less.

On the broader meaning of her reign, of course, the Queen does not try to assert herself rhetorically, or advance her case. A succession of image makers—from Cecil Beaton, Pietro Annigoni, Lucien Freud or Andy Warhol in pictures, and Winston Churchill, Richard Dimbleby, Ted Hughes or Gyles Brandreth in words—have provided color and glitter. But given the amount of time and attention paid to the monarchy, there has been precious little intellectual argument made for it, beyond a rather desperate clutch back at Victorian hand-me-downs. The vivid arguments have been on the other side, from writers such as Willie Hamilton and Tom Nairn. The case for monarchy, similarly, needs to be rethought, generation by generation. It cannot afford to become something generally liked but privately acknowledged as inconsequential.

Modern monarchy can be a system that places a family at the top of the social pyramid as a kind of release valve. If they do the job well, their behavior gratifies and pleases many people because it doesn't seriously demean anyone else. The little formalities of bowing, curtsying, and "ma'am"-ing are no longer obeisance to the mighty. They are simple politeness. One man who has worked closely with her says the Queen and the Duke have "the humility of the hereditary principle; because they know they have done nothing to deserve getting to their position, it poses a huge obligation of duty on them, to fulfil this extraordinary thing that has happened to them. It makes them in a funny way dutiful, almost humble." The British electorate, adds one Palace adviser, is prepared to admire the grandness of the British monarchy because it believes its members understand they are as individuals not special: "they want a communism beneath the skin, and that is what she gives them." The more one observes the Queen, the truer this perception feels. She understands that the respect given her is first for the sovereign and only second for the individual, though she must also realize how much her individual service is now admired.

Serving as the British monarch is a vocation for the Queen, but it is also a job. At eighty-five she always knows where the cameras are and always directs her lightbulb-on smiles to them. She dresses to stand out. When it rains, she uses see-through umbrellas so she can be observed and photographed. She is acutely aware of the opportunities and pitfalls for picture making: when visiting Norway to open a British Council exhibition of large, explicit nudes by the painter Lucien Freud, she told one of the organizers that she had spent some time making quite sure "I was not photographed between a pair of those great thighs."

One of the Queen's quiet successes has been her favorable press coverage. In general, the more journalists observe her at work, the more they admire her phlegm and grit. Ann Leslie, a reporter who rarely takes prisoners, says she is amazed at the Queen's readiness to affect an interest in airplane engines and foreign leaders when she would much rather be talking about horses or simply resting. On one sweltering day in Bangkok, Leslie says, "I was watching the jet engine parts makers and they were glowing because they got the impression somehow that, although she was very dignified—and she's not going to gush, because gush is not her default mode—that she really did care about them and their engine parts. And I thought, this woman is bloody brilliant." That experience, multiplied, is the real reason why the Queen has weathered the prejudices of newspaper proprietors and the storms of newspaper wars so successfully.

The Queen loathes being late, not least because punctuality is part of what allows her to be seen by as many people as possible. She has never looked for personal publicity, given interviews or tried to explain her side of the story. She has never "confessed" or reinvented herself. When something hurtful or wrong is reported she bites her tongue. As a young woman she was a global superstar, but she does not play to the media in a gushing way and certainly does not court them. Monarchy is a parade of images—castles, state occasions, flags, anthems, ritual celebrations. But the Queen, in the modern self-conscious sense, has no image.

Yet she is anything but ordinary; after all, there is nothing ordinary about her life, circumstances or sense of duty. She is one of the richest people on the planet, attended by staff from her earliest years, whose private pursuits, from breeding racehorses to shooting, are not ordinary. She had no school education, has no middle-class friends, and has never had to ask herself how to earn money. Nor are her interests middle-class. She may keep her breakfast cereal in Tupperware boxes, watch the same television programs as the rest of the British and enjoy gossip, but as the "fount of honor" she is far more interested in titles, orders, uniforms and decorations than most of her subjects. The royal family lives in a world where precise rankings of this Cross or that Order really do matter—which is not, perhaps, the most engaging feature of the institution.

Still, the Queen is well aware that the grandeur, the gilt and the wealth, the history and the pomp, surround a family that has been accidentally selected by history to fill a special national position. Had ancient battles gone the other way, or now-forgotten people changed their faith, or had different marriages occurred, other people entirely would have been the Queen and the Duke. When was the last time in European history that someone became a monarch purely by virtue of his personal qualities? Napoleon, perhaps—and look how long his dynasty lasted. Chance put this Queen on her throne. In a brutally competitive world, many will find that a kind of consolation. Today, democracy and monarchy are no longer in opposition. Odd as it might seem, they support each other.

Epilogue: The Future

The year 2012 marks the Queen's Diamond Jubilee. The British are good at looking back. Perhaps a little too good: nostalgia is the vice of an old nation. Yet the jubilee does allow stocktaking of a useful kind. Britain has been strongly marked by monarchy. Without the Queen, that odd alliance of fifty-four countries—rich and poor, democracies and despotisms—known as the Commonwealth would probably not exist. Without the survival of her dynasty, the Windsors, there would be no slightly mysterious "Crown" powers used by the British state. It is true that monarchies exist all around the world, from absolute ones in the Arab world to informal family ones in Scandinavia and Spain. But the British monarchy, in its relative wealth and splendor, and its continuing attachment to an important nation, makes Britain a slight oddity among her natural allies and partners—the republics of the United States, France, Germany, India and Pakistan—never mind China, Brazil and Russia.

If we have lived through an American century, then it must have been a republican century too. Passionate royalists play what feels like a trump card, by pointing out various dunderheaded or merely controversial politicians who might have been elected president of a republican Britain instead. Would we have been better off with a president X or Y? It's impossible to know, but we can reasonably guess that we would elect someone whom at least half the nation cordially loathed. After serving his or her term, the British president would then return to civilian life—to join the board of a bank, perhaps, or travel the world charging £50,000 a time for speeches to conferences of plastics manufacturers. We would all know that, and it would not feel the same.

A fair account of the Queen is likely to end up supporting her case, and therefore a case for monarchy. You would have to have an elephant-hide layer of republican resentment to resist. Besides, the scale of reinvention required to turn a monarchy into a republic is only likely after a big break with the past. The United States, rising up as a new nation, was the exception. France, Russia, Germany and China became republics because of some shattering trauma, involving social collapse and revolution. Since no sane person would wish any part of such a trauma on a stable country, it follows that republicanism in today's Britain is a sideshow, an intellectually respectable but dimly theoretical position. The monarchy may fall. A future King or Queen may make such bad decisions, or have such bad luck, that an infuriated country rises up, tears down the state, and insists on a clean break. But if we lose the monarchy, the British will have much worse to worry about at the time.

The monarchy could, however, be radically curtailed. That would probably happen if a future monarch put himself at the center of political argument and then lost it. (Winning the argument, however, could be just as dangerous.) Britain might then choose to draw up a constitution that formally limited the Crown's existence to a few pages of legalese. Parliament could simply take away the traditional lands and wealth that remain as the Crown Estate. Politicians could easily tax the Windsors in such a way that, within a short space of time, they would find themselves severely reduced.

Countries come with history attached, good and bad. What matters is what they make of it. The British monarchy has been impressive and useful because it has been popularly supported— and mostly more popular than the elected government of the day. That has been possible because of its human popularity, and because it is *not* the government of the day. The monarchy has long provided a kind of national bedrock; in turn, for most of our lifetimes, we have had Queen Elizabeth II as a kind of mysterious, half-seen shadow relative of us all.

⤜⳺⤛

What lessons does the Queen's success have for her son? Modesty is one. Her view of her role has been that she is a symbol, and that symbols are better off keeping mostly quiet. After the first excitement of her Coronation she was never the center of a frenzy of national optimism, so she was never in the firing line during a spasm of national self-loathing. If this is a strangely passive record of achievement, one has only to think of what trouble an activist, opinionated monarch might have got into during the 1960s, or the Thatcher years, or when New Labour was going to war in the Middle East.

The lesson of modesty goes deeper. The Queen's style of monarchy has buried much of a sense of self, as we understand that today. Many of us have been brought up, explicitly or not, to believe that personal development and "being oneself" in the most vivid way possible is the highest human good. To develop one's talents, to be successful, to end richer or at least wiser than when one started—in the minds of many, achieving these goals is what gives life meaning. Not for the Queen: professionally and socially, there is nowhere further to go. She finds meaning through vocation or calling. Not so long ago many people defined themselves by their role; whether a farmer or a shoemaker, you were, in essence, what you did. The Queen still is what she does. There is only a little space (though an interesting space) between Queen Elizabeth II and the woman who lives her life.

For her heir, the Prince of Wales, it is very different. He has had to carve out a life, a role, for himself. Prince Charles is a puzzle: well meaning, shrewd, ambitious to do good, he is also a more prickly and self-conscious person than his mother. This may be a problem when he becomes King. We have become used to self-abnegation in our monarch. Prince Charles, already summoning ministers to see him and firing off letters to government departments, is not much in favor of self-abnegation. Indeed, around him there is a new theory of monarchy quietly being discussed, one that suggests that the sovereign ought to serve as the nonexecutive chairman of the national company. In this role, the chairman should challenge, balance and make up for the deficiencies of the rest of the board—those pesky and often incompetent elected politicians who can only think in the short term. If Parliament brings itself into contempt by fiddling expenses or igniting other scandals; if ministers dodge difficult long-term problems; if the public has lost its allegiance to the old political ideologies—why then, a modern monarch may step forward and help.

Over the past sixty years, the Queen has taken a much more cautious attitude. Thoughtful, hardworking, and psychologically shrewd, she has offered politicians a great store of memories about the business of state. She does not sit on the real board, but she is listened to, and provides continuity, in the way that an elderly chairman and onetime founder of a global company might be listened to. The more the "board"—the parliamentary government—is in disrepair, or struggling, the more attentive the listening is. Why does she sit for hours each day, patiently reading her red boxes? It is a question of credibility. If she is to be a good head of state, she must know state's business, just as a nonexecutive chairman must read the paperwork before a board meeting.

Princes Charles, like his mother, is a hard worker, and he too is well practiced at feigning interest, week after week, when out and about. Yet if monarchy has influence, Prince Charles might ask, should it not be used for good? Charles is said to have a plan for his first six months as King. Among other things he might look at the honors system; he might question whether it is still appropriate to invest good citizens with the Membership or Order of a defunct British Empire; he might wonder whether there are a few too many members of the official royal family. We do not know his opinions on these matters but we can be sure he has some, and that he would want to make a mark. As he ages, friends observe, he grows more like his father, who once seemed his opposite. The Duke of Edinburgh, says one who knows them both, is a poetic, sensitive man who has spent his life going to great lengths trying to hide it. The Prince of Wales, by contrast, is a tough, cutthroat, rather ruthless man who goes to great lengths to hide that.

The eventual passing of the Queen will be one of the greatest tests for the Windsor dynasty so far. Outside Britain, one or more countries of which she is head of state—Australia or Canada, for instance—may see the end of her reign as providing the opportunity to shift to native presidencies. Even the Queen's role as Head of the Commonwealth, which she has guarded jealously, does not pass automatically to her heir. It has no constitutional standing and is in the gift of the political leaders of the Commonwealth nations at the time. It may be that her passing will not lead to a break of any kind, but the odds are that it will.

Inside the United Kingdom, a number of changes surely cannot be resisted for long. An obvious one is the Coronation Oath, which at the moment requires the new sovereign to do his utmost to maintain "the Protestant Reformed Religion established by law" and the "doctrine, worship, discipline and government" of the Church of England. Though the proud royal title of Defender of the Faith is an intellectual absurdity that was granted by the Pope to Henry VIII before he broke with Rome—some Defender!—the title has been taken to refer to the defense of Protestant Christianity in its Anglican and Presbyterian forms. And under the 1701 Act of Settlement, Roman Catholics (persons "who shall profess the popish religion") are barred from ascending the throne.

Prince Charles has publicly said that he wants to be a "Defender of Faith" in general, not simply one faith. Indeed, it is hard to see how he could tolerate either the continuing ban on Catholics or the current Coronation Oath. The former is offensive to a strong and important part of the British people; the latter is out of alignment with Charles's sympathy for Islam and other non-Christian faiths. And if Charles does insist that the Oath be revised, that would immediately place a question mark against the continued status of the Anglican Communion as a state church, especially since Anglicanism is already in severe decline.

Prince Charles has already pushed the boundaries of what Royals are supposed to do. He has raised an astonishing amount of money for good causes such as helping preserve rain forests and giving young people a new start. Almost all of this work is done away from the limelight because of his despair about the likely effect of media exposure. Millions of people share his environmental and culturally conservative views, and they are poorly reflected in the ordinary, democratic politics of modern Britain. But it is naive to claim that he stays out of politics. He is a political man, whose political vision usually happens to be rather wider than the current debates at Westminster. He is also not afraid to irritate Downing Street, as he did during both the Thatcher and Blair regimes. More recently, he showed his firm disapproval of Chinese behavior in Tibet by boycotting official visits by the Chinese president.

Here, then, is a man of strong views and considerable energy, albeit not the greatest organizer, who has raised important questions about religion, the environment and human rights, and who has tried to use his unusual position to bring together politicians, business people and campaigners to change things for the better. Thanks to the coalition government headed by David Cameron, the Prince has been given his wish for much greater financial independence, and possibly much greater monarchical wealth, too. As King, he would be in a remarkably strong position. The problem is that he cannot campaign for particular issues in any meaningful way and also be the above-the-fray head of state. As King, his job would be not only to receive a Chinese president, but also to do his best to make the man or woman feel genuinely welcome. As King, if his ministers brought him planned legislation involving, say, wind farms that would blight a part of the landscape loved by sportsmen, he would be required to smile graciously and sign. As King, if his government agreed to a deal with a South American nation that meant further destruction of an invaluable ecosystem, he could say nothing at all.

Could the man who is now Charles, Prince of Wales, stomach being the man who would be King Charles III, or George VII? If a hereditary monarchy means anything, it cannot break its own rules, so it is highly likely that he will succeed his mother. And since Charles long ago distanced himself, physically and emotionally, from the Queen's court, it is also highly likely that his succession would be followed by a dramatic clearing-out of the current Buckingham Palace staff. Some have even put forward the radical notion that the Royal family in his reign might leave Buckingham Palace entirely, leaving it as a kind of grand official government hotel and center for events. The King would base himself not in London, but at Windsor Castle. Whether this happens or not, Charles has a strong desire for his reign to be different, and to make his own way as monarch, just as he has in his current life. One thing is certain: assuming he lives longer than his mother—and he has at times wondered aloud if he will—Prince Charles will become a very interesting King.

Whenever one mentions the word "abdication" at Buckingham Palace, faces wince and mouths tighten. "I don't suppose the Queen has ever entertained the thought," comes the reply. Or: "She doesn't know what the word means." Or, harking back to Uncle David, "The Queen's view is that you couldn't have two abdications in one lifetime." It is not quite true that the Queen has not entertained the thought. She has discussed abdication privately with loyal and very senior figures, though she has gone on to declare against it. For her, if it can possibly be done, the job really is for life. Yet the Queen is a pragmatist. More and more of her work now will be passed over to her son, and to her grandsons too. The formal duties are becoming a little more tiring all the time. She will travel less. Prince Philip, having retired from some of his jobs, has said he wants more time to relax, and as he grows ever older the Queen wants to be with him as much as possible. Should she be unable to carry on in great old age, there is a Regency Act. Some pronounce it "perfectly serviceable" whereas others say it "needs revisiting," but in any case it would allow Prince Charles to dissolve Parliament, give royal assent to bills, and read out Queen's speeches. One source says of abdication, "I wouldn't actually rule it out, at the end of the day. If she got to a point where she was very old, and very tired, it could come to be the sensible view. A lot depends on the public."

It always has. So far, the British public's view of the Diamond Queen is sparklingly, crystal clear. The longer she reigns, in good fettle and spirits, the better for what remains, despite everything, her lucky country.

Notes

Part One: Dynasty Is Destiny:
How the British Monarchy Remade Itself

1. Kenneth Rose, *King George V*, Weidenfeld & Nicolson, 1983, p. 167.
2. James Pope-Hennessy, *Queen Mary*, George Allen and Unwin, 1959, pp. 480–81.
3. Harold Nicolson, *King George V*, Constable, 1952.
4. Frank Prochaska, *The Republic of Britain*, Allen Lane, 2000.
5. Rose, *King George V*, chapter 6.
6. Pope-Hennessy, *Queen Mary*, p. 494.
7. Prochaska, *Republic of Britain*.
8. John Wheeler-Bennett, *King George VI*, St. Martin's Press, 1958, p. 145.
9. Nigel Nicolson (ed.), *The Harold Nicolson Diaries: 1907–1963*, Weidenfeld & Nicolson, 2004, entry for August 17, 1949.
10. Pope-Hennessy, *Queen Mary*, p. 494.
11. Prochaska, *Republic of Britain*.
12. John Gore, *King George V: A Personal Memoir*, John Murray, 1941.
13. J. R. Clynes, *Memoirs*, quoted in Pope-Hennessy, *Queen Mary*, p. 534.
14. Sir Arthur Bryant, *King George V*, Collins, 1936.
15. Edward, Duke of Windsor, *A King's Story*, Cassell & Co., 1951, pp. 132–33.

16. Sir Alan Lascelles, *In Royal Service: Letters and Journals 1920–1936*, Hamish Hamilton, 1989, p. 50.

17. Ibid., p. 88.

18. Ibid., p. 109.

19. Nicolson, *Diaries*, entries for May 25, 1929, and July 10, 1940.

20. King George VI's own words, from a memorandum on the abdication crisis he wrote, and which is reproduced in full in John Wheeler-Bennett's official biography, *King George VI*.

21. Ibid., p. 294.

22. Mark Logue and Peter Conradi, *The King's Speech*, Quercus, 2010, p. 62.

23. Kenneth Rose in *Kings, Queens and Courtiers*, Weidenfeld & Nicolson, 1985.

24. Eleanor Roosevelt's diary, June 9, 1939, Roosevelt archives, quoted in Wheeler-Bennett, *King George VI*, p. 382.

25. From the Broadlands Archive, quoted in Philip Ziegler, *Mountbatten*, Collins, 1985, p. 457.

26. Ibid., p. 680.

27. Wheeler-Bennett, quoted in Harold Nicolson's diary, March 1954: see Andrew Roberts, *Eminent Churchillians*, Weidenfeld & Nicolson, 1994.

28. William Shawcross, *Queen Elizabeth, the Queen Mother: The Official Biography*, Macmillan, 2009, p. 167.

29. Ibid., p. 75.

30. Ibid., p. 165.

31. Ibid., p. 187.

Part Two: Lilibet

1. David Cannadine, interview with author.

2. Harold Nicolson, *Diaries and Letters*, ed. Stanley Olson, part 3, Weidenfeld & Nicolson, 1980, p. 338.

3. Marion Crawford, *The Little Princesses*, with an introduction by A. N. Wilson, Duckworth, 1993, p. viii.

4. William Shawcross, *Queen Elizabeth, the Queen Mother: The Official Biography*, Macmillan, 2009, p. 336.

5. Lady Cynthia Asquith, *The King's Daughter*, Hutchinson, 1937, pp. 96–97.

6. See Philip Eade, *Young Prince Philip*, Harper, 2011, p. 111.

7. Gyles Brandreth, *Philip and Elizabeth*, Century Books, 2004, p. 181.

8. Shawcross, *Queen Elizabeth*, pp. 523–24.

9. Ibid., p. 532.

10. Robert Lacey, *Majesty*, Sphere Books, 1977, p. 179.

11. See Nigel Dempster, *H.R.H. The Princess Margaret*, Quartet Books, 1981, p. 5 onward.

12. Taken from Margaret Rhodes, *The Final Curtsey*, Calder Walker Associates, 2011.

13. See David Cannadine, *The Decline and Fall of the British Aristocracy*, Penguin, 2005.

14. Basil Boothroyd, *Prince Philip, An Informal Biography*, Dutton, 1971, p. 24.

15. Michael Sissons and Philip French (eds.), *Age of Austerity: 1945–1951*, Penguin, 1964, p. 138.

16. Ben Pimlott, *The Queen*, HarperCollins, 1996, p. 170.

17. Elizabeth Longford, *Elizabeth R*, Weidenfeld & Nicolson, 1983, p. 141.

Interlude: The Queen in the World

1. John Wheeler-Bennett, *King George VI*, Macmillan, 1958, p. 722.

2. Robert Lacey, *Majesty*, Sphere Books, 1977, p. 260.

Part Three: The Queen at Work

1. David Cannadine, interview with author.

2. Harold Macmillan, *The Macmillan Diaries: The Cabinet Years*, Macmillan, 2003, p. 140.

3. Private conversation.

4. Lord Moran, *Winston Churchill, The Struggle for Survival: Diaries 1940–65*, entry for May 15, 1954.

5. Macmillan, *Diaries: The Cabinet Years*, p. 208.

6. Peter Hennessy, interview with author.

7. Quoted in Jonathan Dimbleby, *Richard Dimbleby*, Hodder and Stoughton, 1975, pp. 236ff.

8. *The Spectator*, February 27, 1953.

9. Asa Briggs, *Sound and Vision: The History of Broadcasting in the United Kingdom*, vol. 4, Oxford University Press, 1995, pp. 420ff.

10. *Time and Tide*, June 6, 1953.

11. *New Statesman*, June 6, 1953.

12. Dimbleby, *Richard Dimbleby*, p. 246.

13. See the roundup in *Time and Tide*, June 13, 1953.

14. For details, see Harry Hopkins, *The New Look*, Secker and Warburg, 1963, pp. 296–97.

15. *New Statesman and Nation*, May 30, 1953.

16. Macmillan, *Diaries: The Cabinet Years*, p. 208.

17. Moran, *Churchill, The Struggle for Survival*, p. 377.

18. Ibid., p. 399.

19. Macmillan, *Diaries: The Cabinet Years*, p. 150.

20. Richard Cockett, *Thinking the Unthinkable*, HarperCollins, 1994, p. 127.

21. D. R. Thorpe, *Eden*, Chatto & Windus, 2003, pp. 124–5.

22. Robert Lacey, *Majesty*, p. 298.

23. D. R. Thorpe, *Eden*, pp. 584–5.

24. Robert Rhodes James, *Anthony Eden*, Papermac, 1987, p. 595.

25. Elizabeth Longford, *Elizabeth R*, p. 255.

26. Ben Pimlott, *The Queen*, HarperCollins, 1996, p. 332.

Interlude: *Britannia* and the Waves

1. Interview with Alan Titchmarsh for ITV, broadcast May 2011.

Part Four: Off with Her Head! The Queen in the Sixties

1. Ben Pimlott, *Harold Wilson*, HarperCollins, 1992, p. 113.

2. Anthony Howard (ed.), *The Crossman Diaries*, Methuen, 1979, p. 283.

3. Philip Ziegler, *Wilson: The Authorised Life*, Weidenfeld & Nicolson, 1993, p. 214.

4. Peter Hennessy, *The Secret State*, Penguin, 2010, p. xxxv.

5. Peter Hennessy, interview with author.

6. Tony Benn, *Out of the Wilderness: Diaries 1963–67*, Hutchinson, 1987, p. 14.

7. Ibid., p. 55.

8. Ibid., p. 232.

9. Richard Crossman, *The Crossman Diaries*, Hamish Hamilton/Jonathan Cape, 1979, p. 30.

10. Richard Crossman, *The Diaries of a Cabinet Minister*, vol. 2, Hamish Hamilton/Jonathan Cape, 1976, pp. 43–44.

11. Ibid., p. 121.

12. Ibid., pp. 249–50.

13. Ibid., p. 510.

14. Crossman, *Crossman Diaries*, p. 346.

15. Ibid., p. 594.

16. Willie Hamilton, *Blood on the Walls*, Bloomsbury, 1992, p. 15.

17. *Guardian* parliamentary report, December 15, 1971.

18. Ian Smith, *The Great Betrayal*, Blake Publishing, 1997, p. 86.

19. Edward Heath, *The Course of My Life*, Hodder & Stoughton, 1998, p. 483.

20. Sir Anthony Jay, interview with author.

21. See Asa Briggs, *Competition: The History of Broadcasting in the United Kingdom*, vol. 5, Oxford University Press, 1995, p. 917; Cawston's entry in the *Dictionary of National Biography*; and Elizabeth Longford, *Elizabeth R*, Weidenfeld & Nicolson, 1983, pp. 220–21.

22. *New Statesman*, June 17, 1969.

23. *Spectator*, June 28, 1969.

24. *New Statesman* profile, June 27, 1969. Though anonymous, it reads very like the prose of Mr. Alan Watkins.

25. Ann Leslie, interview with author.

26. Harry Arnold, interview with author.

27. Gore Vidal, *Point to Point Navigation*, Little, Brown, 2006.

28. Heath, *The Course of My Life*, p. 308.

29. Ibid., p. 318.

30. Ibid., p. 394.

31. Interview with the author.

32. Philip Howard in *The Times*, June 8, 1977, special edition.

33. Roger Berthoud in *The Times*, June 4, 1977.

34. See Kenneth O. Morgan, *Callaghan, A Life*, Oxford University Press, 1997, p. 511.

35. Timothy Knatchbull, interview with author.

36. Jonathan Dimbleby, *The Prince of Wales*, Little, Brown, 1994, p. 266.

Interlude: Money

1. Ben Pimlott, *The Queen*, HarperCollins, 1996, p. 534.

2. Dorothy Laird, *How the Queen Reigns*, Hodder & Stoughton, 1959, p. 332.

Part Five: Into the Maelstrom

1. Margaret Thatcher, *The Downing Street Years*, HarperCollins, 1993, p. 18.

2. Peter Hennessy, *Having It So Good*, Allen Lane, 2006, p. 235.

3. Robert Lacey, interview with author.

4. Jonathan Dimbleby, *The Prince of Wales*, Little, Brown, 1994, pp. 322–24.

5. Lord Hurd, BBC interview.

6. Alastair Campbell, *The Alastair Campbell Diaries*, vol. 1, Hutchinson, 2010, p. 621.

7. Tony Blair, *The Journey*, Hutchinson, 2010, p. 133.

8. John Birt, *The Harder Path*; see Tina Brown, *The Diana Chronicles*, Century, 2007, pp. 350ff.

9. Blair, *The Journey*, p. 142.

10. Ibid., pp. 148–49 and 260–61.

11. Gyles Brandreth, *Something Sensational to Read in the Train*, John Murray, 2009, p. 649.

12. *Guardian*, January 24, 2002.

13. See Robert Blackburn, *King and Country*, Politico's, 2006, pp. 32–33.

14. Margaret Rhodes, *The Final Curtsey*, Calder Walker Associates, 2011.

15. David Starkey, *Crown and Country*, HarperPress, 2010, p. 492.

Selected Bibliography

There is a vast literature about the Queen and her family. Madness and exhaustion would have followed any attempt—at least by this author—to read everything. The various political and other memoirs and general histories I have used are referred to where they are quoted from directly. But the following is the list of books about the Queen and other Royals that I have found particularly helpful.

Beaverbrook, Lord, ed. A. J. P. Taylor, *The Abdication of King Edward VIII*, Hamish Hamilton, 1966.

Blackburn, Robert, *King and Country*, Politico's, 2006.

Bradford, Sarah, *Elizabeth*, William Heinemann, 1996.

———, *George V*, Weidenfeld & Nicolson, 1989.

Brandreth, Gyles, *Philip and Elizabeth, Portrait of a Marriage*, Arrow Books, 2004.

Brown, Tina, *The Diana Chronicles*, Century, 2007.

Dimbleby, Jonathan, *The Prince of Wales*, Little, Brown, 1994.

Donaldson, Frances, *Edward VIII*, Weidenfeld & Nicolson, 1974.

Eade, Philip, *Young Prince Philip*, Harper, 2011.

Hibbert, Christopher, *Queen Victoria, An Intimate History*, HarperCollins, 2000.

Hoey, Brian, *Mountbatten*, Sidgwick & Jackson, 1994.

Lacey, Robert, *Majesty*, Hutchinson & Co., 1977.

————, *Royal: HM Queen Elizabeth II*, HarperCollins, 2002

Longford, Elizabeth, *Elizabeth R*, Weidenfeld & Nicolson, 1983.

Morton, Andrew, *Diana, Her True Story*, Michael O'Mara Books, 1993.

Pimlott, Ben, *The Queen*, HarperCollins 1996.

Plumtree, George, *Edward VIII*, Pavilion, 1995.

Pope-Hennessy, James, *Queen Mary*, Allen & Unwin, 1959.

Rose, Kenneth, *King George V*, Weidenfeld & Nicolson, 1983.

————, *Kings, Queens and Courtiers*, Weidenfeld & Nicolson, 1985.

Shawcross, William, *Queen Elizabeth, the Queen Mother*, Macmillan, 2009.

Vickers, Hugo, *Elizabeth, the Queen Mother*, Random House, 2006.

Wheeler-Bennett, John W., *King George VI*, St. Martin's Press, 1958.

Zeigler, Philip, *King Edward VIII*, HarperCollins, 1990.

————, *Mountbatten*, HarperCollins, 1988.

Acknowledgments

The book was written while writing and filming a three-part BBC television series about the Queen, which will be broadcast for the anniversary of her accession, in February 2012. It is not, however, "the book of the series," but a separate endeavor. Nor is it in any way officially authorized. The text has been read by the Palace to correct errors of fact but there has been no access to the Royal Archive, nor any restrictions about what I could say. I would, however, like to record my profound thanks to the Queen's helpful, sensible and friendly staff at Buckingham Palace who have opened doors and corrected mistakes. I would like to thank members of the royal family, past and present royal servants, family friends, White-hall officials, many politicians and journalists for their candid help too. Many of them did not want to be identified by name and I have tried to respect all promises of confidentiality. I have not splattered the text with knowing asterisks and the irritating footnote "private information." What follows is based on my best efforts to record facts and views given to me by people in a position to know, and based as well, of course, on some of the vast pyramid of books about the

Queen, her reign and her family that already exist. (Published sources are referenced in the backmatter.)

I could not have written this without the help of the London Library, which is the nearest thing I have to a spiritual home. Nor without the expert help of Gilly Middleburgh or the help and encouragement of the BBC team, including Nick Vaughan-Barratt and Sally Norris. Of the many people who have been particularly kind, I would like to mention the team at the Buckingham Palace press office who have been unfailingly pleasant and helpful; Lord Janvrin and Lord Fellowes, the Queen's former private secretaries; the Earl of Airlie, Lord Luce, Charles Anson; Peter Hennessy, friend and pinnacle of modern British history writing; Sir Gus O'Donnell, Lord Wilson, Lord Armstrong of Ilminster, Lord Turnbull, Mary Francis, Philip Astor; my terrifyingly successful agent, Ed Victor; my wife, Jackie Ashley; Philippa Harrison, who expertly edited the rough manuscript; and the team at Macmillan headed by Jon Butler and Georgina Morley.

Many years back, I would have confidently described myself as a republican. This was mainly because I thought it would make me seem clever. As a strategy it was doomed. "Get over yourself," I thought, and long ago jettisoned the elitism of antimonarchism in a profoundly pro-monarchy country. The majority are not always right, God knows; but when they raise a glass or a mug to the stability and reassurance Queen Elizabeth II has brought during difficult decades, they express genuine common sense. I have followed the Queen during some of her many duties, and talked to those closest to her, from ladies-in-waiting to friends of the family and members of the royal family too. And honestly, the more you see of her in action, the more impressed you are. She has been dutiful, but she has been a lot more than dutiful. She has been shrewd, kind and wise. Britain without her would have been a grayer, shriller, more meager place.

Index

popularity of monarchy and, 5–6
post-WW II social world and, 85–86
prime ministers and, 11, 113–17, 132–35
Privy Council and, 179–80
Privy Purse and, 235–36
reign of, and length, xii–xiii, 6, 9–10, 308, 312
reign of, and lessons for Charles, 319–21
reign of, and meaning of monarchy, xv, 308–16
relationship with children, 232
relationship with Philip, 69, 150, 309
Rhodesia and, 188–92, 212–13, 228
role of, xiii–xiv, 4, 8–10, 219–20
Rose biography of George V and, 26
royalists vs. republicans and, 221–25
royal traditions and, 15, 61–62, 311–12
security of, 233–34
Silver Jubilee and, 142, 221, 223–29
silver wedding anniversary and, 221, 224
South Africa and, 249–50
speech by, on 21st birthday, 90, 131, 202
speeches by, xiv, 2, 12, 14–15, 86–87
staff of, 6–7, 38, 186
State Opening of Parliament and, 10
state visits and, 10–11, 101, 108–9
Suez affair and, 142–45
taxes and, 242
Thatcher and, 115–16, 245–51, 255
title of, on accession, 117–18, 119–20
traditional tastes of, 206–7
Uganda and, 192–94
visits and travel, 14–15, 103
visits Australia, 106, 217
visits Canada, 98, 219
visits Caribbean, 205
visits China, 206
visits Commonwealth, 104–7
visits Dresden, 103
visits East Africa, Australia and New Zealand, 98–100
visits Ghana, 153–54
visits Jamaica, New Zealand, Australia and Canada, 288–89
visits Morocco, 103
visits Quebec, 217–19
visits Republic of Ireland, 2–3
visits Russia, xiii
visits South Africa, 87–90
visits UAE and Oman, 107–11
visits U.S., 4, 98, 140
William's marriage to Kate Middleton and, 299–304
Wilson and, 115–16, 134, 137, 169–70, 176, 181, 184, 188, 214, 220–21
Windsor Castle fire and, 264–65, 268
Windsor family name and, 136–37
WW II and, 47, 80–87
Yeltsin and, 164–65
Elizabeth, Queen Mother (*formerly* Elizabeth Bowes Lyon, wife of George VI, mother), 4, 6
background of, 54–59, 302
Civil List and, 240
death of, 59, 287–88
Diana and, 263, 277
Elizabeth's birth and childhood and, 63–64, 67, 72
Elizabeth's marriage to Philip and, 88
George VI's stammer and, 44
marries George VI, 25, 42–43, 56–59, 93, 187–88, 211
personality of, 55–56, 59, 247
visits Australia, 59, 64
visits Canada, 125
visits South Africa, 89–90
visits U.S., 47
WW II and, 80
Emirates Airline, 108
Empire Day, 89, 119
Empire Exhibition (Wembley), 43
Enigma intercepts, 47
Epson Derby, 307
Esher, Lord, 28–29
Eurobond market, 139
European Economic Community (EEC), 153, 213–14, 225
European Union, 255

Fagan, Michael, 233
Fairlie, Henry, 147
Faisal, King of Saudi Arabia, 101
Falkender, Marcia Williams, Lady, 221
Falklands War, 166

About the Author

ANDREW MARR, a bestselling author and award-winning journalist, hosts *The Andrew Marr Show* on BBC. His best-known book, *A History of Modern Britain*, was accompanied by a BBC television series that won one of British television's most prestigious prizes. He and his wife live in London with their three children.